The Basque Poetic Tradition

 The Basque Series

OTHER BOOKS BY GORKA AULESTIA

Basque-English Dictionary

English-Basque Dictionary,
   with Linda White

Basque-English English-Basque Dictionary,
   with Linda White

Improvisational Poetry from the Basque Country

Escritores vascos

Erbesteko euskal literaturaren antologia

GORKA AULESTIA

The Basque Poetic Tradition

Translated by Linda White
Foreword by Linda White

University of Nevada Press ▲▲ Reno & Las Vegas

The Basque Series
Series Editor: William A. Douglass

University of Nevada Press, Reno, Nevada 89557 USA
Copyright © 2000 by University of Nevada Press
All rights reserved
Manufactured in the United States of America

Library of Congress Cataloging-in-Publication Data
Aulestia, Gorka, 1932–
The Basque poetic tradition / Gorka Aulestia ; translated by Linda
White ; forword by Linda White.
p. cm. — (The Basque series)
Includes bibliographical references and index.
ISBN 0-87417-283-7
1. Basque poetry—History and criticism. I. Title. II. Series.
PH5290 .A926 2000
899'.921009—dc21 00-008196

The paper used in this book meets the requirements of American
National Standard for Information Sciences—Permanence of Paper for
Printed Library Materials, ANSI Z39.48-1984. Binding materials were
selected for strength and durability.

First Printing
09 08 07 06 05 04 03 02 01 00
5 4 3 2 1

To my sister Lorea

CONTENTS

FOREWORD

Within the field of letters, Basque literature emerges as a small literature created, nurtured, and studied by larger-than-life individuals. The author of these essays is a member of that group, a memorable man with a grand, sweeping personal style that cannot always be captured on paper. Gorka Aulestia Txakartegi was born in Ondarroa, Bizkaia, on December 11, 1932. He grew up hearing both Bizkaian and Gipuzkoan Basque (in spite of being schooled during the Franco years), and his familiarity with two dialects served him well later in life as he embraced Batua, the Unified Dialect. Aulestia studied philosophy and theology as a young man preparing for the priesthood, then pursued a degree in social economics at the University of Deusto in Bilbao. In the United States, he completed an M.A. in French literature, then another in Spanish literature, and in 1987 received his doctorate in Basque Studies (Language and Literature) at the University of Nevada, Reno, with a dissertation entitled "El Bertsolarismo: literatura oral improvisada del País Vasco." Aulestia's publication list includes eight books, ninety-one articles, and numerous conference papers and book reviews—an admirable contribution to scholarship, but even more inspiring when viewed in the context of his teaching duties. He has taught many subjects over the years, but none with greater gusto than the course in Basque literature that he delivers as Professor of Basque Literature at the University of Deusto, EUTG, in Donostia-San Sebastián. Since 1996 he has been a member of Euskaltzaindia, the Academy of the Basque Language.

In the current volume, Gorka Aulestia provides us with fourteen essays on the Basque poetic tradition. As a literary critic, he keeps a respectful eye on the past and its traditions while providing an accurate, factual, and highly informative picture of each author's life and production. Aulestia's unpretentious approach to literary criticism (in effect, each essay stands alone as a minihistoriography) is especially valuable to students of Basque literature who have taken up the field for the first time. Yet the volume of information presented in each piece provides the experienced scholar with reliable, honest, and often firsthand personal knowledge of the writers in question and their contributions to Basque literature.

The observations on these pages span over a decade of ruminations about Basque poetry. The inclusion of certain poets and the exclusion of others speak more to a chronology of the author's interests than any statement regarding the ultimate ranking of the poets within Basque literature.

In his introduction, Aulestia begins with a brief overview of Basque literary historiography, in which he comments on works about Basque literature that literary scholars will find useful. Next, he provides a "Survey of Basque Poetry," highlighting major poets from the beginning of Basque written literature through the twentieth century. In "Bertsolaritza and the Basque Diaspora," Aulestia examines his specialty, *bertsolaritza* (improvisational oral poetry), from the perspective of the theme of Basque emigration. "Pastorales" examines a traditional form of folk theater-in-verse and offers the novice a succinct description of the art form and its milieu, as well as information on plots and themes, along with a brief history of the pastorale in the Basque Country.

The essays that follow examine individual poets, providing biographical sketches and histories of their productivity. "Bernard Detxepare—Medieval or Renaissance Writer?" addresses a favorite topic for discussion regarding the priest from Behe-Nafarroa. In "Jose de Aristimuño, Alias Aitzol: A Martyr to the Basque Cause," Aulestia pays tribute to the efforts of the Basque nationalist writer whose life and work in behalf of Basque poetry were cut short by the Spanish Civil War. The lengthiest treatment in the collection is "Nicolás Ormaetxea, Alias 'Orixe' (1888–1961): The Life and Work of a Controversial Writer," in which Aulestia provides a remarkably evenhanded examination of the subject, given his evident fondness for the artist and his creations. In his essay on Lizardi, "Jose Mari Agirre, Alias 'Lizardi': A Lyric Poet," Aulestia paints a picture of a man searching for himself through his art, a man beset by enemies and an artist of great potential and depth, lost to the world at the age of thirty-seven after changing Basque poetry forever.

In "Esteban Urkiaga, Alias 'Lauaxeta' (1905-1937): A Modern Poet of the Pre-Civil War Period," Aulestia's familiarity with the Bizkaian dialect allows him a special window on the poetry of Lauaxeta, an artist who, for many years, received less attention than he deserved because of what the author terms the "secret flavor" of his dialect. "Salbatore Mitxelena and Bitoriano Gandiaga: The Franciscan School" offers a view of the literary contributions of two Franciscans from the renowned Arantzazu Sanctuary. In "Jon Mirande: A Nonconformist Writer," Aulestia cites some of the most scintillating and intriguing passages of the "bad boy" of Basque literature, whose Parisian upbringing and subsequent reclamation of his native language and culture, even to the assumption of paganistic rhetoric, make him one of the most fascinating and most abused artists in Basque literature.

Aulestia's essay "Gabriel Aresti: The Poetry of a Fighter" concentrates on Aresti's social poetry. "Juan Mari Lekuona: A Bridge Between Cultured Poetry and Popular Literature" provides us with a retrospective on sixty-five years of devotion to Basque literature and scholarship by a major Basque writer/poet/teacher, an essay enriched by Aulestia's personal acquaintance with and admiration for Lekuona. And finally, we return to the subject dearest to Aulestia's heart, bertsolaritza, in the final essay, "Marcel Jousse and Manuel Lekuona: Two Pioneers of Oral Literature."

The various essays in this volume contain elements that, if read all at one sitting, might seem repetitive, but like all great teachers, Gorka Aulestia relies on the value of repetition and restatement to pass along certain sidelights while he focuses on different individual topics and writers. These seemingly repetitive elements, however (such as historical notes regarding Sabino Arana), make the essays highly useful as independent works. As such, literary scholars will find them invaluable as frank, reliable sources of information not available elsewhere in the English language, written by one of the foremost experts in the field.

LINDA WHITE

PREFACE

On July 4, 1975, I headed across the arid terrain of Nevada to attend the Elko Basque Festival for the first time. I was accompanied by William A. Douglass, coordinator of the Basque Studies Program at the University of Nevada, Reno. One of our topics of conversation was the need for adequate Basque- and English-language materials for the Basque language and literature classes I was soon going to teach at the university.

As the 1976 school year began, I informed Douglass of three urgent necessities: a Basque-English/English-Basque dictionary, an English-language grammar of Basque (or Euskara), and an English-language history of Basque literature in English, because the few existing materials were insufficient to attain our academic objectives.

From January 1976 to September 1979, I could do little to realize these projects because of my teaching obligations (in Basque, Spanish, and French) and my studies (I was pursuing a master's degree in French and Spanish literature). On September 1, 1979, however, I initiated the project of the first Basque-English dictionary project while teaching at Washington State University in Pullman. Pullman's short, cold winter days and long, dark nights (made even darker by the eruption of Mount Saint Helens on May 17, 1980) offered me the perfect opportunity for launching two of the three projects William Douglass and I had discussed on the way to Elko. In that claustrophobic environment, whenever the tedious work on the dictionary allowed me a brief respite, I began to write about Basque literature. Thus was born my first article about Bernard Detxepare in 1979.

After my return to Reno in August 1980, I used the extensive resources of the Basque Studies Program library to write most of the chapters in this book, which started out as notes for my students of Basque literature. In March 1989, after fourteen years in America, I returned to Euskal Herria (the Basque Country), where I completed chapters 5, 12, and 13 on Jose de Aristimuño, alias "Aitzol," Juan Mari Lekuona, and Marcel Jousse and Manuel Lekuona.

At the beginning I never thought those articles and students' note pages would become a book. My priority was to prepare teaching materials for students who, for the most part, were completely ignorant of Basque literature. But as the number of articles multiplied, I began to consider the possibility of a book of literary essays aimed for American readers.

I felt there were no problems with regard to the selection and order of the subject matter; since I was not attempting to write a sequential history of Basque literature, I could choose a poetic subject here, a prose subject there, and write about the authors whom I judged to be outstanding in Basque literature. I did have problems, however, with the form in which I was to deal with my topics. Should I delve deeply into each subject and run the risk of my readers getting lost in a foreign literary forest, or should I expound on each subject as simply and clearly as possible without losing sight of the fact that I was writing for an intelligent and fairly well-educated audience? I opted for the second choice, preferring to follow the wise counsel of the great bertsolari Ignacio Eizmendi, alias "Basarri," who stated, "I would prefer not to compose verses at all than create them in such a manner that they be incomprehensible to the common people."

I hope that my books *Improvisational Poetry from the Basque Country* and this current volume, with their special emphasis on Basque oral literature and Basque-written poetry, will serve to fill the need, already identified in 1975, for surveys of the field of Basque literature. With faith and optimism for the future, I trust also that in the next few years there will follow a third volume dealing with Basque writers who have made their mark in prose.

In conclusion, I would like to acknowledge the help and encouragement of three people without whom this book would not have been possible: Dr. William A. Douglass, Dr. Linda White, and Dr. Mertxe de Renobales, my wife.

INTRODUCTION

On more than one occasion I have been asked about the best reference books in the field of Basque literature. This motivated me to create a short annotated bibliography, which I have divided into four parts: (1) histories of Basque literature in Basque, (2) histories of Basque literature in Spanish, (3) histories of Basque literature in French, and (4) bilingual history of Basque literature.

Literary history did not become a systematized and independent discipline until the nineteenth century, with the appearance of modern nations and linguistic nationalism. The study of Basque literature is still in its formative stages, because Basque literature possesses characteristics that make it difficult to compare with other literary traditions. First, the great periods of the history of major Western literatures do not apply to Basque literature, because it developed relatively late. Second, Basque literature has been basically a handmaiden of linguistic necessity. The primary protagonist of this literature has been Euskara, a minority tongue even within the borders of the Basque Country. Euskara has been largely excluded from public life, its proponents have been dominated and persecuted on occasion,[1] and it is still undergoing the process of standardization. Only about 35 percent of nearly three million Basques speak the language today. Basque has been spoken more extensively, but it has never transcended its status as the language of peasants, the private tongue of family and personal relations. Until recently it has never been the medium of formal education, nor has it ever been a language that could compete with Latin or with French and Spanish. Even during the apogee of the Kingdom of Navarre in the eleventh century, arguably the triumphant political moment for Basques, the language was not used for official dealings.

The scarcity of universities and academies has been one of the principal causes of the lack of written literature in Basque. If only 35 percent of Basques speak the language, only 15 percent know how to write it. Most of those who have used the language constantly still prefer Spanish or French for writing down their ideas. At times, the University of Oñate was spoken of as a center of cultural influence, but its sway was very limited. Moreover, this university was more a creation of a Renaissance patron of the arts than a response to any felt need of the Basques.

Basque literature is also a latecomer. The first book in the language dates from 1545. Written in the midst of the Renaissance, its meter reminds us of the *cuaderna via*[2] and other meters used in the Middle Ages. Moreover, Basque literature is divided along geographic lines into two parts, the literature of Iparralde (the North) and that of Hegoalde (the South) just as the Basque Country is itself divided between the two states of Spain and France.[3]

This division has spawned several notable differences. In the northern zone, where Basque is spoken along with French, the cultivation of Basque literature predates the literature of Hegoalde by more than two centuries. While Iparralde has produced writers like Bernard Detxepare and Leizarraga, in Hegoalde writers like Baltasar Etxabe have struggled to demonstrate (always in Spanish) that it is possible to write, for example, the "Hail Mary" in Basque.

Last, Basque literature is, to a large extent, religious in both content and authorship. Very few sixteenth- to nineteenth-century laymen appear on the list of Basque writers. Most authors were clerics who wrote on religious themes from a point of view that was more didactic and apologetic than literary. The religious literature of the sixteenth century was dedicated to the fight against Protestantism recommended by the Council of Trent. The majority of Basque classics from the seventeenth and eighteenth centuries are also religious in nature and were written with specific goals in mind— to preach and to defend the beauty of the Basque language. This aesthetic prose later gave rise to the narrative and, at the beginning of the twentieth century, the novel.

When speaking of the history of Basque "literature," I do not limit my study solely to literary aesthetics. If we were to follow that approach, the history of Basque literature would be truly short, since, until the late-nineteenth century, very few books written in Basque deserved to be regarded as "literary."

HISTORIES OF BASQUE LITERATURE WRITTEN IN BASQUE

Nicolás Ormaetxea, Alias "Orixe" (1888-1961)

Orixe's "Euskal-literatura'ren atze edo edesti laburra" (A short history or background of Basque literature, 1927) comprises twelve short articles that were published in the Basque magazine *Euskal esnalea* in 1927.[4] It does not purport to be a complete history; its originality lies in the fact that it centers on three Basque writers around whom, from the seventeenth to the nineteenth centuries, the most important Basque literary movements formed. These were Pedro Daguerre, alias "Axular" (1556-1644), Father Manuel de Larramendi (1690-1766), and Sabino de Arana y Goiri (1865-1903).[5] In these articles Orixe demonstrates a profound knowledge of Basque literature. In addition to being one of the best Basque writers of the twentieth century,[6] his ideas about the different authors he studies are precise and profound.

Jon Etxaide (1920-1998)

Etxaide was without a doubt one of the best Basque prose writers of the twentieth century. His abundant production (including the novels *Joanak joan* [The past is already gone, 1955] and *Gorrotoa lege* [Hatred is law, 1964]) is an expression of the literary prowess of this simple, hardworking man.

His *Amasei seme Euskalerriko* (Sixteen sons of the Basque Country, 1958) is not a complete history of Basque literature but an interesting study of sixteen of the best early Basque writers (from the sixteenth through the nineteenth centuries). The author has carefully chosen writers from both Iparralde and Hegoalde and provides information on the life, work, and style of each. His deep knowledge of the subject makes this a very useful book for Basque-speaking readers.

Ibon Sarasola (1946-   )

Sarasola's *Euskal literaturaren historia* (History of Basque literature, 1971) possesses very important characteristics. First, it is the first overview of Basque literature ever written in Basque. Second, it is the first book that attempts to contextualize Basque literature within the social and economic infrastructure of the Basque Country. Moreover, it has been translated into Spanish, which makes it more accessible.

Ibon Sarasola is a young Basque writer of whom much is expected in the fields of Basque lexicography, linguistics, and literature. His ideas occasionally seem a bit dogmatic and iconoclastic, but he is noteworthy for being the first to apply the sociological method to the Basque literary field.

Santiago Onaindia (1909-1996)

Onaindia's *Euskal literatura* (Basque literature, 1972) is an extensive, though unfinished, history of Basque literature. To date six volumes have been published.

The author's intention is to cover all Basque authors, from the great to the lesser-known. Onaindia establishes his method from the outset, studying every author's life and work, and literary criticisms of their works. When examining their styles, he pays excessive attention to linguistic features, which prevents this history from reaching the analytical level we might desire. His treatment is organized by centuries and is further divided according to the different provinces and dialects of the Basque Country. We have here an extremely valuable work by a Basque Carmelite who is dedicated more to the collection and explication of the Basque works of others than to his personal literary output.

Mikel Zarate (1933-1979)

Zarate was without a doubt one of the Basque writers who best understood the problem of standardizing the Basque language as well as the method for doing so. His native dialect was Bizkaian, but he mastered the rest of the dialects to arrive at a clear, popular, and elegant unified Basque. His literary production written during his final years is impressive.[7]

In addition to being a good poet and writer of prose, Zarate was an excellent educator who was concerned about his students and dedicated to finding ways to reach the humblest of audiences. To that end he limited his history of literature to the writers of his native province of Bizkaia.

Bizkaiko euskal idazleak is divided into four parts: (1) the early Basque writers; (2) writers of Larramendi's era; (3) writers of the Arana y Goiri school; and (4) modern writers. Zarate used the same pattern for each study: a biography, a list of works, and selected texts. At the end of each section there is a short vocabulary to aid in the comprehension of the texts. In spite of its apparent simplicity, this book is very useful because of the author's thoughtful evaluations of Bizkaian writers.

Joshe Erzibengoa (1942-   ) and Patxi Ezkiaga (1943-   )

Erzibengoa and Ezkiaga's *Euskal literatura* (Basque literature, 1975) is a simple history comprising three volumes. It was intended only as an aid for the thousands of students at the *ikastolak* (Basque schools) who wished to venture further into the Basque language. Erzibengoa and Ezkiaga briefly study the life and works of several writers. Critical comments and a few very short bibliographic listings complete the book. The first volume treats the sixteenth and seventeenth centuries, the second, the eighteenth century, and the third deals with the whole of the nineteenth century.

Enrike Zabala

As the title of the work indicates, *Euskal literatura alfabetatzeko* (Basque literature for beginners, 1979) is intended as a primer on Basque literature. Its format is simple, and it presents nothing new or original. It follows the methodology of Erzibengoa and Ezkiaga's manual — presenting each author's life, a list of works, a criticism, sample text, and a short bibliography.

Karmelo Etxenagusia (1932–   )

Etxenagusia has learned to combine his priestly duties with his great love of Basque literature, about which he has written three books. During the difficult years of Franco's dictatorship, he prepared mimeographed pages to use in teaching Basque literature courses at the Seminary of Derio near Bilbo. In his first book, *Euskal idazleen lorategia* (Garden of Basque writers, 1969), he studies the most important Basque writers, and it is the fruit of those mimeographed pages from the late 1950s.

In 1980 Etxenagusia copublished a second book, *Euskal idazleak bizkaieraz: antologia, testu azterketak, ariketak* (Garden of Basque writers in the Bizkaian dialect: anthology, textual analysis, and exercises) with J. Cortazar and A. Etxebarria. This book deals mainly with writers born in Bizkaia. However, he does not limit himself to the geographic boundaries of the region, as does Zarate, but extends his area to encompass all Basque writers who wrote in the Bizkaian dialect, regardless of their native province. Thus, for example, we find Gipuzkoan authors such as Esteban Garibay and Orixe included. The objective of the work is to provide insight into Bizkaian literature and to serve as a manual for students at the Basque Summer School at Derio.

The book is divided into four parts: (1) a study of the oral literature (old songs, *bertsolariak* [Basque troubadours], and proverbs); (2) the classic writers of the seventeenth and eighteenth centuries; (3) the renaissance of Basque literature from the end of the nineteenth century through the Spanish Civil War (1939); and (4) the modern era (1940-1980). It ends with a section dedicated to the methodology of the critical study of literary texts.

Etxenagusia's third book is entitled *Iparraldeko euskal idazleak* (Writers from Iparralde, 1981) and is basically an anthology of texts by writers from Iparralde. The introduction is devoted to oral literature, with emphasis on the old songs and the bertsolariak of that region. Each author's section is preceded by biographical data, and there is a short vocabulary list at the end.

These three books have one important element in common: all are intended as student manuals. Because of their pedagogical nature, they are more collections of texts than critical histories of Basque literature.

HISTORIES OF BASQUE LITERATURE WRITTEN IN SPANISH

Koldo Mitxelena (1915-1987)

Mitxelena's *Historia de la literatura vasca* (1960) is the first complete, systematic history of Basque literature.[8] In spite of its brevity, it is one of the best for its depth, precision, and methodology. There is little biographical data and no extraliterary material here, not even an anthology of literary texts, yet the book is outstanding for its synthesis. It has served as a model for many of the histories of Basque literature that have been published since.

Luis Villasante (1920-   )

Villasante's *Historia de la literatura vasca* (first edition published in 1961) is, in some respects, more complete than Mitxelena's history. It is larger and contains more biographical data, more information, and more bibliographical items. This history is divided by century, thereby preventing a systematic study by genre. It is further divided into two parts, one dealing with writers from Iparralde and the other with those from Hegoalde. This precludes any global view of the nation's literature and obfuscates the relationship between the two literatures. Occasionally, the inclusion of an author strikes me as inappropriate. For example, Miguel de Unamuno is included, but his contribution to Basque literature is practically nil. In the second edition (1979) there is an appendix of authors who died after the publication of the first work, but the book still lacks a section dedicated to the study of contemporary authors.[9]

Bernardo Estornés Lasa (1907-1999)

Estornés Lasa has published five large volumes of the *Enciclopedia general ilustrada del País Vasco* (1981) devoted to Basque literature. To a great extent, he follows the trail blazed by Villasante, but this work contains a good anthology of Basque texts, which is also translated into Spanish, and provides an abundance of material on Basque literature.

Luis Mari Mujika (1939-   )

Mujika attempts in *Historia de la literatura euskerika* (1979) to follow the sociological method used by Ibon Sarasola. Before studying the different authors, he places them within the historical, sociological, and ethnic context of their century. Mujika is one of the most prolific authors of recent years, but some of his works appear too hastily conceived. The parts of his history dedicated to Detxepare; Pierre Topet, alias "Etxahun"; Esteban Urkiaga, alias "Lauaxeta"; Jose Mari Agirre, alias "Lizardi"; and Orixe are more substantive than are the remainder. He treats some great writers, like Domingo Aguirre and Ebaista Bustinza, alias "Kirikiño," rather superficially, and, at times, his opinions come across as iconoclastic and personal. This history concludes in 1936 with Orixe.[10]

Patri Urkizu (1946-   )

Urkizu's *Lengua y literatura vasca* (1978) contains two parts: a brief presentation of Basque as a language and a history of Basque literature. Following the traditional approach, Urkizu divided the work by genres (poetry, novel, theater, and essay). In spite of its brevity, this book is notable for its selection of texts, excerpts of which are also translated into Spanish. This book was written as a high school textbook.

HISTORIES OF BASQUE LITERATURE WRITTEN IN FRENCH

Francisque X. Michel (1809-1887)

Michel's *Le Pays Basque. Sa population, sa langue, ses moeurs, sa littérature et sa musique* (1857) is a voluminous book in which there are four interesting chapters on Basque writers. The first three chapters are dedicated to Detxepare, Arnauld Oihenart, and Axular. The fourth chapter describes several other Basque writers in much less detail. Given the book's publication date, these chapters are all the more interesting. This is the work of a great writer who knew the Basque Country well; his criticisms are the result of deep and serious analysis.

Pierre Lafitte (1901-1985)

Lafitte's *Le basque et la littérature d'expression basque en Labourd, Basse-Navarre et Soule* (1941) is a very structured book divided into two parts, oral and written literature. The author studies only a few writers from Iparralde within their historical and social context. Although the book is brief, Lafitte's ideas are interesting and well founded.

A BILINGUAL HISTORY OF
BASQUE LITERATURE

Joan Mari Torrealday (1942–   )

Torrealday's *Euskal idazleak, gaur: Historia social de la lengua y literatura vascas* (Basque writers, today: 1977) is a large volume on literary history up to 1975. This history presents all that has been said about the writers and their works and analyzes that information from the sociological perspective of Robert Escarpit of the University of Bordeaux. There is no personal or in-depth criticism. The book is an important reference because it provides an excellent overview. It is written mostly in Basque, but each page contains a Spanish translation of the Basque ideas being studied.

ADDITIONAL STUDIES

To conclude, I offer a list of additional books that are of some interest for the study of Basque literature: Joan Amenabar (ed.), *Euskal poesia kultoaren bilduma, 1880–1963* (Survey of Basque educated poetry, 1880-1963), 2 vols.; Nicolás de Cortazar, *Cien autores vascos;* Jean Haritschelhar, *Être basque;* Juan Mari Lekuona, *Ahozko euskal literatura* (Oral Basque literature); Manuel de Lekuona, *Aozko literatura* (Oral literature), vol. 1 of *Idazlan guztiak* (Complete works); Ignacio Omaechevarria, *Euskera;* Juan San Martín, *Escritores euskéricos* (Basque writers) and *Literaturaren inguruan* (About literature); Ibon Sarasola, *Euskal literatura numerotan* (Basque literature in numbers); and Martín de Ugalde, "El exilio en la literatura vasca: problemas y consecuencias," in *El exilio español de 1939.*

CHAPTER ONE

Survey of Basque Poetry

There is a fairly widespread notion that the Basque language has no literature, but the facts are otherwise. In the last twenty-five years histories of this literature have increased dramatically, including one study comprising six volumes.

Basque *oral* literature is both ancient and original. Within it, there are two genres: the *pastorales* (a form of popular theater from the province of Zuberoa) and the *bertsolaritza* (a type of improvised sung verse). I shall discuss both in the following chapters. In contrast, written Basque literature had a late start.

Largely religious in nature until the twentieth century, written literature can be divided into works written in four dialects of Basque spoken in two different states, France and Spain. Before the twentieth century, Basque literary prose was essentially pragmatic, its themes largely religious, linguistic, or apologetic (in defense of the language). Only poetry was able to transcend those extraliterary goals in its search for aesthetic beauty.

The first book of Basque poetry, *Linguae vasconum primitiae per Dominum Bernardum Dechepare Rectorem Sancti Michaelis Veteris* (The first fruits of the Basque language by Bernat Detxepare, rector of Old Saint Michael's), was published in Bordeaux in 1545—the year of the inauguration of the Council of Trent. This work consists of fifteen poems totaling 1,034 lines in fifty-two pages, with a short prose foreword (21 lines) by the author. The poems focus on three main themes: religion, love, and the Basque language. Poems 1 and 2 have religious themes and make up the first and longest part of the book (449 lines). The second part (403 lines) contains ten poems (numbers 3 to 12) about love. Poem 13 describes the author's life in 102 lines. The fourth and last part contains poems 14 and 15 (59 lines), in which Detxepare praises his native Basque language.

The outstanding Basque writer of the seventeenth century was the poet Oihenart (1592–1667). With the exception of Garibay (1533–1599), Oihenart was the first nonreligious Basque writer—a rare exception in the first two centuries of written Basque literature. He was born in Maule, Zuberoa, was one of the most important Basque intellectuals of his era, and was knowledgeable in Basque, French, Latin, Spanish, Greek, and Italian. He also studied law in Bordeaux.

Oihenart is better known as a historian and collector of Basque expressions and maxims than as a poet. Nevertheless, his contribution to Basque poetry is notable, though his work often appears conceptual, cold, intellectual, and technical. He knew a great deal about the European poetry of his time and was the first critic of Basque poetry. His book, *Art poétique,* analyzes and applies the general rules of poetic art to Basque poetry.

Of greater importance to Basque literature is *Les proverbes basques recueillis par le sieur d'Oihenart, plus les poésies basques du même auteur* (Basque proverbs gathered by Mr. Oihenart, with Basque poems by the same author), published in 1657. As the title indicates, the book contains two parts. The first, one of the best collections of its kind, presents 706 Basque maxims gathered by Oihenart. This part is translated into French, apparently by Oihenart.

The second part of the book, entitled "O. ten gaztaroa neurtitzetan" (The youth of O. [Oihenart] in verse), contains twenty-nine poems, including the famous "Ezkontidearen hil-kexua" (Lament on the death of a spouse), written on the occasion of the death of his wife, Joanne. There are also fifteen poems that deal with youth, an elegy on the death of his wife, five religious poems, five short essays, and two poems written in praise of two Zuberoan poets. Most of them are also love poems in which Oihenart extols the physical beauty of the women he loved.

Oihenart wanted to be an innovator; thus, he criticized the poets who came before him, especially Detxepare and Joannes Etxeberri of Ziburu, for using the traditional fifteen-syllable rhythm and for not being precise with regard to elisions and synaloephas.

Oihenart did not write in his native dialect (Zuberoan) but in a mixture of Nafarroa Beherean and Lapurdin, and his Basque is pure, with few foreign or borrowed words. In his attempt to write cultured poetry he used many verb forms, especially synthetic ones not current today, and he sought out rich rhymes, synaloephas, elisions, and varied rhythms.

Oihenart was more concerned with formal structure than with sentiment, and at times his poetry comes across as rigid and puristic, reminding us of the much later poetry of Lauaxeta (1905–1937).

Oihenart's rhymes are rich and complex. He used hyperbaton, enjambment, and dieresis, which makes comprehension difficult. He also employed many neologisms, some of which, like *neurtitz* (verse), have passed
into the modern language, making a dictionary absolutely essential for even
a native Basque speaker.

In his use of the theme of love, Oihenart reminds us of Detxepare, but
his sensual feeling is not as deep as is that of the earlier Basque poet. Sometimes Oihenart's poetry lacks emotion and shows no flair for popular expression, thereby giving the impression of having been constructed in a
laboratory rather than springing from the heart. Despite their deficiencies,
his efforts must be considered a very positive attempt at Basque poetic reform.

In the eighteenth century there was no Basque artist of consequence in
written poetry, although there was a wealth of important figures in oral
genres, especially in Iparralde.

In the nineteenth century, in the province of Zuberoa, the legendary poet
and bertsolari Etxahun (1786–1862) figured prominently. He is one of the
most original popular poets in all of Basque literature. In the manner of the
French poet François Villon, Etxahun penetrated human suffering. He was
the poet of the "I"; his works are laden with all the romantic characteristics
of love, hate, jealousy, and desire for revenge, and his satire is violent and
very personal. Etxahun's suffering and hatred give depth to his poetry. At
times, he resorts to bitter humor and sarcasm, and his verse is caustic and
biting; sadness and disillusionment surface in poems of aching desperation. Some of his best poems are autobiographical: "Urxaphal bat" (A turtle-
dove); "Ahaide delizius huntan" (On this delicious air); "Mundian maleru-
zik" (The unfortunates of the world); and "Etxahunen bizitzaren khantoria"
(The song of Etxahun's life).

Etxahun possessed an extraordinary natural talent, and his contact with
nature compensated for his lack of higher learning. His keen sense of observation, a gift that inspired caricatures of persons and things he disliked,
allowed him to view things precisely, and his work reveals a command of
the Zuberoan dialect uncommon among the majority of Basques. He chose
the *mot juste* in every case. His mastery of language is most obvious when
he portrays either characters or situations in brief, colorful brush strokes.

In general, Etxahun's rhymes are assonant and not rhythmic. He did not
use enjambment. In this respect, he falls within the tradition of the bertsolariak. All of this is complemented by his depth of feeling and the beauty of
his imagery, especially in his elegiac and satirical poems. His style is inimi-
table, and his language is difficult for those who are not natives of Zuberoa.
Furthermore, his work is not easy to translate.

Etxahun intended his poems to be sung rather than read. Therein lies the
great difference between the popular poet (bertsolari or *koplari*) and the cultured one (*olerkari*), who writes a verse after he has had time to refine it. Etxahun knew the popular eighteenth-century Basque melodies and availed
himself of them. Those few of his poems that have survived are of great

value to popular Basque poetry and are proof of the exceptional and, in many ways, unique stature of this bard from Zuberoa.

Jean-Baptiste Elizanburu (1821-1891) was born in Sara, Lapurdi. The Basque poetry competitions organized by Antoine d'Abbadie encouraged his literary vocation, and during the 1860s he won many first prizes in poetry. Some of those poems have passed into the realm of folk song: "Nere etxea" (My house), "Agur herriari" (Hello to my hometown), and "Lau andren besta" (Four ladies' celebration). His poem "Solferinoko itsua" (The blind man of Solferino) is one of the best poems of the nineteenth century.

When Elizanburu dealt with his favorite themes—the countryside, the farm, the Basque language, religion, family—his verses employed a popular style. He was a great master of Basque and an expert at versification; his language is clear and his verses musical and harmonious. Sometimes, however, his poetry is plastic, perhaps excessively ideal, and it lacks the depth and naturalness of Etxahun's and Detxepare's work.

Gracian Adema, alias "Zalduby" (1828-1907), wrote a great deal, especially poetry, on both religious and profane subjects, his patriotic poems being especially notable. "Zazpi Eskualherriek" (The seven Basque provinces), a symbolic song that proposes the unification of the seven Basque provinces into one nation, deserves special mention. He was also a great defender of the Basque language.

Adema was a musician and a poet, and his poetry is meant to be sung. He was very careful with his technique, and he constantly polished his poetry without abandoning its spontaneous inspiration. He uses many different rhymes. His Basque is popular yet pure, luxuriant yet economical, and his style is compact.

During the nineteenth century in Hegoalde the Second Carlist War (1872-1876) and the loss of the old liberties greatly sobered Basque life. These circumstances, however, stimulated and paved the way for the literary renaissance of the first half of the twentieth century.

The Bizkaian poet Felipe Arrese Beitia (1841-1906) was a product of this environment. He wrote many poems, elegies, odes, and sonnets and won fourteen first prizes in Basque poetry competitions, beginning with his poem "Ama Euskeriari azken agurrak" (Final farewell to the Basque language). Arrese Beitia's poetry is more heartfelt than cerebral. His language is popular and vigorous, and he uses many idiomatic expressions. His work falls somewhere between educated poetry and the popular poetry of the Basque troubadours, and although it does not reach the heights attained by more conceptual poets like Lizardi (1896-1933), Arrese Beitia's poems are colorful and highly polished.

In Hegoalde, two literary focal areas emerged in Donostia and Bilbo. In Gipuzkoa the work of José de Manterola (1849-1884) was very important. He awoke and nurtured in his readers a need to conserve and cultivate the Basque language. Thus the literary floral games began, and Basque troubadourism reached very high levels.

There was also a politico-literary awakening in Bizkaia, thanks to the founder of modern Basque nationalism, Arana y Goiri (1865-1903). Arana y Goiri issued a clarion call to his compatriots to search for their Basque roots and recover Basque culture, especially the language. This return to what was genuinely Basque fit perfectly with the romantic spirit of the nineteenth century, a spirit that avidly sought local color, regionalism, and new nationalism within the old Europe.

Arana y Goiri was born in Abando, in what is today Bilbo, to Basque parents. In 1882 he transferred the Carlist ideas inherited from his father to his emerging Basque nationalism. Arana y Goiri is noteworthy more as a stimulus of literature than for his own literary merit, and he gave impetus to a Basque movement whose influence is felt even today. His excessive use of neologisms give his poems an artificial luster, but despite this deficiency, his work became the fountain that nourished the next generation of poets, such as Orixe; Lizardi; Lauaxeta; Juan Arana, alias "Loramendi"; and Kepa Enbeita, alias "Urretxindor." At the center of his poetry lies his main preoccupation—his defeated country.

Before the Spanish Civil War interrupted the literary history of Hegoalde, a number of events made possible a renaissance of Basque poetry. Especially important were the creation of Euskaltzaindia, the Academy of the Basque Language, in 1919, the establishment of the *lore-jokoak* (Basque floral games and poetry competitions), and the *txapelketak* (championship competitions for Basque troubadours) promoted by the priest Aitzol (1896-1936). Prominent among the poets of this period are Orixe, Lizardi, and Lauaxeta.

Orixe was noted for the lyrical-mystical poetry in his *Barne-muinetan* (In the marrow, 1934), for his poems "Igan beti nire lelo" (May my song be always in you, 1951) and "Getsemani" (Gethsemane), and for his epic poem of almost 12,000 lines, *Euskaldunak* (The Basques), which was written in 1935 but not published until 1950. *Euskaldunak* is a large collection of poems in which Orixe depicts rural life in a small Basque village.

Lizardi is considered by many critics the single greatest lyrical Basque poet, in spite of his scanty production. He wrote only one book of poetry, *Biotz-begietan* (In the eyes of the heart), published in 1932. A classical poet and an intimate of nature who used very concise language, Lizardi was an excellent observer who became one with the countryside and expressed nature's hidden messages.

Lauaxeta was the most modern poet of this group. He wrote two books of poetry, *Bide-barrijak* (New paths, 1931) and *Arrats-beran* (At sunset, 1935). The title of the first volume of forty-one poems demonstrates Lauaxeta's fondness for renewal. His themes and his poetic language reflect especially the influence of the French Symbolists. The language of his second book is stylistically more elaborate and uses more symbolic suggestion.

Loramendi (1907-1933) stands out among the Generation of 1930 despite his death early in the decade. In 1932, competing with the best poets of the day, he won first prize in poetry in Hernani for his poem "Barruntza-Leioan" (Looking inside).[1] He wrote some sixty poems, of which the best twenty-seven were published in *Olerkiak ta idatzi guziak* (Complete poetry and prose, 1960). Loramendi was a poet with a potent imagination who wrote with great feeling, and his poetic works exude religiosity, musicality, and a love for the Basque Country, its people, and its language.

This renaissance of Basque literature was cut short by the Spanish Civil War. Franco's troops shot Aitzol and Lauaxeta, and the majority of Basque writers were imprisoned or forced into exile. During the ten years following the war (1939-1949), the publication of Basque-language books was forbidden in Hegoalde. Among the few books published from exile were *Urrundik* (From far away, 1945) and *Gudarien egiñak* (The actions of Basque soldiers, 1947) by Telesforo Monzón (1904-1981). These collections showcased Monzón's late romantic and patriotic poetry. *Urrundik* was published while the author was in exile in Mexico and was the first Basque-language book to appear in Spain after the Civil War. In it, the poet demonstrates the nostalgia of the exile, similar to that demonstrated by the romantic bard Jose María Iparragirre (1820-1881). In some of these poems Monzón reveals his tender side; in others he shows hardness and harshness but never rancor or hatred.

Gudarien egiñak (The acts of warriors) resembles a chanson de geste, and pays homage to the brave Basque soldiers who fought against the fascism of Franco, Hitler, and Mussolini. The book's patriotic poems narrate the exploits and the most important battles in an unequal war. Both books exude optimism, youth, and valor, and it is in his treatment of such themes that Monzón captures the interest of the Basque reader.

Monzón's song-poems are also very important. This is the aspect that allowed his work to become known in spite of political censorship. Monzón understood how to touch the soul of the Basque people. His qualities as a political orator were transformed into those of an imaginative poet who used both poetry and music to create his art.

In 1949 Salbatore Mitxelena (1919-1965) published his religious poem *Arantzazu, euskal-sinismenaren poema* (Arantzazu: Poem of the Basque Christian faith), based on the history of the sanctuary of Arantzazu in Gipuzkoa. He also wrote other poems, such as "Bizi nahi" (Desire to live), "Erri bat gurutzebidean" (A people at the crossroads), and "Aberriak min dit eta minak olerki" (My country gives me pain and the pain [gives] poetry), in which he exposed his passionate soul. He was the best interpreter of the pain and sorrow of the post-Civil War years. There was little stylistic innovation in his poetry, which was generally epic in nature, but his Basque was easy to understand.

Two other notable poets of the post-Civil War period deserve mention—Nemesio Etxaniz (1899-1982) and Juan Ignacio Goikoetxea, alias "Gaztelu" (1908-1983). Both of them advanced Basque literature from classical to modern poetry.

In the religious poetry of this period, the work of Jean Diharce, alias "Iratzeder" (b. 1920), stands out. His complete works, *Biziaren olerkia* (Poetry of a lifetime, 1983), includes his earlier poetry, such as "Pindar eta Lanho" (Sparks and fog, 1957).

Although Iratzeder has written ten plays and many articles, his specialty is poetry—the two outstanding themes of which are religion and the Basque Country. He is a Basque mystic, reminiscent of Saint John of the Cross, for whom poetry was love, music, peace, and happiness. Iratzeder's religious verse, however, also chronicles his inner turmoil. His love for the Basque Country focuses on the Basque people, their language, and the beautiful sea off the coast.

Iratzeder's poetry is mystical, lyrical, and elegiac, and it is notable for its sincerity and strength. He creates his own meters, although on occasion he uses those of the bertsolariak. He writes in his native dialect, Lapurdin, and his Basque is of the popular variety, but very elegant.

After 1950 some Basques began to express a desire for a total break with traditional culture, including Basque poetry. Euskadi Ta Askatasuna (ETA, Basque Country and Liberty), the Basque independence movement, was born during this decade, and existentialism, Marxism, and Freudianism were spreading among Basque youth. Out of this context arose the "breakaway" poets Jon Aiphasorho Mirande (1925-1972) and Gabriel Aresti (1933-1975).

Mirande (discussed in greater detail in chapter 10) was one of the great pioneers of modern Basque poetry. A decade later, in Hegoalde, Aresti (see chapter 11) continued the "rupturist" renovation that Mirande had initiated in Iparralde.

In the 1960s there arose a group of good poets who followed many different tendencies, from the spatial poetry of J. A. Arce, alias "Hartzabal" (b. 1939), to surrealist and symbolic poetry. These poets were bound by their fondness for new poetic forms, delicate lyricism, and a strong sense of social satire.

In his five published collections of poetry, Bitoriano Gandiaga (b. 1928) evolved from religious poetry to describing the Basque people's struggle for survival. He is a Franciscan priest who, from the isolation of the remote sanctuary of the Virgin of Arantzazu, Gipuzkoa, makes himself heard through the sincerity and beauty of his poetry. In *Elorri*[2] (Hawthorn, 1962) he speaks of his inner self in contact with nature, where he finds God. In *Hiru gizon bakarka* (Three men alone, 1974), a volume of social and political poetry, he urges his small nation to refuse to disappear. *Uda batez Madrilen* (One summer in Madrid, 1977) tells of the complex world of a large modern city. In *Denbora galdu alde* (In defense of leisure, 1985), Gandiaga's sincerity is impressive, and this free-verse work is of great interest, particularly for its autobiographical insight.

Generally speaking, Gandiaga's poetry reflects Franciscan mysticism: his intimacy with nature and his love for animals and all small creatures were

Christian in their humanism and existentialism. By temperament, Gandiaga is artistically demanding. He cultivates a high-quality poetic technique, and his Basque is lively and popular, yet highly polished. The influence of Lauaxeta and Lizardi is noticeable. For a lyric poet, his language is concise and forceful. He eschews wordiness and facile moods and seeks out images and symbols consonant with the psychology of the Basques, such as the image of *txakoli* (a Basque wine) as a symbol of the Basques who wish to live as Basques but cannot. Many of his poems are suitable for singing.

Juan Mari Lekuona (b. 1927) is a poet who prefers quality to quantity. He has published only three collections of poetry. The first, *Muga beroak* (Hot frontiers, 1973), contains the best poems of the first twenty-five years of his poetic production. In Lekuona's second book, *Ilargiaren eskolan* (In the lunar school, 1979), the poet uses the techniques of fiction and imagery, as well as those of surrealism. His style is highly personal, and his language is compact and sometimes elliptical. The vocabulary used in this book opened the door to a new era in modern Basque poetry.

Lekuona's last book, *Mimodramak eta ikonoak* (Gestures and icons, 1990), is the most difficult to understand but perhaps the most beautiful of the three works of poetry he has published to date. The book portrays six moments in the cultural history of the Basque Country.

Between 1968 and 1982 Xabier Lete (b. 1944) produced three collections of poetry concerned with the hopeless circumstances of his people during the Franco era. His denunciation of social and political injustice is clearly defined, and he is noted for his imagery and his lyricism when describing love and the Basque Country.

After the end of Franco's long dictatorship (1939–1975), Basque poetry set aside its vengeful message and sought new and autonomous forms. It became above all an aesthetic medium for personal expression. This transition was not the result of poets' sudden lack of interest in culture or the Basque Country but was simply a return to experimental avant-gardism and an effort to create a literary language with aesthetic form. In this regard I must mention two poets, José Irazu, alias "Bernardo Atxaga," and Joseba Sarrionandia.

Bernardo Atxaga (b. 1951) is the most representative figure of this group, as is reflected in his two poetry collections, *Ziutateaz* (About the city, 1976) and *Etiopia* (Ethiopia, 1978). Along this same aesthetic line, and following closely in Mirande's footsteps, is Sarrionandia (b. 1958). In *Izuen gordelekuetan barrena* (Through the hiding places of terror, 1981), Sarrionandia gives us a suggestive poetry full of metaphors.

I must also mention three female poets: Arantza Urretabizkaia (b. 1947), Amaia Lasa (b. 1948), and Tere Irastorza (b. 1961). These poets are currently writing about the lives and problems of women in the Basque Country.

CHAPTER TWO

Bertsolaritza and the Basque Diaspora

The Basques have long been characterized by their tendency to emigrate, especially to America. Although they are greatly attached to their native land, there exists in the Basques a tremendous desire to explore, to better their situation in as yet unknown places, and to seek luck as they test fortune. It is not a coincidence that the first man to sail around the world was Basque.[1]

Two forces—the one centripetal and the other centrifugal—exist simultaneously in the Basque.[2] The former allows Basques to maintain their ties with their native land, but the latter has made the Basques one of the peoples of Western Europe with the greatest tendency to emigrate. Their diaspora has been generated by internal conflicts, by persecution, and by wars in the Basque Country. The ominous aftermath of the French Revolution, for example, forced many Basques from Iparralde to flee to the Americas. The same thing happened in Hegoalde after the two Carlist Wars (1833-1839 and 1872-1876). Many Basques, especially the young, were obliged to cross the Atlantic and seek refuge in Latin America and the United States.

The diaspora is reflected in different ways in Basque art. Thus, for example, the Basque songbook contains songs that have emigration as their main theme, along with nostalgia, sadness, and, at times, humor and the desire to make one's fortune, as we see in the following popular song:

> Ameriketara joan nintzan
> xentimorik gabe.
> Andik etorri nintzan maitea
> bost milloien jabe.
> Txin, txin (bis) diruaren otsa
> Aretxek ematen dit
> maitea biotzean poza.[3]

> I went to America a poor man, without a cent, and I returned with five million. The sound of clinking money warms my heart.

Another popular song expresses the desire for a better life and for change:

> Amerikara noa
> nere borondatez
> emen baño obeto
> bizitzeko ustez.[4]

> I'm going to America of my own free will, with the hope of living better than here.

Within bertsolaritza there is also reflection on the people's emigration. This form of verse improvisation echoes the concerns of the Basque people and the events in their lives. The bertsolari is a voice for the people.[5]

I will not try to analyze the nature of this artistic phenomenon here; I will simply describe it in terms of its role as a medium for transmitting the theme of Basque emigration. Nor will I attempt to analyze the types of melodies, rhythms, rhymes, and improvisation that constitute the essence of Basque troubadourism. Instead, I will try to shed some light on how Basque troubadours have mirrored this centripetal and centrifugal force, a combination of attachment to the homeland and desire to seek one's fortune outside the Basque Country.

In order to do this, I will first discuss the professional bertsolariak who were in the Americas and whose art reflected the world of the diaspora: Pello Otaño (or Pedro María Otaño in Spanish); José Elizegi, alias "Pello Errota"; Fernando Aire, alias "Xalbador"; and Iparragirre. Second, I will analyze the verses of nonprofessional bertsolariak. Although the artistic quality of their work does not meet the same standards as that of the first group, analyzing their work will serve our objectives by opening new doors in the interpretation of the Basque diaspora.

PELLO OTAÑO (1857-1910)

We may refer to Pello Otaño as *the great bertsolari* of Basque emigration. He was born in the little Gipuzkoan village of Zizurkil and later moved to Donostia. He dedicated some of his best verses to that city, the capital of Gipuzkoa. In 1875, while he was still very young, he sailed from the port of Pasaia and went off to be a sheepherder in Argentina. Fortune must not have smiled on him, for in 1889 he returned to Donostia, where he married and had three children. Twice more he returned to the pampas to seek his fortune and settled in the city of Rosario (Santa Fe). There he and his wife had three more children.

He worked hard at sheepherding and occasionally taught Basque language at Laurak Bat, the Basque center of Buenos Aires. He also wrote the lyrics to an opera entitled *Artzai mutilla* (The shepherd) set in 1900 in the capital of Argentina. He slipped on the stairs of his house in 1910 and died at the age of fifty-three. He never achieved his fondest dream, to have his bones laid to rest in the shade of the walnut tree on the family farm in the Basque Country:

> Bañan joan nai det ostera,
> Euskal-lurreko zuaizpe artan
> Nere ezurrak uztera.[6]

> But I want to return once more to die beneath my tree in the Basque Country.

Before leaving for Argentina the first time, Otaño composed the famous verses "Aita-semeak" (Father and son) in strophes using the *hamarreko txikia* meter (ten lines of seven and six syllables alternating). In six strophes he relates the departure of a son leaving for America. His Christian father gives the young man last-minute advice at the foot of a cross. These verses are famous for their depth of feeling and are still sung today in the Basque Country:

> Lagundurikan denoi
> gugatik il zanak . . .
> Orain gurutze onen
> oñean esanak
> ondo goguan artu
> biaituzu danak.[7]

> Counting on the help of He who died for us . . . Remember well what I am about to tell you at the foot of this cross.

The father begs his son always to remember his family, the place where he was born, Euskara, and the Christian religion that he learned at home:

Seme izan goguan
Zeure gurasuak
Eta uzten dituzun
Senide gozuak;
Jayo ziñan tokiko
Mendi ta basuak,
Euskerazko otoitzak
Edo errezuak,
Erakutsiak zure
Amatxo gaxuak.[8]

Son, remember your parents and the beloved relatives you
leave behind, remember the place where you were born, its
mountains and forests, and the prayers in Basque that your
beloved mother taught you.

In the last strophe the father sums up his message in a single word: *eus-kalduna*. He pleads with his son not to forget what he heard at the moment
of farewell—always be Basque no matter where you are:

Iritxi da ordua
Joan bear dezuna
Badakizu ait-amak
Emen dauzkatzuna;
Ez dezazula aztu
gaur neri entzuna.
Itz baterako au da
Eskatzen zaizuna:
izan zaitez nonnai ta
Beti euskalduna.[9]

The time has come for you to leave, you know your parents
will be here; do not forget what you heard from me today. In
a word, this is what I am asking you: always be Basque no
matter where you are.

Otaño had a great desire to see new lands, but when he arrived in Argentina he had to settle for a little corner of the New World, a sheep ranch.
From a remote, treeless piece of the pampas he wrote the following nos-
talgic lines, expressing his *herrimin* (homesickness). Next to his shepherd's
hut there was a solitary ombu tree (the national tree of Argentina), the sight
of which reminded him of the walnut tree on his family farm and the woods
where he spent his youth. That ombu tree was his oasis. He personified it,
treating it as his best friend. He promised always to remember it but wanted
to return home to the Basque Country to rest eternally under the shade of
the tree on his family farm:

Euskal-Erriko lur maite artan
Jayo nintzan baserrian,
itzal aundiko intxaur arbol bat
dago gure atarian . . .
Denak utzi ta etorri nintzan
Lur au ikusi nai nuan! . . .
Oraiñ artzantzan Ameriketan
Arrantxo baten onduan,
eguna igaro larrian eta
jiratzen naizen orduan,
nere begiak gozatzen dira
Aldameneko ombu'an.

Txabol ondoko ombu laztana
maitatzen zaitut gogotik
eta biotza erdibitzen zait
nere burura ekartzen dezun
oroimen gozuagatik.
Zure itxura nai det ikusi
ez dizut eskatzen frutik
ni emen bizi naizen artean
Arren! Egon zaite zutik!

Nere lagunik maitatuena
ombu laztana, zu zera,
argatik nator zure kolkora,
ni malkuak isurtzera
iduriturik naramazula
atariko intxaurpera . . .
Beti izango zaitut goguan
bañan joan nai det ostera,
Euskal-lurreko zuaizpe artan
nere ezurrak uztera.[10]

In a place in the Basque Country on the farm where I was born there is a walnut tree that stands next to the door of the house and gives wonderful shade.

I came here, leaving everything behind, because I wanted to see this land! Now I find myself in America working as a shepherd on a ranch. When I return home after a hard day at work, I rest my eyes on the ombu tree that grows nearby.

Beloved tree near my hut, I love you with all my heart, and that heart is torn by the sweet memories that you evoke in me. I want to keep looking at you. I will ask no fruit of you while I live here. Please, remain standing!

You, my beloved ombu, are my best friend; that is why I come to you to shed my tears, thinking that you will carry me back to the tree by the door of my farmhouse . . . I will always remember you, but I want to return once more, to die beneath my tree in the Basque Country.

In 1889, at the age of thirty-two, Otaño was living in Rosario. His years in Argentina had not dimmed his memories of his beloved Basque Country. He corresponded with his relatives, especially with his uncle José Bernardo. Since they were both bertsolariak, their letters were always written in verse. In some of those verses, entitled "Ameriketatik osaba Jose Bernardori bialduak" (Verses sent to Uncle José Bernardo from America), Otaño sings about the beauty of Donostia while expressing the nostalgia caused by living far from the Basque Country:

Milla zortzireun larogei eta
bederatzi da aurten
orra ogeita amabi urtek
nola arrapatu nauten . . .
Errosario Santa Fen . . .

Gu geienian gabiltza emen
esna ere ametsetan
beti pentzatzen berongan eta
Euskalerriko gauzetan
askok dionez bizi gerade
txit toki aberatsetan
bañan ez dago Donostiarik
gure lurrian bestetan.

Ameriketan ikusten ditut
zenbait euskaldun "andare"
bizi diranak beren lurrari
aitormenik eman gabe
bañan ez dute ezagutzen
oiek barkatuak daude
Nik Donostia eskatuko det
paraisora joan ta ere.[11]

The year is 1889 and look how these thirty-two years have found me, in the city of Rosario, Santa Fe.

Often we walk around here as if in a dream, even though we are awake, thinking about you and the Basque Country; according to many, we live in a precious place, but a city like Donostia is found only in our country.

In America I live with many "pretend" Basques who go through life without giving their homeland a second thought, but they are excused because they do not know her. I will always choose Donostia, even when headed for Paradise.

Otaño left the Basque Country after witnessing the tragic outcome of the Second Carlist War. He experienced firsthand the frustration caused by the definitive loss of the *fueros*. He was saddened both by the oppression of his country and by the regression of the Basque language. For that reason, he tried in his poetry to urge native speakers living in the Basque Country to preserve the Basque traditions. Using simple similes like the bandanna, scissors, and a tree and its branches, Otaño describes in emotional verses the reality of a nation divided by a river and a border:

Oialtzat artu zagun euskera
goraizitzat Bidasoa
ibai koskor bat besterik
ez da utsa balitz itsasoa
elkarren urbil daude zazpiak
muga deitzen da pausoa
zergatik izan bear eztegu
famili bakar osoa.

Arbola baten sainetatikan
sortzen diran landariak
bezela gera Bidasoaren
bi aldetako jendiak
Berdiñak dira gure jatorri
oiturak eta legiak
ama euskerak magal berian
asitako senidiak.

Ama euskera bere semiak
gu Ameriketan zenbat
arkitzen geran ta urrutitik
maitiago degu an bat
emen ez dago Bidasoarik
ta beste trabikan ainbat
ama maitia indartu dedin
bizi bedi zazpiak bat.[12]

Let us take the Basque language for a bandanna and the Bidasoa River for a pair of scissors; it would be no more than a stream if the sea were empty; the seven provinces lie next to each other, the pass is called a border, there is no reason why we cannot form a single, united family.

All of us on both sides of the Bidasoa are like new shoots born on the branches of the same tree. We have the same origin, the same customs and laws; we are brothers that our mother, the Basque language, has nursed at the same breast.

Mother Basque, some of your children are here in America. Even though we are far away, we love the one we are far from even more. Here there is no Bidasoa to divide us, nor so many difficulties; may the seven provinces live on so that our dear mother will regain her health.

Unamuno's aversion to the language of his ancestors is well known. In his day, he was rejected by Arana y Goiri, Lizardi, Aitzol, Lauaxeta, and Pedro Basaldua. Otaño, a defender of the Basque language and a fervent Basque nationalist, also rejected Unamuno, the philosopher from Bilbo:

Esaera zarra da
inoiz jakintsuak
egin oi dituztela
txit gauza txatxuak,
zailak dira bildutzen
ondra ta protxuak,
nola ez du pentsatu
au gure maixuak?

Guk nai diogulako
euskarari fidel,
zuk ipintzen diguzu
bekoskua goibel
asko dakizularik
gaizki zaude Migel
ezin biurtu leike
amorrairik igel.

Ezagun da erritik
urruti zaudena.
Ezta gaitza euskaldunak
eskatzen dutena
baizik izan dedilla
ongi mundu dena
ta utzi deigutela
ostu zigutena.

Bilbao'tik irten da
Salamanka'raño
Noraño joan zerade
zu, Migel, noraño?
Gu etorriagatik
beste munduraño,
uste det alderago
gaudela zu baño.[13]

There is an old refrain that says that at times wise men do absurd things. It is very difficult to combine honor and profit. How can it be that our teacher has not thought of that?

Because we are loyal to the Basque language, you frown at us. You think you know a lot, but you are mistaken, Miguel; the trout cannot turn into a frog.

It is well known that you live far from your country. The Basques are not asking for anything bad. They want the whole world to be well, and they want what was taken from them returned.

You left Bilbo and you went to Salamanca. How far have you gone, Miguel, how far? Even though we have come to another continent, I believe that we are closer [to the Basque Country] than you are.

JOSÉ ELIZEGI, ALIAS "PELLO ERROTA" (1840-1919)

Another great nineteenth-century Basque bard to cross the Atlantic was Pello Errota. The miller from Asteasu, Gipuzkoa, was a completely different type of bertsolari than Otaño. Pello Errota can be placed in the same category with such great improvisers as Juan F. Petrirena, alias "Xenpelar" (1835-1869), and Joxe Manuel Lujanbio, alias "Txirrita" (1860-1936). The three of them belonged to a group of bertsolariak who received no scholarly training. They did not know how to write. They were noteworthy for their capacity for improvisation and their barbed humor.

In 1895 the Basques living in Argentina issued an invitation to Pello Errota. From the news that he sent to his family, we know that the boat on which he traveled made a stop in Dakar. We also know that in Buenos Aires he lodged at the Fonda de Buena Sopa. He was greatly surprised by the length of Buen Orden Street in Buenos Aires, especially in comparison with the streets of his own village.

What surprised him even more was the religious indifference of the Basques in Argentina. Although there were many churches and convents in Buenos Aires, the Basques did not attend Mass. Furthermore, they mocked him when he went to church and considered him crazy for doing so. Pello Errota reflected this climate in several bertsoak (verses) that he sent to his relatives, and he promised them that he would continue to practice his religion:

Ikusitzen banaute
sartutzen elizan
atzetikan burlaka
txoratu al naizan,
nik berdin korritzen det,
lenagoko gisan
baita segituko're
ez bildurrik izan.

Oi t'amairu urte ontan
konfesatu gabiak
Pellok ikusi ditu
atso ta aguriak,
zer ikasiko dute
aien landariak?
erremedi ditzala
guztion Jabiak.[14]

If they see me enter a church, they laugh behind my back and
ask me if I've gone crazy; I continue practicing in the old way
and will continue to do so, don't worry.

Pello saw women and men who had not confessed in thirty-
two years; what would their children learn from them? May
God remedy this situation.

Pello Errota spent ten months in Argentina. In 1895 his Basque friends
held a banquet and presented him with a gold watch to honor his skill as
a bertsolari. But the little miller did not like the atmosphere there and returned to his native village in 1896.

Other problems related to the Basque diaspora waited for him in the
Basque Country. He was usually asked to compose verses about family
problems or specific events, such as the wedding of a *mutilzarra* (bachelor).
On one occasion, he was asked to bring to account and ridicule a thieving
old man. Pello Errota's anonymous verses were posted on the door of the
house belonging to the old thief's wealthy fiancée, thereby informing the
young woman of the bad deeds of her suitor.

The event that inspired these verses occurred in Cárdenas, Cuba. A
young man from Asteasu saved 10,000 pesetas working as a servant. He
turned over half of it to his master and hid the rest. His master asked to bor-
row the 10,000 pesetas with a promise that they would be returned to him.
Papers were signed to that effect, but the servant recovered only 1,500 pesetas. His boss refused to pay the rest and disappeared from Cárdenas. Both
men returned to the Basque Country, and the servant took the opportunity
to expose his former boss with verses composed by Pello Errota:

Emen gustora ez nengoen ta
Juan nintzaden Cuba-ra
Cardenas deitzan erri eder bat
paraje aietan bada,
Amabost urte kunplitu ziran
ni juan nintzalarik ara,
esango'izuet ango diruak
egin zidaten jornara.

I did not like it here and I left for Cuba. There is a beautiful town called Cárdenas in those parts; fifteen years have passed since I went there. I'm going to tell you what happened to the money I earned there.

Milla duro nik gordeta neuzkan
B. orren etxian
estuasun bat zuela eta
aiek eskatu zizkian,
baietz agindu nion orduan
serbitu nuen tranzian,
artzeko pronto izan zan baño
buelta daduka atzian.[15]

I had a thousand duros tucked away in B's house. He asked me for them, explaining that he was having financial problems; then I promised him that I would give him the money while I was a servant there; he took it quickly, but he did not return it to me.

FERNANDO AIRE, ALIAS "XALBADOR" (1920-1976)

This unfavorable impression of everyday life for the Basques in America was in dramatic contrast to the positive impression Xalbador formed on his trip to the United States. Xalbador was without a doubt the best bertsolari from Iparralde, and one of the best in the history of bertsolaritza.

He was born in Urepel, Nafarroa Beherea, and was a shepherd for many years. His son Mixel is also a shepherd and spent several years in Los Banos, California.[16] Xalbador visited his son when he was living in the western United States.

In *Odolaren mintzoa* (The language of the blood) he tells us about his trip to America in twenty verses, "Ameriketako itzulia" (The trip to America). He relates his joy on deplaning at the Los Angeles airport in "Xori ori ez baita Jainkoaren obra" (Because that bird is not one of God's creatures). After listing his relatives in the tenth verse, he cites all the places he visited (Chino, California; Idaho; and San Francisco, California).

Xalbador was very favorably impressed, especially by the atmosphere that he encountered in the different Basque communities and in the Basque centers. Hearing Basque spoken by so many of his émigré compatriots was to a great extent the cause of his happiness. The impression he received contrasted sharply with the sad experience in so many town squares in the Basque Country, where Euskara was no longer heard. Xalbador felt that this example was something Basque Americans could offer many Basques in the Old Country. He thought that there might come a day when, in order to maintain the Basque identity, it would become necessary to go to America:

> Hau ere erran gabe ez nitaike pasa,
> hango biltokietan ikusten den gauza:
> garbi agertzen da han euskaldun arraza,
> denak gure herriko kantu eta dantza,
> gaur ez da hain euskaldun gure aunitz plaza.

> I cannot go on without mentioning something that is seen in the Basque centers in America: the Basque race is clearly seen there, everyone united by our songs and our dances; so many Basques are not visible today in our own town squares.

> Han argia ikusi euskaldun haur asko
> entzun ditut euskaraz gu bezala mintzo,
> berexkuntzarik gabe neska ta mutiko,
> amodio dutenak herri hunendako.
> A zer erakaspena hemengoendako!

> There I observed many Basque children speaking like us in Basque, girls and boys alike, who love the Basque Country. What a lesson for the Basques from here!

> Gauza hortaz egin dut aunitz pentsamendu
> Gure erri maitean zer ikusten dugu?
> Gureak diren gauzak ditugu higuindu:
> beldur naiz "izaite" hau nahi bada zaindu,
> guk ere behar dugun herritik urrundu.

> I have thought a lot about this problem. What do we see in our beloved country? We have scorned that which is ours; I fear that in order to preserve our identity, we also will be obliged to leave the Basque Country.

> Utzi dut Amerika, eremu haundia,
> orai etxe xokoan ai zer gozaldia!
> Lehen ere aldi bat ninzan ibilia;

nola jartzera noan urtez estalia,
beldur naiz hau nuela azken itzulia.[17]

I have left the vast American continent and find myself at
home. What a delight! I have also traveled once before; I fear
that this trip will be my last, because I am growing old.

Xalbador foresaw his death as he wrote those last lines, for he was already
ill. While all the Basque Country was paying homage to him in Urepel on
November 7, 1976, he passed away, moments after hearing the final chords
of "Gernika'ko arbola" (The tree of Gernika) for the last time.

JOSÉ MARÍA IPARRAGIRRE
(1820-1881)

Iparragirre was not just a bertsolari; rather, he was
a mixture of bard, singer, and musician. Nevertheless, we can include him
in this list of professional bertsolariak who were in America and whose
work reflected the world of the diaspora.

Few have sung about the return of the *indiano* (a Basque who migrated to
America and usually returned rich) to his native land with as much feeling
as Iparragirre has. His sentiments focus on three types of love: love of one's
mother; love of one's wife; and love for the Basque Country and its liberties.
The nostalgia he felt for the Basque Country after wandering throughout
Europe and America for several years inspired his tendency toward romantic emotion. In his work we perceive a kind of folkloric world view in
which a love for the Basque countryside, customs, and history prevails. Iparragirre's life was a living history of intermittent loneliness where the word
agur (good-bye) played a decisive role, as we see from some typical lines
of verse, for example, from "Agur Euskalerria'ri" (Farewell to the Basque
Country) and "Agur, nere biotzeko amatxo maitea" (Good-bye to my beloved mother).

Iparragirre's works also reflect the vicissitudes of Basques during the
nineteenth century in Europe and in America. In 1834 he enlisted with
the Carlist troops. At the end of the First Carlist War he fled to France, after
the treason of Bergara (a peace treaty sealed by the embrace between General Espartero, a Liberal, and the Carlist general Maroto). In 1848 he sang
the "Marseillaise" in Paris and was applauded with patriotic fervor. In 1853
in Madrid he sang "Gernika'ko arbola" as well. Because of the political
situation at that time, Spain was not ready to accept the message of uni-
versality and liberty expressed in the Basque hymn, and Iparragirre was
imprisoned: "Giltzapean sartu naute" (They put me in jail).

After traveling with his guitar through France, Portugal, Italy, and En-
gland, in 1858 Iparragirre decided to go to Argentina. In Buenos Aires he

married a young Basque girl, Angela Kerexeta, who had embarked with him at Bayonne in 1858. Although they had met in Tolosa, Iparragirre did not want to get married in the Basque Country "because the priests had asked for a lot of paperwork to marry us."[18] Angela was seventeen years old and Iparragirre was thirty-eight. The wedding took place on February 26, 1859, before the Basque priest Francisco Javier Lardizabal.

Iparragirre went from Argentina to Uruguay, where he planned to herd sheep. But his understanding of ownership and liberty was such that, when the sheep got lost and did not return to the corral, he did not go after them but just said, "They, too, love liberty, and I want even the sheep to have fueros."[19] He would stay in camp and pass the hours sitting on the grass and creating verses.

Iparragirre spoke three languages—Basque, Spanish, and French—but he wrote only in Basque. He also spoke Basque with his wife. One of his greatest compositions as a bertsolari is "Ezkongaietan" (During the engagement), in which he expresses a dual reality: the chimera and dreams of youth contrasted with the reality of everyday life:

> Ezkongaietan zerbait banintzan
> ezkondu eta ezer ez:
> eder zalia banintzan ere
> aspertu nintzan ederrez,
> nere gustua egin nuen da
> orain bizi naiz dolorez.[20]

> When I was courting I was something, but after getting married, I'm nothing; even though I loved beauty, I grew bored with beautiful things, I did what I pleased, and now I live in pain.

When Iparragirre received news of the loss of the fueros in 1876, he spent days pining and weeping. In 1877 he was in constant yearning for the Basque Country and obsessed with the desire to return there. He left his wife and eight children and returned to Euskal Herria, thanks to money collected for his trip by friends from the Laurak Bat Basque Center in Buenos Aires. When he arrived in the Basque Country he composed the following lines, which have been transformed into a song that still moves many Basques who return from America:

> Ara nun diran mendi maiteak,
> ara nun diran zelaiak,
> baserri eder zuri-zuriak,
> iturri eta ibaiak . . .

> O! Euskal-Erri eder maitea,
> ara emen zure semea,
> bere lurrari mun egitera
> beste gabe etorria,

Zuregatikan emango nuke
pozik, bai, nere bizia;
beti zuretzat, il arteraño,
gorputz ta arima guztia.[21]

There are the beloved mountains, there are the meadows, the
white farmhouses, the fountains and the streams . . . Oh, beloved Basque Country! Here is your son, who has come for
no reason other than to kiss the land. For you my life I would
happily give; I am yours body and soul until death.

Iparragirre also created several *bertsoak* (stanzas) about the diaspora,
among them "Ameriketa-tik Urretxuko semeai" (From America to the children of Urretxu) and "Euskal-erria eta America" (The Basque Country and
America). The best known is entitled "Agur Euskal-Erria'ri" (Farewell to
the Basque Country), the first verse of which follows:

Gazte gaztetandikan
erritik kanpora
estranjeri aldean
pasa det denbora.
Erri-alde guztietan
toki onak ba-dira,
baiña biotzak dio:
"Zoaz Euskal-errira."[22]

While I was still very young, I left my country, traveling
through foreign lands most of the time. It is true that there are
beautiful places everywhere, but my heart says to me: "Go to
the Basque Country."

After returning from America Iparragirre always carried a photograph of
his family with him; however, he sent them only two or three letters. On
April 5, 1881, he died in his beloved Basque Country.

OTHER BERTSOLARIAK

None of the other nonprofessional bertsolariak at-
tained the artistic stature of Pedro Mari Otaño or Xalbador, but the stories
they tell about the diaspora are just as interesting as the messages of the
greatest Basque bards. In this brief analysis I shall discuss their ideas—
what they actually say—more than the form in which these ideas are expressed. My goal is to describe how the Basque bertsolariak view the diaspora as they sing about their travels, work, wages, problems, and homesickness.

Juan José Alkain, Alias "Udarregi" (1829-1885)

Among those bertsolariak who are considered "classic" is the bard from Usurbil, Gipuzkoa—Udarregi. A thousand anecdotes are told about his prodigious capacity to improvise verses and about his memory.[23] It was his father, however, who went off to Buenos Aires, leaving his entire family in the Basque Country. His father was sixty years old at the time, so we have to marvel at his pluck. His business must not have gone well, because he spent what little money he had and was forced to return home. He died in his native village of Usurbil in 1883 at the age of ninety.

Very little is known about the capacity of Udarregi's father to improvise verses, but the few strophes that remain of the son's work are related to the Basque diaspora. In them, the bard of Usurbil describes his distressing situation:

> Sei arrua ta erdi banintzan,
> Orain jetxi naiz bostera,
> au da munduko diferentzia
> egun batetik bestera;
> sosik baneuka Euskalerri'ra
> joango nintzake ostera,
> zer estadutan arkitzen naizen
> korputza erakustera . . .
> familia daukat urruti,
> andriak ez nau erruki,
> izurratu nau ederki![24]

If I once weighed 162 pounds, I am now down to 125; there is a world of difference in me from one day to the next; if I had some money I would return to the Basque Country, to show them the physical state I am in . . . My family is far away, my wife has no pity on me, she really did it to me!

Jean Etcharren

Another old bertsolari associated with Basque emigration is Jean Etcharren, a native of Irulegi, Navarre. In 1901 he embarked for the Americas from the port of Santander. First he arrived in Cuba, then he moved on to Mexico and finally to California.

He describes his travels in his verses, mentioning such things as his failure to receive a warm welcome from the black women in Havana. He sought his fortune in Mexico but still had little luck, and he left for San Francisco in the company of Basque friends. He also mentions his life as a sheepherder in California:

Ni Habanako irian . . .
Andre beltz heyek zalapartaka
Ihes ene aintzinian . . .
Itzuli nintzan ordian
Ahalgeturik bidian.

Handik gero itsasora . . .
Juaiteko Mejikora . . .
Yin zitzautan gogora
Juaiteko San Franziskora
Eskualdun maiten ondora.

Artzain naiz Californian
Bakarrik bortu gainian.[25]

In the city of Havana with those noisy black women who fled
before me . . . Unable to do anything else I chose a new path.

From there I traveled by sea to Mexico. . . . I got an urge to go
to San Francisco, where my dear Basque friends were going.

I am a sheepherder in California, alone in the mountains.

Nicolás Lujanbio (1877-1958)

America caught the attention of Basques in the
nineteenth century. The two Carlist Wars further weakened the economic
status of the Basque farms, but fortune smiled on many in the United States.
Furthermore, almost everyone had a relative waiting across the Atlantic.
Such was the case with the bertsolari Nicolás Lujanbio, who had seven
cousins in Buenos Aires. As soon as his military service was completed, he
sailed for Argentina. Many young Basques were lured by the siren song of
living the good life and getting by without much work. Lujanbio gives us
some details of his voyage:

Ameriketan iñork dionez
bada amaika leku on,
eta ara buelta bat egin gabe
iñola ezin naiz egon.

Burdeos'tikan martxatu giñan
bapore "Cordillerian"
Argentina'ko Buenos Aires'en
ateratzeko idian;
galdu etsiyak ibilli giñan
Dakar aldeko parian,
itxaso dana asarretuta
etzan atsegin urian,

egun batzuek triste xamarrak
pasa ginduzen birian.[26]

Like some people say, there are many beautiful places in
America, and I cannot stay anywhere without going there.

We set sail from Bordeaux on the ship *Cordillera* expecting to
land at Buenos Aires; we wandered half lost through the region of Dakar, the sea was rough, not calm, we spent some
sad days en route.

Lujanbio also remarked on the differences in the way the women
dressed. Accustomed to the Basque woman's fashion of covering her body
completely, he was compelled to note the distinct contrast of the mini-
skirted Argentine women:

Argentina'n badabiltza
neskatxa-kuadrillak,
tontuak engañatzen
bastante abillak;
soñeko motzak eta
bistan pantorrillak,
petxuaren gañian
oien lore-pillak! . . .
eroturik dabiltza
oiekin mutillak.[27]

In Argentina there are groups of girls who are quite capable
of fooling silly boys; dressing in short skirts and showing
their calves, bunches of flowers adorning their breasts . . . the
boys go crazy over them.

Nevada's Bertsolariak

This *dolce vita* contrasts sharply with the hard life
that other Basques led in the desert hills of Nevada. The difficulty of the
sheepherder's job and his way of life—the loneliness, cold, snow, rain, and
the kind of food he ate—were described in bertsoak written by a sheepherder in 1911. This anonymous bertsolari wrote his verses as a warning to
other potential sheepherders from the Basque Country:

Personian sonbria
illian birritan
ikusiko bagendu
gagoz gu pentsetan.

We yearn to see even a human shadow twice a month.

Ogei urte orain dira
ni jaio nintzala,
gaztia izan arren
eginda neu zarra;
gorputzian badaukat
ulia ta bizarra
berbetan aztutia
izango da txarra.

I was born twenty years ago, but in spite of my tender age I
look like an old man, my hair goes uncut and I am unshaven,
but the worst of it is that I forget how to talk.

Uda partia bada
arbola tartian
Koltxilla bat botata
lo lurren ganian,
izarra tellatutzat,
edurre danian,
pastoriak egon biar du
olango lanian.

In the summertime he sleeps among the trees, on a blanket
spread on the ground, with the stars for his ceiling; even
when it snows, this is how the sheepherder lives while doing
this job.

Otsua eta gukarra
alkate basauntza,
eta alboko arbolan
santzoka gabontza;
pastore gizajuak
lurrian lo otza,
esan lei nai duela
eman eriotza.

There are wolves and predators, large bucks, and in a nearby
tree a night owl hoots; the poor sheepherder sleeps on the
cold ground; he might prefer to die.

Indarra ta arroza,
zentenia ogi,
orixe izaten da
bai gure janari[28]

Our food consisted of beans, rice, and rye bread.

Sheepherding in the mountains of Nevada was left, for the most part,
to Basques. Many bertsoak were written by these Basque sheepherders.

Sometimes old sheepherders advised the new ones and told how they suffered from their solitude. For example, we have Pablo Yanzi, a sheepherding bertsolari who sent the following verses to his nephew, who was also sheepherding in Nevada:

Kalamidade oiek lenago
dauzkat neunek pasatuak

I myself suffered these calamities long before you

Udan lan arraxa izanikan
neguan beti nekia,
artzaiak izaten du mendiyan
ibilli biar aundiya;
askotan elurra azpiyan eta
gañetik berriz uriya,
barrena auleriyak artua,
bizkarra berriz buztiya,
ara nolakua den artzai
gizajo oriyen bizia.

In the summer the work is easy, but in the winter, it is hard; the sheepherder must walk a lot in the mountains, often with snow on the ground and rain coming down; he is weak on the inside and his back is wet; this was the lot of these poor sheepherders.

Ezagutzen det nolakua den
Amerika'ko Nortia,
orko oiturak artu bitarte
naiko paraje torpia;
bañan gaztiak or lana egiñez
irabazten du dotia,
gero kate gorri bat zintzilik,
ezpañetan bigotia,
patrikan txeke aundi batekin
Europa aldera trotia.[29]

I know how it is in the northern part of America; it's an inhospitable place until you get used to it; but by working there, a young man earns money so he can return quickly to Europe with a gold chain, a big mustache, and a big check in his pocket.

The nephew replied by sending verses to Pablo Yanzi declaring that the sheepherder's sacrifices were rewarded economically, because in sheepherding one lacked neither meat nor money. He went on to wish that everyone in Spain lived like those in America:

Egia da orko oroipena
ez dala anztutzen errez,
bañan zartzarako ari gera
patrikak betetzen urrez.

It is true that it is not easy to forget one's memories of that
place, but we are growing rich for our old age.

Egia da ibiltzen gerala
ondo bustirik bizkarrak,
artzaiak mendian izaten ditu
onak bezelaxen txarrak;
neguko elurrak kentzen ditu
udaetako sukarrak,
ok ta geiago izaten ditu
artzaiak igaro biarrak,
bañan guztiak anztutzen ditu
emengo okelan indarrak.

It's true that our backs are often wet; the sheepherder must
spend both good and bad moments in the mountains. The
winter snow chases away the summer heat; the sheepherder
must endure this and much more, but the good meat in this
place makes you forget everything.

Zakurrak ere gizen dauzkagu
gere sobriak emanta,
ez degu oinbeste jan biarko
geren errira juanta.

Even our dogs grow fat on our leftovers; we would not have
as much food if we returned to our villages.

Gere bizitzaz ez dadukagu
ezer esanik batere,
egunaz lana, gabaz lo egiñ
ondo jan ta edanak gaude . . .
obe lukete Europa'n denak
modu onetan baleude.

We complain about the conditions of our life; we work in the
daytime and sleep in the nighttime, we eat and drink well . . .
I wish all those in Europe lived this way.

Ogi zuria, zato ardua,
okela beti eltzian . . .
otaz gañera urre gorriak
lanan saria artzian.[30]

We never lack white bread, or wine in a goatskin bag, or meat in the pot . . . what's more, we earn gold for our work.

Not everyone was as happy as young Pablo Yanzi in the mountains of Nevada. The sheepherder's way of life was quite different in Nevada and California. David Aranburu, born in Lesaka, Navarre, in 1928, wrote the following lines in a letter to friends in California. Aranburu felt the need of a woman:

> Enteratu nauk ondo
> bizi zeratela
> jan-eran ederrakin,
> nekerik eztela;
> neskatxakin gozatuaz
> nai zuten bezela . . .

I know that you live well, eating and drinking well with no problems, enjoying young girls whenever you wish . . .

> Gu emen gabiltza geure
> onetik aterik
> illabetiak neska bat
> ikusi gaberik;
> nik eztiat agontzen al
> denbora luzerik,
> gañera au osasunak
> gonbeni ote dik?
> gutxiago irabaziaz
> neskakin obe dik.[31]

Here we run around half crazy without seeing a girl for a month at a time. I can't bear much time without them, and what's more, is it good for one's health to be without them? It's better to earn less money and be able to be with girls.

Several Basque-sheepherding bertsolariak were known by the name "Nevada Sheepherder." Some were from Bizkaia, others from Navarre, some from Nafarroa Beherea. Every one of them reflects on the state of his spirit, although, occasionally, their experiences are very different. The first lines by a "Nevada Sheepherder" appear in the second volume of Santiago Onaindia's *Milla euskal-olerki eder* (A thousand beautiful Basque poems, 1954). From the language he used, it seems that he was probably from around Baigorri. In every case, the sad sheepherder expresses his desire to someday return to the Basque Country:

> Hemeretzi ehun-ta berrogei ta zortzian
> Sor-lekua utzi dut adin ederrian.
> Orain emen naiz bizi Nevada-mendian,

Gogoa illun eta penak biotzian,
Desertuetan artzain bakartasunian.[32]

In 1948 I left my country while still a young man. Now I live in the mountains of Nevada, dispirited and heavy-hearted, as a lonely sheepherder in the inhospitable desert.

This young sheepherder resented living alone. He guarded his flock day and night. He missed Sunday Mass. He found no entertainment in the Nevada mountains. And he did not want to grow old there:

Nehor ikusi gabe zazpi-zortzi egun . . .
Gau-egun oroz nago artaldea lagun.
Ez dira jostatzeko emengo lekuak . . .
Orko oroitzapenak ez tut ahantziko.
Zonbait urteño ditut emen pasatuko.
Hitz-emaiten dauziet huntaz segur nago;
Ni segurik ez naiz ez emen zahartuko.[33]

I go without seeing anyone for seven or eight days . . . I guard the flock night and day. There is nothing to do for fun in these places . . . I will not forget my memories of home. I promise you, I am sure that I will not grow old here.

As the Basque proverb says, "Urrutiko intxaurrak urrez, bertara joan ta ezer ez," which translates literally as "Distant walnuts look golden, but when you approach them they are nothing," we see repeatedly in these expressions of the Basque sheepherders' experiences in Nevada that not everyone was paid in gold and not everyone had more than enough to eat. The same was true for those in Argentina.

Argentine Bertsolariak

The following verses were composed in 1932 by Bautista Galarregi, who relates his suffering on the plains of Argentina. He made a mistake when he saw some rich indianos in the Basque Country and decided to emulate them. Sheepherders could no longer earn the kind of money they once did, and the situation was very sad for them. They had lived better in the Basque Country. Many twenty-year-old men looked like grandfathers in Argentina:

Arjentina'tik Españi'rako
nai nuke nik adierazi
ango jendia onera etorri
ta nola geraden bizi;
or pentsatzen da Amerika onek

baditula milla grazi,
etorri ezkero dirua erraz
egiten dala irabazi,
orain egiak jartzera nua
nai ditubenak ikasi.

I wanted to send a message from Argentina to Spain explaining how those of us who came here live; there you think that everything is free in America, that you can earn a lot of money here as soon as you arrive. Now I am going to tell the truth to those who wish to learn from my experience.

Milla beatzireun urte pasata
oi ta amabigarrenian . . .
zazpi urte dira pasatutxoak,
nua zortzigarrenian,
hotel batian sartu nitzala
andik etor nitzanian,
eta geroztik ementxe nago,
beti ari naiz lanian.

The year 1932 is over . . . I have spent seven years here and in my eighth year I am going to the hotel I entered when I arrived from the Basque Country; from now on I will be here working constantly.

Beste eratan bizitzen nintzan
Españi'n nengoanian . . .
Ni baño ere gaizkigo dauden
asko dira Amerika'n
erdi jantzirik, gosiak eta
dirurik gabe patrikan . . .
Emen ez dago alaitasunik,
bakarrik dago tristura.[34]

I lived much better when I was in Spain . . . There are many here in America who live worse than I, half naked, hungry, with no money in their pockets . . . There is no happiness here, only sadness.

Australian Bertsolariak

Basque immigration was not limited to the American continents; it extended all the way to Australia. It is generally believed that Basque immigration to Australia dates from the 1950s, but we have a verse from 1927 that expounds on the difficulty of the work there. Our bertsolari was a fellow from Mutriku who set sail on a French ship. The voyage was terrible, but his stay in Australia was no better because of the loneliness and hard work:

> Ortik onera pasatu ditut
> lur ta itxaso luziak,
> prantzes barkuak ekarri nindun
> irugarrengo klasian;
> gutxi jan eta padezituaz
> egarri eta gosiak,
> nunbait merezi izango nitun
> kastigu onek guztiak.

I crossed earth and ocean to come here in a French ship on which I traveled third class; little to eat, and suffering a lot from thirst and hunger, I must have deserved that punishment somehow.

> Kalabazia tomatiakin
> dirade gure janari,
> ta errekan geldi daguan
> ura gañetik edari.

Our food was reduced to squash and tomatoes, and we drank the stagnant river water.

> Ondo kostia da emen orain
> irabazten dan dirua,
> egun luzia lanerako ta
> beti eguzki berua;
> lendik ez nitzan listua baino
> ia galdu zait burua,
> txerriari ere ez diot opa
> olako bizi-modua.[35]

The money I'm earning now has cost me a lot, working all day in the full sun; before, I was not smart, and now I am going out of my mind; I wouldn't wish this life on a pig.

U.S. Bertsolariak

Many of the Basque men who contracted out as sheepherders were simple peasants with no experience in the field. Most people in the United States think that the majority of Basques are shepherds, but in reality less than 1 percent of the Basque Country's inhabitants herd sheep. Among the inexperienced herders, a few, such as the fellow from the treeless fields of Urbia near Arantzazu, Gipuzkoa, related their experiences in verse.

In Oregon in 1965 the following sheepherder wrote verses in which he remembered the Virgin of Arantzazu and sang and spoke in Basque with other herders about the problems they had with predators:

Piztirik txarrenak artzak
eta Koioteak
gauetan ezin utzi
zabalik ateak,
eta sarritan egiten
diguten kalteak;
tiro batzuek tirata
egin bear pakeak.[36]

The worst animals are the bears and the coyotes. We cannot leave the doors open during the night because of the damage they often do; we must shoot at them to keep them from panicking the flock.

The verses of these Basque sheepherders echoed throughout the Basque Country. Sometimes from the pages of the magazine *Aránzazu* they encouraged people to remain true to Basque ethnicity. Occasionally, there were verses by professional bertsolariak, such as Manuel Lasarte, a great versifier famous for the quality of his rhymes. He composed verses describing the departure of a son going off to America:

Len ere Amerikan
badira euskaldunak,
zu zuazen bezela
artzantzara junak;
emen gelditzen gera
maite zaitugunak,
zugatik alegiñak
egin ditugunak.[37]

There are other Basques who have gone to America as sheepherders, as you are doing now; we who love you stay behind, we who have done all we can for you.

In conclusion, I should clarify that the cases of Basque emigration presented here exemplify but a fraction of the flood of Basques who immigrated to different continents. These immigrants are modern versions of those brave sailors who accompanied Christopher Columbus on his first voyage or who crossed the seas in search of whales. Basques carry a sense of adventure in their veins and have always sought out work and danger. They belong to an ethnic group that was among the first to populate the North and South American continents. In fact, several Latin American cities and capitals were founded by Basques. Even when performing the most difficult tasks, such as sheepherding and sugarcane cutting, the Basques earned a reputation for being hardworking and diligent. As an echo of public events, bertsolaritza reflected and recorded deeds performed by a small nation whose slogan is "Eman da zabal zazu, munduan frutua" (Give and extend your fruits throughout the world).

CHAPTER THREE

Pastorales

The Basque nation possesses a rich oral tradition. As evidence of this, we can point to the bertsolariak; the *ihauteriak* (carnivals), the *xaribariak,* or burlesque farces; and the *pastorales,* or popular theater that incorporates verse, music, and dance. Of all the types of rural theater that were in vogue in France toward the end of the fifteenth century, only the Basque pastorale has survived.

The Basque pastorale is a story taken from life and told in versified dialogue. It probably had its origins in medieval mystery plays and is performed in the open air during the summer in the province of Zuberoa.[1]

Historically speaking, Basque written literature is quite young, and until the end of the nineteenth century it was dominated by religious themes and writers. As a consequence, Basque theater would be a meager genre indeed were we not to take the pastorales into account. According to some critics, such as Georges Hérelle, the pastorale, which he thought would not survive the erosion of time, has ceased to be a phenomenon exclusive to one province and has become a form of national Basque theater.[2] It is the most spectacular and well-attended type of artistic performance in Zuberoa, and, as a result of a series of innovations to be discussed shortly, it has been revived without the loss of its essential characteristics.

In this chapter I will describe the essence and qualities of the pastorale, analyze its development in general, and conclude with a section on both its history and its future.

CHARACTERISTICS

The Basque pastorales, especially the old ones, cannot be compared with classical theater because the integrity of their action, time, and place are not maintained, and because traditionally there were no divisions into acts or scenes. Such structure was introduced only at the beginning of the twentieth century. The verses of the pastorale are always sung, never recited. Also, dichotomy is an essential element, since the characters always represent the struggle between good and evil. The simple staging uses a single set.

The technique used in pastorales is similar to that of the *misterios* in that the action is continuous rather than divided into acts and scenes. Within only a few scenes we witness the birth, life, and death of a character. Furthermore, the absence of props allows the stage to become a bucolic countryside, a battlefield, or a palace, depending on the action.

Bipolarization of the stage is also a source of simplification. The protagonists all enter by a door on one side of the stage, and the antagonists use a door on the other. The characters never represent a particular being or behavior; that is, there are no character studies, as there are in classical and modern theater. The attitudes of the characters are rigid and their movements abrupt. There is an evident Manichaean division among them.

Poetry

The majority of the old pastorales do not have a single identifiable author but were written by anonymous groups of writers. The language used was generally the Zuberoan dialect, although many words are borrowed from French.

The style of the pastorale can seem dry and monotonous because of its verse type and assonant rhyme. With the exception of the two modern pastorales by Junes Casenave (b. 1924),[3] the plays are written in verses of four lines each with no set rhythm and employ assonant rhyme in the even-numbered lines. This form of writing reflects the Zuberoan literary tradition's scarcity of rich consonantal rhyme in popular poetry.[4] Furthermore, this type of poetry was composed to be sung, not recited.

Music

Music constitutes an essential part of the spectacle of the pastorale. Song, of course, is necessary to the delivery of the lines, but instrumental music provides rhythm for the dances and battles as well as for fillers between the dances.

The majority of the melodies were drawn from old songs and are quite somber in tone. Some are French marches. Others lend themselves to choral arrangement thanks to the occurrence of frequent caesuras that permit the singers to breathe. Formerly, the only musical instruments used were the flute and the drum, but today there is greater variety, and other instruments, including the clarinet and the trombone, are employed.

Dance

Rhythmic movements and dance are essential, for in the pastorale seldom does a performer sing while standing still. Battles, in which rhythm and dance predominate, are also common. These rustic dances, symbolizing the conflict between good and evil, are a spectacle in themselves and lend color to the action.

The Participants

The *errejent* is the key man in the pastorale. His tasks are to study the manuscript in depth, recruit performers, assign each actor the role that best suits him, and direct preparations such as the construction of the stage. On the day of the performance, the errejent is always on the stage, seated at a table by the protagonists' door. From there he directs the work by means of red and blue flags used to signal the entrances of the band. In this way he controls all movement on the stage. He also serves as a prompter. In the preparation of the old pastorales, his was a key role because most of the actors could neither read nor write, and they spent long winter afternoons memorizing hundreds of lines.

The Hero

The *süjet* plays the hero. He must possess physical stamina, a good memory, a strong voice, and stage presence.

Georges Hérelle, a critic who specializes in the pastorale, divides its characters into three worlds: the divine, the satanic, and the human. In the *divine* world, neither God nor Christ appears on the stage of the pastorale. On the rare occasions when God speaks, he does so from behind the curtains. In the *satanic* world, Satan and six devils act as buffoons and dancers. These roles require much agility and dancing talent. The devils are dressed in red jackets, white pants, and red berets trimmed with small bells. Traditionally, there were two devils. One of them carried a whip and the other a hook to carry the antagonists (the Turks) off to hell.

The devils serve three functions. First, they play the role of tempter, hoping that people will fall into sin so they can carry them off to hell. Second, they serve as a diversion for the audience, which laughs at their noisy interruptions and grotesque commentaries on women and the clergy.[5] Finally, they provide the dancing that the people like so much. In fact, the audience usually enjoys the dancing and the süjet's excellent voice more than the poetry of the pastorales.

The *human* world is, by far, the most important, and it is divided into two groups: the protagonists, or "good guys" (Christians, angels, clerics, etc.), who dress in blue, and the antagonists, or "bad guys" (Turks), who wear red jackets and yellow pants. The latter wave their arms and move about quickly, while the former maintain their dignified composure at all times. The angels advance with short steps, their hands pressed together in an attitude of prayer, and the Christians always appear noble and dignified.

The Stage

In the old days, the stage was built in the public square and consisted of a wooden platform balanced on barrels. Curtains were hung at the back. Improvised seating for the audience surrounded the stage and made it easier to hear. Women sat apart from men, in keeping with the bipolarization of the pastorale. Today the stages are wider, often erected on a fronton (handball court), and microphones are employed. Seating is provided for three thousand to four thousand spectators.

The stage is built two weeks before the presentation. It usually measures eight meters in depth and ten in width (thirty by twenty-four feet). At the back of stage center there is a small bandstand, which accommodates four or five musicians. Under the bandstand is the door to be used by the chorus of angels and clerics. On the audience's left there is usually a blue door for the entrance and exit of the Christians, and on the right is the red door for the Turks and devils. This door is crowned with the figure of a little devil puppet that moves frantically when the evil characters enter the stage.

Common Characteristics

Certain characteristics are common to all pastorales. First, this is popular theater created *by* and *for* the people, especially the young; no professional actors are involved. Any young person from any little village in Zuberoa can act in a pastorale as long as he or she possesses certain qualities: the ability to speak the Basque language, a good voice, a good memory, the dedication needed for attending rehearsals, and the agility required for the dances. Today, given the problems of exodus from the region and the gradual loss of the language, young people from several villages join to create a pastorale. In the past, the youth of a single village would take charge of the event, and the task would fall to a different village every year. Thus, about every thirty years, a village was expected to produce a pastorale.

A festive atmosphere is also important to pastorales. In the past, a *munstra* (parade) would precede the play in the morning. On horseback and on foot, the actors, musicians, and leaping devils would pass through the different villages in an attempt to drum up attendance. The pastorale lasted seven hours. Today, a small parade takes place immediately before the play.

THE PLOT

Immediately after the munstra, the play begins with the *lehen pheredika* (first sermon). This prologue generally contains more than twenty-five verses and has three objectives: it greets the audience; it explains the plot, exhorts the spectators to prepare themselves, quiet down, and pay attention to what they are going to hear and to see during the following hours; and it announces the arrival of the actors in two or three verses and calls once more for the attention of the audience. A lone actor sings the entire first sermon, moving from right to left across the stage and delivering the lines in a somber, rhythmic way.

After the three acts that form the major part of the four hours of a modern pastorale, we arrive at the *azken pheredika* (end of the play). This epilogue contains three parts: it thanks the audience for paying attention and apologizes for any errors committed during the performance; it offers a short summary of the plot and expounds on the moral of the play; and, finally, it says farewell to the spectators, wishes them a good night, and admonishes them to remember the lessons learned from the pastorale. This epilogue is generally shorter than the lehen pheredika. While delivering it, the orator, accompanied by the other actors, moves upstage and downstage, toward and away from the audience.

HISTORY OF THE PASTORALES

For many centuries critics ignored this literary phenomenon because of the scarcity of written manuscripts, the difficulty of the Zuberoan dialect, the paucity of obvious literary value, and the questionable authenticity of the Basque flavor in texts sprinkled with French words.[6] It was not until the nineteenth century, an era charged with romanticism and a longing for local color, that critics began to notice the pastorales. Idealized concepts of the ancient world and of the Middle Ages caught the attention of the Romantics, who were eager for fantasy to help them escape their melancholy.

Thus, in the nineteenth century a few ethnologists, historians, and members of the literary community began to take a serious interest in the phenomenon of the Basque pastorale. Among the more notable were Wilhelm von Humboldt, J. Augustin Chaho, Francisque X. Michel, Julien Vinson, and Georges Hérelle, the last of whom was responsible for preserving the most important and most complete pastorales.

Von Humboldt gives us this reference: "The Zuberoan dialect is mixed with a frightening proportion of French words and is quite impure, but the pronunciation is more beautiful, more delicate than that of other dialects, like a flute. . . . Only in Zuberoa are genuine Basque theatrical spectacles common, called here pastorales."[7]

Chaho, a unique witness to the pastorales because he was born in Zuberoa, gives us some interesting insights into the phenomenon. His romantic, and occasionally exaggerated, version of the facts does not lessen the value of his opinion of the pastorales. He says:

> He speaks to us afterward with admiration for the pastorales that the young people compose and present in the valley of Zuberoa. Aside from a few episodes taken from the Bible, the plots of these unique theatrical works are composed of memories of the Crusades and the war against the Moors. Plot development is simple, merely reproducing (in historical order) the life of a great man or the tales of war. . . . The theater is built in the open air. The presentation begins invariably with a long prologue or recitation, the musical prosody of which brings to mind the monotonous singing of the Greek classics; the rhymed quatrains following one after the other render the dialogue monotonous. The costumes of the actors, their brilliant projection, furious gestures, and simulated battles provide a strange spectacle, incoherent but at times quite original, in which breathes the genius of the people along with their ingenuous energy and the varied contrasts that always accompany the infancy of art.[8]

These two writers, along with the others cited above, give us only a partial view of the pastorale. Later, the excellent ethnographer Hérelle made a global study of rural theater in France and Italy, including the Basque pastorales. Hérelle did not know the Basque language, which makes his efforts all the more admirable. Accompanied by an interpreter, he attended presentations given over a period of fifteen years (1899–1914) in Zuberoa. Hérelle's study represents a milestone, so much so that we speak of a time *before* and a time *after* this great historian. His efforts, described in several books, offer us the most complete study of the pastorale.

For Hérelle, the origin of the Basque pastorale goes back to the mystery plays of the Middle Ages. Contrary to those who claimed that the pastorale was introduced in the Basque Country in the eighteenth century, he maintained that it originated much earlier. Because of the distinct similarities between French *mystères* in the Middle Ages and Basque theater, and because of their antagonistic treatment of the Moors, who took Constantinople in 1453 and shortly thereafter devastated Europe, Hérelle maintained that the Basque pastorales originated at the end of the fifteenth century.

Unfortunately, he could not prove his claims, but recent discoveries confirm his contention. Among ancient documents uncovered recently, there is one of summary importance that dates to the middle of the sixteenth century—a letter from Arnauld Oihenart to a parish priest in Lapurdi. In it the title of a pastorale, *Artzain gorri* (The red shepherd), and its possible author, Juan de Etchegaray, are mentioned. This forces us to conclude that the pastorale was known in the Basque Country at least as early as the sixteenth century.

Historically speaking, it is equally evident that the true pastorale of the twentieth century began after Hérelle's time. The most important author of modern pastorales was Pierre Bordazaharre, alias "Etxahun Iruri" (1908–1979), who wrote nine pastorales beginning in 1953. His works contain three constants: There is always action; that action takes place in the Basque Country; and the principal character dies, providing the opportunity for a final dramatic scene. Etxahun Iruri's principal merit stems from the fact that he steeped himself in Basque history. Of his nine pastorales, eight are directly related to the history of the Basque Country. They deal with the lives of Etxahun Koblakari (1953), Matalas (1955), Berterretx (1956), Sancho Azkarra (1965), Txikito Kanbo (1967), Pette Bereter (1973), Ximena (1979), and Iparragirre (1980).[9] The heroes of the modern Basque pastorale are not Napoléon, popes, or kings, but simple countrymen like the revolutionary priest Matalas, who was beheaded in the time of Louis XIV, or the popular oral poets Etxahun and Iparragirre.[10] It is also significant that the French flag that used to preside over the presentations has been replaced by the *ikurriña* (Basque flag).

Junes Casenave is another modern writer of pastorales. He was born in Santa Grazi, Zuberoa; is a priest in Saint Palais, Nafarroa Beherea; and has several pastorales; *Santa Grazi* (1976), *Ibañeta* (1978), *Pette Basabürü* (1982), *Zumalakarregi* (1989), *Santa Kruz* (1992), and *San Mixel Garikoitz* (1994). The heroes of the first two works are not specific persons but represent collectivities.

Hérelle's pessimistic prediction that popular Basque theater was condemned to disappear like its cousins, the Breton and Flemish theaters, has proved false. Today there is growing interest in this kind of theater throughout the seven Basque regions. More than 8,000 people gather each year for the presentation of a new pastorale. Moreover, the phenomenon of the pastorale has evolved historically and without interruption, facilitating its continuation in Zuberoa.

Among the most notable changes, I should point out a general shift in attitude on the part of the clergy. It is very likely that the authors of the early pastorales were priests at a time when theatrical performances dealt with religious themes and were presented in church. After the French Revolution, however, the pastorale moved out of the ecclesiastical realm, and new characters were introduced, specifically Satan and the devils. Their indecent language respected neither women nor priests. It is quite possible that this was one of the reasons that, in the nineteenth century, absolution was denied those who had participated in a pastorale. Fortunately, the church's hostile attitude toward the pastorales has been changing, mostly attributable to the silent but effective work of certain clergymen like Pierre Lafitte and Junes Casenave.

We can also note a significant change concerning the participation of women in the presentation of pastorales. Until a few years ago women could not participate in pastorales with men. They had to take part in works in which all the characters were female, as in *Ximena* (1979).

Even the length of the pastorale has been modified. In the old days the pastorale used to last seven to eight hours and together with the munstra, the whole day was filled. The munstra has disappeared, except for a short parade prior to the presentation of the play. The pastorales now last no more than four hours. The modern pastorale has ably converted itself into an afternoon play.[11]

The centering of themes around Basque topics, the growing numbers of spectators, modern sound equipment, and a libretto written in Basque—with translations into Spanish and French—are all improvements that have helped the pastorale spread and have increased the understanding of this form of popular theater. The Basques see in it not only an artistic expression of popular literature but also a treasured and unique heritage that they must preserve.

CHAPTER FOUR

Bernard Detxepare — Medieval or

Renaissance Writer?

Most cultures have a special appreciation for their earliest literary works, which link the people to their historical and spiritual roots.[1] The French *Chançon de Roland* and the Spanish *Cantar del Mio Cid* are two clear examples of such works.

In the Basque Country, *Linguae vasconum primitiae,* by Detxepare, the first book published in the Basque language, has been gaining popularity, particularly in recent years. A number of Detxepare's poems have been set to music and recorded by leading Basque singers such as Pantxo ta Pello, Oskorri (Gabriel Aresti adapted some of Detxepare's poems to music for this group), and Maite Idirin. Promoters of the Basque language have adopted as their slogan Detxepare's "Heuskara, jalgi adi mundura!" (Basque language, go out into the world!).

Despite varying opinions about the merit of Detxepare's work, he is generally regarded as the founder of Basque literature. Some scholars compare his work, at least partially, to *libro del buen amor* by the Spaniard Juan Ruiz, archpriest of Hita, and see similarities between the lives and works of the two authors. Others find parallels between Detxepare and the French Renaissance writer Rabelais.[2] In this chapter I shall discuss Detxepare's work and examine the differences and similarities between him, Rabelais, and Juan Ruiz.

Most of the documents relevant to Detxepare's life were destroyed when fire struck the Parliament of Pau in 1761. His birth date, birthplace, and the date of his death are unknown. The title page of his book indicates that he was the parish priest of Saint Michel le Vieux (Eiheralarre in Basque), which lies two miles (three kilometers) from Donibane-Garazi in Nafarroa Beherea. One of Detxepare's poems tells of a stay in prison. Despite documents discovered by José M. Huarte in 1926 that give information about this period of incarceration, most of the details of the poet's life remain obscure. The fact that his book was not welcomed, perhaps because of the perceived immoral tone of some of its poems, might have contributed to the lack of information about him.[3]

It is safe to say, however, that he was born in the last quarter of the fifteenth century, probably around 1480. The correct spelling of his name is debated, since it appears in different forms in his book—Dechepare, Echaparere, Etxeparekoak. The initial d is probably not part of his true name but a consequence of Latinization. If this is correct, his name was probably Echepare or Etchapare. Modern orthography suggests Detxepare, and that is the form we will use here.

Detxepare's life has been the subject of much speculation, sometimes leading to peculiar conclusions. Genaro Sorarrain Ogarrio describes Detxepare as a sly priest, fond of women and good food—perhaps reflecting Sorarrain's attempt to find similarities between Detxepare and Ruiz.[4] One of the documents Huarte discovered, however, states the opposite. In this document, Detxepare's parishioners describe him as a priest of good reputation and capabilities and express their desire to have him appointed general vicar of Donibane-Garazi.[5]

One of the most controversial questions about Detxepare's life is the reason for his stay in jail. Certain scholars have attributed his incarceration to the erotic aspects of some of his poems, but this hypothesis is implausible because the book was not published until after he was released from prison. Although the specific charges against him are not known, they are likely to have been political in nature. The historical context in which he lived can give us a better understanding of this and other aspects of his life.

Detxepare was born in Navarre, a kingdom that had been independent of France and Spain for many centuries. The capital of the kingdom was Iruñea/Pamplona, but the kings lived in Pau, where the parliament met. Navarre was divided into six counties. The sixth county, Ultrapuertos, in the region of Cize, lies in today's French department of Pyrenées-Atlantiques. It was here, in Cize, that the Detxepare family had its roots.

Around the middle of the fifteenth century bloody factional conflict broke out in this region between the Agramonteses (pro-French) and the Beamonteses (supporters of the king of Castille).[6] The Detxepare family, as nobles loyal to Castille, enjoyed many privileges and opposed efforts by the Agramonteses to suppress them. These political problems undoubtedly influenced Detxepare's life and work, turning him into a faithful and vocal supporter of the kings of Castille. Poem XIII reflects these political struggles, which were the most likely reason for his arrest and incarceration.

Detxepare's book has a long title: *Linguae vasconum primitiae per Dominum Bernardum Dechepare Rectorem Sancti Michaelis Veteris.* The book is not dated, but the printer's colophon indicates that it was published in Bordeaux in 1545. The volume contains fifteen poems totaling more than 1,000 lines in fifty-two pages, with a short prose foreword (21 lines). The poems can be divided into four parts. Poems I and II—which have religious themes—compose the first and longest part of the book (449 lines). The second part (403 lines) contains ten poems (III through XII) about love. Poem XIII describes the author's life in 102 lines. The fourth part contains poems XIV and XV, 59 lines, in which Detxepare praises his native Basque language.

The subject of poems XIV and XV is introduced in the foreword. The appearance of the printing press early in the Renaissance elevated the Romance and indigenous languages over Latin, and Detxepare saw himself as a pioneer in making his native language more universally accessible. During the Middle Ages oral literature prevailed in the Basque Country, and only a few fragments of the poetry from this period were written down. The Basques themselves used their language primarily as the medium of daily discourse, but it was not developed as a written medium and was thus neglected, since it did not reflect all aspects of daily life. Before 1545 a few sentences in Basque appeared in Perucho's song in the *Tercera Celestina* (1539) by G. Gómez and in Rabelais's *Pantagruel* (1532), but no one had attempted to produce an entire book in this language. In his foreword, Detxepare addressed a lament on the lack of books in Basque to Bernardo Lehete, one of the king's lawyers at the Parliament in Bordeaux: "Miraz nago, jauna nola batere ezgen asayatu bere lengoaje propiaren laboretan heuskeraz zerbait obra egitera eta skributan imeitara"[7] (I am very surprised, sir, that nobody has written any book in Basque for the good of his language).

Very naïvely, Detxepare aimed to promote the Basque language so that it would be known all over the world (poems XIV and XV). His foreword, full of words derived from Latin and rococo sentences, is of poor literary quality, but for the first time a Basque writer had created written literature in his own language. Unfortunately, his example was not frequently followed until much later.[8]

Detxepare's religious poetry reveals him more as a pastor of his flock than as a great poet. In the first two poems in this sequence, he explains what a Christian must believe in to avoid eternal damnation and achieve salvation: God, the Creator; the Virgin Mary and the saints; death and judgment; the Eucharist; and the Cross. His style is poor, except for his description of the Final Judgment, in which the rich metaphors and images of Jehoshaphat's valley, fire, trumpets, hell, and the sun and moon covered with blood depict an apocalyptic end of the world in the manner of Dante. Detxepare's God is not the loving and merciful God of the Mountain of Beatitudes but, rather, the God of Mount Sinai, a stern judge. Some of the verses depicting the Final Judgment appear to have been taken directly from the Christian liturgy, manifesting the clear influence of the Bible and church liturgy on Detxepare's religious poems. Mitxelena notes that "Bekhatu oro publikoki ageriko orduyan" (Then shall all sin be made known):

> Quidquid latet apparebit:
> nil inultum remanebit.[9]

The Virgin Mary, model of women, occupies a prominent place in Detxepare's poetry as mediator and helper. Again, his inspiration is the Christian liturgy, and the parallels between the liturgical texts and his poems are striking:

> Elas, orduyan nola zagoen haren Ama tristia
> Haren ama maitia eta mundu ororen habia,
> Pena hetan ekusteaz bere seme maitia
> Eta hiltzen begietan mundu ororen bizia.[10]

Alas, how must his anguished mother have felt, his beloved mother and the mainstay of the whole world, when she saw her beloved son in such agony, dying before her eyes, the life of all the world.

The second part of Detxepare's book, dedicated to love poems, is superior from a literary point of view. Here the poet uses forceful, descriptive, and at times erotic language to convey his deep, passionate feelings. He seems to be thinking aloud, expressing his feelings sincerely, without any attempt to suppress them. Because his descriptions of erotic love are so vivid, some scholars believe the author had personal experience with the feelings and actions he portrayed so exactly.

In poem III, "Amorosen gastiguya" (The lover's disappointment), the writer compares unfaithful, worldly love to the faithful love of the Virgin Mary. The stanza "Nihaurk ere ukhen dizit zenbait ere amore"[11] (I also had some loves) describes what seems to be Detxepare's experiences in his youth. Mitxelena speculates that he became a priest at age forty because of a failed love affair.

The poet maintains that women are superior to men in all respects.[12] God loved women so much that He chose one of them to become His mother; therefore, men should always praise women, and if someone is tempted to speak ill of them, he should first consider how he was born. It is in this poem that we find the stanza that has made some readers believe that Detxepare really lived what he described:

Munduyan ezta gauzarik hain eder ez plazerik,
Nola emaztia gizonaren petik buluz korririk;
Gizon orrek dagiala hartzaz nahi duyenik.[13]

There is nothing in this world more beautiful and pleasing
than a woman, naked, under the man; her arms wide open,
lying there, for the man to do with as he pleases.

Poem V, "Ezkonduen koplak" (Songs of married couples), depicts the risks and dangers of falling in love with another man's wife. In poem VI, "Amoros sekretuki dena" (Secret lover), the beauty of women is compared to that of the morning star or a clear mirror. In poem VII, "Amorosen partitzia" (Separation of lovers), the poet decides that his lover must be abandoned, but he dislikes this solution because he has no other woman to love. The memory of his lover becomes an obsession in poem VIII, "Amoros jelosia" (Jealous lover). Poems IX and X present lively conversation between two lovers. In poem IX, "Potaren galdatzia" (Asking for a kiss), the man asks his lover for a kiss, hoping that total surrender will follow. In poem X, "Amorez errekeritzia" (Duties of love), the man exposes the reasons for his behavior, and his lover argues with him. Some of the lines of poem XI, "Amorosen desputa" (Flight of lovers), remind the reader of the carpe diem:

Orano, amorea, gazte gituzu;
Jeinkuaz orhitzeko lekhu diguzu.[14]

We are still young, my love;
There is plenty of time to think about God.

Finally, the woman rejects the man, and he is forced to abandon his pursuit (poem XII, "Amore gogorraren despita" [Scorn of the cruel lover]).[15] He concludes that saving his soul is more important than enjoying the favors of women. In general, these love poems are reminiscent of the courtly love themes developed by the Provençal poets—romantic love as a supreme value, the adoration of the ideal woman, and the faithlessness of the lover.

In their intensity and graphic vividness, Detxepare's love poems opened a path that no other Basque writer would follow for almost four hundred years. Until well into the twentieth century, the majority of Basque writers either were priests or belonged to religious orders, and their work was dominated by religious subjects. Not until the 1960s and the resurgence of interest in Basque culture did writers begin to seriously explore the secular and erotic themes that Detxepare developed in 1545.

The third part of the book—poem XIII, "Mosen Bernat Etxeparere kantuya" (Song of Mosen Bernat de Etxepare)—is autobiographical. Here, the author expressed his anger against those who accused him before the king. Knowing himself to be innocent, he decided to go to the king since fleeing would imply his guilt. He was arrested, however. Once in prison, he lamented ever having appealed to the king. He expressed hope that justice would finally prevail and that he would be freed. After a brief consideration of the value of suffering, the poem ends by expressing the writer's strong desire for freedom as a supreme value.

"Kontrapas" (poem XIV) and "Sautrela" (poem XV) are totally different in subject matter from the rest and seem to have been written at a different time. In these poems, the author returns to the themes of the foreword and again expresses his joy that the region of Cize is the first in the Basque Country to elevate the Basque language to its much-deserved status. He celebrates having demonstrated in his book that Basque is as adequate as any other language for expressing profound themes like religion, love, justice, and liberty. Detxepare proclaims the Basque language superior to all others. Although "Kontrapas" is not of high quality, it comes to life as it conveys the spirit of a man in love with his native language:

> Ezein ere lengoajerik
> ez frantzesa ez bertzerik,
> Orain arte erideiten
> Heuskararen parerik.[16]

> No other language, French or any other, is now comparable to the Basque language.

Detxepare wrote in the eastern Nafarroa Beherean dialect spoken in the Cize region, precisely reflecting the popular language and expressions of his time. He almost invariably used the *cuaderna via*, with its four mono-rhythmic verses of fifteen syllables each (two hemistiches of seven and eight syllables, respectively). Only three of his fifteen poems do not follow this pattern: poem X consists of twenty-four stanzas of two lines each; poem XI is written in hendecasyllables; and poem XIV repeats two lines at the end of each stanza. Most of the verses contain caesurae at the division point of the two hemistiches. This subdivision of each hemistich divides the verse into four parts—a poetic pattern that had already passed out of favor among writers more attuned to Renaissance literary values. While Garcilaso de la Vega had already introduced the hendecasyllable in Spain and Rabelais had written his *Pantagruel* in a polished, remarkably flexible prose, Detxepare was still using a medieval meter forsaken by Renaissance writers.

A comparison between Rabelais and Detxepare is, therefore, not appropriate. The two writers were very different, except for the superficial similarities that both were priests, both were enthusiasts of the recently invented printing press, and neither wrote in Latin. The great French writer was very much part of the Renaissance and laid the groundwork for the French Renaissance literary group known as the "Pléiade"—Ronsard, Du Bellay, and others. Moreover, Rabelais's works *Pantagruel* (1532) and *Gargantua* (1534) are written in prose. Indeed, his prose is so splendid that many critics include Rabelais with Voltaire and Hugo as the fathers of French prose. Rabelais helped spread the humanist spirit through France and espoused a love of nature without medieval asceticism. His work was comical and entertaining, and his humor later inspired Molière.

Some critics have pointed out similarities between Detxepare and Ruiz. Two centuries separate these writers, but there are certainly parallels between their lives and their works. Both were priests and archpriests, and both spent time in prison. The few known details about their lives are found in their books. Both writers used the cuaderna via form in most of their poems, which reflect realism, deep feelings, eroticism, imagination, and an extraordinary ability for close observation, all manifested in popular language. Their works are courageous and original, yet the differences between them are significant.

Ruiz led a worldly life. He was fond of women, pleasure, and good food. His *Libro del buen amor* is saturated with sensuality and an earnest desire for immediate pleasure. Sexual love always dominates pure love, following the themes of medieval goliardic poetry and some poems from the *Carmina Burana:*

> Voluptatis avidis
> magis quam salutis
> mortuus in anima
> curam gero cutis.[17]

> Caring more for voluptuous pleasure than for my health, dead in spirit, I think only of my skin.

The Spanish poet regarded the body of a woman as merely an instrument for his own pleasure. He wanted nothing of her but that she be a voluptuous female, expecting only that she "have broad hips, no body hair, and to see her without her top." His four *serranas* and the other women he mentions in his poems, such as Gadea, Chata, Trotaconventos, and Marga Llorente, are portrayed in this way.

Regarding the formal aspects of both books, the Spanish work contains 1,709 stanzas, whereas the Basque book contains only 1,034 lines. Despite the use of several very different genres—narrative, lyric, fable, and satire—the strong personality of Ruiz and the autobiographical nature of his writing give the book a clear unity. Detxepare's work is just the opposite. Here the various parts are independent of one another both in subject matter and chronology. Throughout *Libro del buen amor,* Ruiz uses humor and irony, sometimes in a grotesque manner and in lively and colorful dialogues. Detxepare, on the other hand, uses these devices sparingly in only a few poems. The Spaniard's work reminds the reader of *La Celestina* by Fernando de Rojas, and two centuries before the Renaissance he could be considered a literary pioneer. Standing between the dying Middle Ages and the Renaissance, Ruiz is a significant figure in Spanish literature. The extraordinary quality of his poetry is beyond question. None of this can be said about the

Basque poet. By contrast, the quality of Detxepare's poetry has been questioned by some Basque writers.[18]

Thus, the differences between Detxepare and Spanish and French writers are more significant than the similarities. Although Detxepare lived in the early Renaissance period, he was closer to the writers of the Middle Ages, both formally—through his use of the *cuaderna via*—and in subject matter—God, death, hell, love. Yet Basques can still be proud of the work of Detxepare and can say with him, "Heuskare, jalgi adi mundura!" (Basque language, go out into the world!) Had Basque writers followed his example by writing in their own language, Basque literature would have taken its place among other world literatures long ago. Detxepare's goal is still alive in Basque schools and universities, and the dream of the father of Basque literature is only now becoming a reality.

CHAPTER FIVE

Jose de Aristimuño, Alias "Aitzol"

A Martyr to the Basque Cause

Aitzol was not himself a creator of literary works in Basque. His two books and most of his five hundred or so articles were written in Spanish. Nevertheless, he was a promoter of Basque literature during the pre-Civil War era. His work was so decisive in that regard that the poet Jokin Zaitegi coined the phrase "Generation of Aitzol" to describe the group of writers who made the Basque cultural renaissance possible from 1927 to 1936. Aitzol was the undisputed cultural leader of that decade, the arbiter of beauty in poetic competitions, and the one who efficiently carried on the political and cultural renaissance initiated by Arana y Goiri at the beginning of the century.

Aitzol was born in Tolosa on March 18, 1896, and was assassinated by Franco's troops in Hernani, Gipuzkoa, on October 18, 1936, after being tortured. His crime was his political, social, and cultural commitment to the Basque Country. Many labels have been used to describe him, but I will limit myself to presenting him as a promoter of Basque language and culture, especially in the genres of popular and cultured poetry, the theater, and journalism.

While still very young, Aitzol entered the Seminary of Comillas in Cantabria from which he was expelled in 1918, along with other Basque companions, because of his love of the Basque language. He continued his studies in the Seminary of Gasteiz and became a priest in 1922. From 1917 to 1936 that ecclesiastical center was converted into an important Basque cultural seedbed, thanks to the efforts of two professors: José Miguel de Barandiarán (1889-1991) and Manuel Lekuona (1894-1987).

Aitzol found himself among a group of young seminarians collaborating with the knowledgeable ethnologist Barandiarán. Lekuona, the brilliant literary explorer of the depths of the Basque soul, oriented the student Aitzol toward popular and oral literature. The influence of the book *Le style oral* (1925) by Marcel Jousse would later be very important in Lekuona's studies of bertsolaritza and the world of popular literature in general. Jousse emphasized the importance of the roles of memory and gesture as transmitters of oral culture (see chapter 13).

From August 31 to September 8, 1930, the Fifth Congress of Basque Studies (Eusko Ikaskuntza) was celebrated in Bergara, Gipuzkoa. At that congress, Lekuona gave a lecture on Basque oral literature. Aitzol was not in Bergara but in Donostia, where the lecturer read the second part of his speech. Aitzol followed Lekuona's words with much interest; they left him with the feeling that he had discovered something important and unexpected. The content of the lecture was very simple: the verse is the breath of a people, and the Basque cultural renaissance should base itself not only on written and cultured poetry but also on popular oral poetry. Lekuona's masterly book *Literatura oral euskérika* (Basque oral literature, 1935), the first theoretical work on Basque orality and traditional poetry, would have a decisive influence on Aitzol's plans with regard to bertsolaritza involvement.

In 1927 Aitzol and some companions, including Orixe and Lizardi, founded the Euskaltzaleak society with the goal of promoting Basque culture, poetic competitions, and literature in general. They organized various celebrations to that end: Euskal Olerki Eguna (Day of Basque Poetry, held from 1930 to 1936); Antzerki Eguna (Day of Basque Theater); Kirikiño Saria (the Kirikiño Prize, awarded from 1929 to 1934); Euskara Eguna (Basque Language Day, commemorated from 1927 to 1930); Euskal Aur Eguna (the Day of the Basque Child, commemorated from 1929 to 1934); and Bertsolari Eguna (the Bertsolari's Day, commemorated in 1935 and 1936). Aitzol founded the journal *Yakintza* in 1933, which provided a sense of unity for the activities of the Euskaltzaleak society. He also created the newspaper *El Día* in 1930 in Donostia, to which he contributed daily with a page written in Basque about social issues.

Aitzol was a voracious reader, especially of the literatures of the new nations that were created after World War I. That war destroyed the Austro-Hungarian Empire and redrew the Central European map. Aitzol had a lively interest in the political phenomenon known today as "nations without states," and he analyzed the cases of Finland, Belgium, and the Baltic countries. He carefully studied the problem of bilingualism in Europe and discovered, with Lizardi and others, the importance of, and the urgent need for, the literary unification of Basque.

Aitzol worried about the political future of the Basque Country and researched Basque history, democratic structures, and the *fueros*. He drafted a plan to the members of Euskaltzaleak and the Basque people to deal with the status of minority populations in Europe. In order to achieve autonomy, sovereignty, and independence, he felt a national language was absolutely necessary. It was the best lever that could be given to the people to help them solidify their own identity.

In the specific case of the Basque Country, Euskara and patriotism were intimately linked as the best means for obtaining the social changes sought by the supporters of autonomy and independence. Then there was the question of how to create a cultured poetry that would reach the quality and level of other European countries. In the magazine *Euzkadi* (in Bilbo), Aitzol wrote about the relationship between Euskara and society. In his own journal, *Yakintza,* he insisted on the necessity of cultural renewal, with the Basque language serving as the basis of that reform. He also wrote literary criticism of the poetry of Detxepare, Lizardi, and others. In *La democracia en Euzkadi* (Democracy in Euzkadi) he proposed his political plan, and in *La muerte del euskera o los profetas de mal agüero* (The death of the Basque language or the prophets of bad luck, 1931) he attacked with severity and humor Unamuno, the Baroja brothers, Ortega y Gasset, and others who prophesied the demise of the Basque language. He also dedicated himself to writing prologues for books such as Lauaxeta's *Bide-barrijak,* prologues in which he demonstrated his profound knowledge of European poetry.

Aitzol was a dreamer and a diehard theoretician, but as a loyal Basque he was at the same time very stubborn about making his dreams a reality. He knew how to surround himself with helpful collaborators, whom he inspired with his ideas, his charisma, and his strong personality. In the early years of the Basque cultural renaissance he spoke imaginatively of a grand Basque epic poem that would glorify the Basque language. He believed that the future of the language depended on learned poetry. The destiny of Euskara would be ensured if a masterpiece were created in Basque. Why could the Basque Country not have its *Iliad,* its *Aeneid,* or its *Lusiadas*?

The Basque people felt almost invisible, as if they had fallen asleep after the seven-year, iron-fisted dictatorship of General Miguel Primo de Rivera (1923-1930), which was a very damaging period for the Basque language and its literature. It was necessary to inspire the people from their lethargy by initiating a cultural renaissance, the principal basis of which would be learned poetry.

Aitzol was aware of the positive influence that the poem *Mirèio,* for which Mistral won the Nobel Prize for Literature in 1904, had had in Provence. The year 1930 was the first centennial of the birth of its author, Frédéric Mistral, whom the great Romantic poet Lamartine had named "a true Homer." For that reason, Orixe was charged with the task of translating the poem into Basque.

But a simple translation was not sufficient to fulfill Aitzol's plans, so he decided to be a promoter of young Basque poets by delegating tasks to them and creating poetry competitions. They would be the great pioneers of the cultural revival of the Basque Country.

In order to promote poetry, even though Aitzol was not on friendly terms with Orixe, he gave him the task of writing a national poem that would elevate the prestige of the Basques. This was to be a poem with which all Basques would identify, a poem born of the people that would overflow with their goodness. It was Orixe's mission to deliver the truth to Basque society. Guided by Aitzol's romantic ideas. Orixe wrote his long poem *Euskaldunak. Los vascos* (The Basques) between 1931 and 1936.

During the years 1927–1931 Aitzol was an outstanding supporter of young poets, especially Lauaxeta and Lizardi. It is no coincidence that they were the first two winners of the poetic competitions Aitzol established. Lauaxeta won in Errenteria with "Maitale Kutuna" (Favorite lover, 1930), and Lizardi won in Tolosa with "Baso-Itzal" (Shady forest, 1931). Both were creators of a learned poetry that projected a great change in poetic language. As time passed, Aitzol's help also benefited other poets, such as Loramendi, Zaitegi, Jautarkol, Patxi Etxeberria, and Otamendi.

After 1932 Aitzol's concept of the value of poetry would change drastically. Always alert, he observed that in Europe a debate was commencing over so-called pure poetry. This conceptual poetry, based on the autonomy of its own text, was elitist and difficult for most people to understand. Moreover, it created a problem that was very hard to solve: the commercialization of books whose print runs did not exceed three hundred copies. This written, learned poetry was, as a result, incapable of carrying forth Aitzol's plans and goals. How could he convert such elitist poetry into a changing force for achieving his political goals in the Basque Country? The task was practically impossible. Thus, he began to urge Basque poets to create a more popular and comprehensible kind of poetry, because, according to him, "we writers and poets are on the wrong path." He occasionally even attacked learned poetry directly, converting himself, in the last three years of his life, into an opponent of Basque elitist poetry. One year before his death, the great poet Lizardi complained bitterly about Aitzol's abandonment of learned poetry: "I have not wanted to dissuade any writer fond of an easy style to change his opinion. . . . Given that we have resigned ourselves docilely to our solitude, why do you attack us?"[1]

As time passed, Aitzol's pessimism with regard to learned poetry increased. By 1933 a great change was perceived in him. The Day of Basque Poetry that year was celebrated in Urretxu in honor of Iparragirre. Etxeberria won the competition with his simple poem, "Bost lore" (Five flowers). Throughout the event Aitzol continued to encourage Basque poets to write popular traditional poetry, which he considered the legitimate poetry of the Basque spirit.

The year 1934 marked a new stage, and Aitzol wrote a very significant article in *Yakintza*. His pessimism had become disappointment, and after a long analysis of the theory of popular Basque poetry, he wrote "Eusko olerti-kera berezia (estetika)" (Type of special Basque poetry [aesthetics]), in which he confirms the presence of a genuine aesthetic in traditional Basque literature. The traditional Basque song, he claims, teaches us what poets and writers have not. In the article, Aitzol systematically studies the images of traditional poetry and examines their use and function. At the end of the article he cites more than ten contemporary Basque poets, and then reminds them of the importance of traditional poetry.

There was now only one step remaining—to separate himself entirely from learned poetry and defend the bertsolariak's popular improvised poetry with all his might. In 1935 he organized the first competition for bertsolariak, the Bertsolari Eguna, which attracted a large audience and excellent popular poetry. That same year, when he inventoried the books published in 1934, he cited, with bitterness, two posthumous works by Lizardi and *Barne-muinetan* (In the marrow) by Orixe.

In my view, no one can doubt the importance of this Gipuzkoan priest in the pre–Civil War cultural revival. Nevertheless, I believe that, contrary to what is usually averred, Aitzol's stand against the group of learned poets was unfair, and in any case did not benefit the development of learned poetry among the Basques. It is possible that the principal reason for his position was the importance he placed upon poetry as an instrument of social change and as a lever for achieving the autonomy and independence of the Basques.

His enemies did not forgive him for his work during the last decade of his life. When Franco's troops entered Gipuzkoa, Aitzol was forced into exile in France. A few months later, when he tried to enter the zone occupied by Basque nationalists, he was taken prisoner by one of Franco's warships. The local newspaper in Donostia, *El Diario Vasco*, published an article on October 17, 1936, part of which is cited here: "And caught in this net of minor importance was the fat fish 'Aitzol,' the sadly famous priest 'Aitzol,' the possessed leader of separatist nationalism. . . . A bad Spaniard, a bad Basque, and a worse minister of God."

After being incarcerated, tortured, and shot with two other priest companions, he was buried in a common grave outside the cemetery of Hernani. For forty years his mortal remains lay there, and not even the bishops of his own diocese of Gasteiz celebrated a funeral Mass in his name. But Basques will always remember him as a martyr and a great champion of the Basque cause.

CHAPTER SIX

Nicolás Ormaetxea, Alias "Orixe" (1888–1961)

The Life and Work of a Controversial Writer

Few twentieth-century Basque writers have been as admired and as controversial as has Orixe. Koldo Mitxelena, for example, said that Orixe was "perhaps, in several aspects, the most important author in all of Basque literature."[1] Lafitte, in spite of having publicly maintained a contrary point of view to Mitxelena on one occasion, saw Orixe as "one of the most remarkable artisans in Basque letters."[2] On the other hand, there also exist many unfavorable opinions, one of the harshest among them from Federico Krutwig, who classified *Euskaldunak* as the "apoteosis de la jebada," or the height of ridiculousness.[3]

In the 1940s many authors considered Orixe a demigod: "Orixe zan gure jainko tipia"[4] (Orixe was our little god). Nevertheless, in the last years of his life he fell into disfavor, especially among a certain group of young Basque writers: "Guztion aitormenez irabazia zuen irakasletza eta gidaritza ukatu dio oraintsu batek baino geiagok"[5] (In the end, more than one person denied that he had the qualities of teacher and leader that, in everyone's previous opinion, he had earned).

Orixe's work suffered from a lack of realism because he idealized traditional values and the Basque farmstead. It also suffered from a lack of plot, as is evidenced in one of his best works, *Euskaldunak,* and in his characters' lack of emotion, specifically love. His Basque also failed to win over certain groups of young writers, who considered it somewhat incoherent and not at all appropriate for the unification of the Basque language.

Beyond these literary reasons, his religious tendencies and his ideas about modern culture distanced him from these groups, thus creating a generation gap. His name was linked to conservative movements and, as a result, his work was dismissed in certain sectors, perhaps without being closely read. During the last years of his life, his opinions were discounted as he developed a reputation for being overfond of controversy, a grumbler, and a stubborn old man. Under his crusty exterior no one could see his childlike soul. He was a Quixote ready to attack whenever he thought the beauty of his beloved Basque language was being put on trial.

Almost forty years have passed since his death, and time has provided us with a perspective from which to evaluate his work. In the opinion of Koldo Mitxelena: "Gure ondorengoek, orain pixkaren bat ahazturik badaukate ere, aurkituko dute berriz egunen batean Orixe, harrimenez eta espantuz. . . . Orain da garaia bere lanak hobeto aztertzeko eta zehatzago ezagutzeko"[6] (Although our descendants have forgotten him somewhat, someday they will rediscover him with surprise and admiration. . . . The time has arrived to analyze and familiarize ourselves with his works).

In this chapter I outline Orixe's extensive verse and prose production, both in translation and in Basque, and discuss their content. I also look at his life, his character and ideology, and his literary influences. It is my intention to give only an overview of Orixe's work, using his biography as a guideline. This should lead us to a better understanding of the personality and the work of one of the most prolific, controversial, and best-known writers in the history of Basque literature.

ORIXE'S LIFE AND WORK

Nicolás Ormaetxea was born on the Iriarte farm in Orexa, Gipuzkoa, on December 6, 1888. He was one of a set of triplets whose births increased an already large family:[7]

> Ama gaisoak, aurraldi batez
> titi baiñon aur geiago . . .
> Azken jaioa nintzalako, ni
> besteak baiñon aulago.[8]

> Poor mother, in one birthing she had more children than she had nipples . . . since I was the last to be born, I was the weakest of the three.

The child Nicolás was given over to the care of a wet nurse from Uitzi, a small Navarrese town on the Gipuzkoan border. The poet describes it later: "Belar goxo tartean eper-kabi irudi" (It looks like a partridge nest in the middle of a meadow). Orixe was thus Gipuzkoan by birth and Navarrese by adoption; therefore, he was able to master both dialects, as is demonstrated in his work.[9]

In one sense it can be said that Orixe's first Basque school was a kitchen in Uitzi: "Nere lenbiziko euskal-eskola gure sukalde ua izan zinan"[10] (My first Basque school was that kitchen of ours). He was fortunate to have an excellent teacher in Uitzi. On more than one occasion he affirmed that he never found an equal in the Jesuit schools or other centers of learning that he attended. At age eleven, however, he had to quit school, even though he was a brilliant student: "Aurrena edo bigarren ibiltzen zan beti" (He was always the first or second in school).[11]

Until he was seventeen years old he went to visit his family in Orexa every summer. His nickname, "Orixe," dates from this era.

Cultural and Religious Upbringing (1905-1923)

In 1905, at age seventeen, Orixe entered the Jesuit school in Javier, Navarre. He studied humanities, philosophy, and three years of theology with the Jesuits. He moved on to schools in Loiola, Burgos, Oña, Comillas, Carrión de los Condes, and Tudela. In 1923, at age thirty-five, Orixe had to leave the Jesuit order before he completed his studies to become a Jesuit. The eighteen years he spent with them left an indelible mark: "Jesuiten karrera guzia egina zan. Azken urtea bakarrik etzun maixukin eman"[12] (He spent his entire educational career with the Jesuits except for the last year).

After leaving the order in 1923 Orixe moved to Bilbo to work with Resurrección María de Azkue, the first president of Euskaltzaindia. During Orixe's eight years in the Bizkaian capital (1923-1931), he worked with Azkue, a prominent figure in Basque language and literature; he established and maintained literary contacts with certain Basque writers; and he published the first of three books.[13]

Orixe always professed a great admiration for Azkue. When the aged president of the Academy died, Orixe dedicated a eulogy to him in the form of an article:

> After more than seven years of daily interaction with him, I think I know him well. . . . The great Azkue has died. Great because of his enormous capacity for work and his Cyclopean production. . . . His great trilingual dictionary alone is a work worthy of a collection of men. . . . It is the work for which we are most famous abroad. . . . Another of his monumen-

tal works is *Morfología vasca,* the editing of which I witnessed and was the first to read. . . . The fact that Spencer Dodgson called the Basque language 'Azkuenze' instead of 'vascuence' suggests the author's own love.[14]

Orixe's stay in Bilbo, which I shall discuss in more depth later, was also very important for his mastery of the Bizkaian dialect, a key factor in his translation of *El Lazarillo de Tormes* into Basque as *Tormes'ko Itsu-mutila* (1929).

From 1923 to 1931 he produced abundant prose, but his poetic production ceased for some unknown reason. For more than ten years he wrote no poetry. Some of Orixe's first poems were original, and others were translations. He wrote twenty-six original poems, including "Igesi" (Escaping), "Jesus'en Biotzari" (To the Sacred Heart), "Gabonetarako" (For Christmas), and "Eguerrietako" (Of Christmas). Orixe's early poetic art is generally religious in theme and does not attain the literary level of his later religious poetry, such as *Barne-muinetan* (In the marrow; 1934). It does demonstrate, however, the young Orixe's poetic vein. The purism that reigned at that time had a certain influence on him, and he used neologisms such as *gentza* (peace) and *txadon* (church) that he never used again. He also employed many synthetic verbs.[15]

Among his translations of poetry from this period are the religious hymns and canticles that later served him in the construction of his Basque missal, *Urte guziko meza-bezperak* (Daily missal and book of vespers, 1949), for example, "Adoro te devote" (I adore you devotedly), "Sacris solemniis" (On this great festival), "Stabat Mater" (The mother [was] standing), "Te Joseph celebrent" (Glory to you, Joseph), "Cor Arca" (Heart, chest), and "Maitasun dan tokian" (Where there is love), all published first in the Jesuit magazine *Jesus'en biotzaren deya.*

At times there is a tendency to undervalue the importance of translated works: "Erruz agertzen dira itzulpenak izkuntza landuetan, baiña eztiote itzulpenek ematen literatura bati bere mailla, berezko obrek baizik"[16] (In written literatures there exist numerous translations, but the original works, not the translations, demonstrate the measure of a literature). Certainly the best translation of a book, if not a proof of the author's literary capacity, is at least a testimony to the translator's knowledge of two languages. After acquiring a solid foundation in French, Latin, Greek, and Hebrew, plus a profound knowledge of several Basque dialects, Orixe was prepared to carry out any translation from those languages.

His translations fall into two categories: literary fragments and complete works. Among the first group are several short pieces from such authors as Homer, Horace, Virgil, Prudencio, Eusebio Nieremberg, Cervantes, Fray Luis de León, and Saint John of the Cross. He also translated contemporary authors such as Joan Maragall.

A summary of his translations will give us an idea of Orixe's capabilities in this field:

1. "Nekazaritza" (Agriculture) or "Beatus ille" (Happy [be] the one) by Horace (65 B.C.). Horace's obscure syntax does not lend itself easily to translation, but Orixe proved himself to be a great Latinist with his translation of this panegyric of country life.[17]

2. "Gogo Lotia" (Dormant soul), or the *Coplas* of Jorge Manrique. The translation of these famous lines is an example of Orixe's skill:

> Nuestras vidas son los ríos
> que van a dar en la mar,
> qu'es el morir;
> allí van los señoríos
> derechos a se acabar
> e consumir.
>
> Ibai dira gure bizitzak, ba doazi
> itsaso dan eriotzera:
> Ara doa jabego guzi
> zuzen-zuzen itotzera.[18]

Orixe translated only the first three verses of the *Coplas*. He knew the Spanish classics very well, and his translation mirrors perfectly the serene melancholy and interpenetration of individual and universal sorrow expressed in Manrique's work.

3. One of Orixe's favorite Spanish writers was San Juan de la Cruz, whose *Noche oscura, Cántico espiritual,* and *Llama de amor viva* represent the peak of mystical love poetry. Orixe translated parts of these three works under the titles *Gau illuna, Jainkoaren maite leloa,* and *Maite-sugar bizi.*

4. Fray Luis de León was another classic Spanish author Orixe translated. His translation of "De la vida del cielo" (Life in heaven), or "Zeruko bizia," is one of the best fragments of the Spanish poet's work.[19]

5. Orixe also translated a difficult work by Juan Eusebio Nieremberg called *Vida divina y camino real de grande atajo para la perfección.* He gave it the Basque title "Jainkozko biziera ta ongienera eldutzeko lasterbide bikaina" (The divine life and an excellent shortcut to perfection). Orixe took on the difficult task of translating this ascetic work for two reasons: He considered it important to Christian life, and he wanted to demonstrate the possibilities of the Basque language in spite of the difficulties presented by the original work.[20]

Orixe's translations of fragments are numerous, so I will limit myself to a brief list:

1. "Zaldia" (The horse) is taken from Virgil's *Third Georgic,* lines 75–88. Virgil wrote in hexameter, which Orixe adapted for Basque.

2. "Lasterkariak" and "Burrukalariak" are two fragments taken from the last canto of Homer's *Iliad*.

3. Orixe translated two fragments of Aurelio Prudencio's Latin *Kathemerinon*.

4. Another of Orixe's favorite books was Miguel de Cervantes's *Don Quixote de La Mancha*, a parody of the chivalric novels. The Basque writer translated chapter 9, which he entitled, "Euskaldun bipilak eta Manchatar bizkorrak izan zuten burrukaldi lazgarriaren ondarra" (Wherein concludes the stupendous battle between the gallant Bizkaian and the valiant native of La Mancha).

5. *Salmutegia* (1967) is the translation of the 150 psalms of King David from the Old Testament. Both *Salmutegia* and the psalms were the work of poets and former shepherds. According to Manuel Lekuona, who wrote the prologue to *Salmutegia* (p. vii), Orixe was the appropriate translator for this work:

   > Gure egunetan ezin arkitu zitekean Salmoen itzultzale egokiago ta jatorragorik, Orixe baño.[21]

   > In our time we could not find a more appropriate writer than Orixe to translate the *Psalms*.

6. "Bei itxua" (The blind cow) is a brief fragment from one of the best works in Catalonian poetry, *La vaca cega*, by Joan Maragall, a poet from Barcelona.

7. Orixe translated the Gospel according to John from the Greek as *Itun berria, lau ebangelioak*. This Gospel is the most difficult to translate, because it deals with problematic themes such as divinity and the incarnation.

8. *Leoi-Kumea* (Little lion) is an adaptation of a French book written for children. Orixe managed to adapt his translation to a child's level and mentality.

9. *Gizonaren eskubidegai guzietaz aitorkizuna* is a translation of the Declaration of Human Rights, or the Charter of the United Nations.[22]

ORIXE'S STAY IN BILBO (1923-1931)

Orixe spent nearly eight years in Bilbo, where he translated two works into Basque and wrote one of his best books in the Gipuzkoan dialect.

Tormes'ko Itsu-mutila (*El Lazarillo de Tormes*) is the only translation Orixe did in the Bizkaian dialect. Because of its apparent simplicity, this classic Spanish literature is a true work of art. Its humor and satire are moderated by an ingenuous charm. The vocabulary used is sober but colorful and pica-resque. The narration is interesting because of its autobiographical tone and its realism.

Orixe was able to re-create all the freshness, mischievousness, and hu-mor of the work's antiheroes by using precise sentences and simple, but appropriate, vocabulary. Moreover, he demonstrated an uncommon knowl-edge of the Bizkaian dialect, although it was occasionally obvious that he was not a native Bizkaian because of his use of certain Gipuzkoan and Nava-rrese words. For example, he uses *izketa* (conversation) for *berbeta* on page 9, *atara nintzala* (I went out) for *urten nebala* on page 13, *oinbeste diru bilduta* (after accumulating so much money) instead of *oinbeste diru batuta*, *zikoitz* (stingy) for *zeken*, *burni* (iron) for *burdin* on page 17, *ozka egiten* (biting) for *aginka egiten* on page 27, and *itz egin* (to speak) for *berba egin* on page 85.

At the end of *Tormes'ko Itsu-mutila* there appear a few of Orixe's special touches. He took the liberty of changing an obscenity, *hideputa* ("son of a whore" is translated as "son of an evil mother"), in the first chapter, delet-ing eighteen lines in the third chapter (which tell of a bath taken by a page with two "loose women" in the cool waters of a river), and two clauses in the fourth (which describe a friar of the Order of Merced whom two women claim as their relative).

Orixe did not content himself with these changes. In chapter 7 he switched from translator to coauthor by eliminating the original chapter, because it told of the sexual relations of the archpriest of Salvador and the wife of the guide. He wrote a new chapter in the old Spanish spoken in that era. With Orixe's changes, the work ends like a fairy tale as the guide marries the blind man's niece.

Orixe justified his changes by quoting his conscience, which gives us a glimpse of the young Basque writer's narrow-mindedness: "Kritikuak be-girapena zor ei deutsoe yaubearen idazti yatorrari; nik ostera begirapena zor deutsot neure buruari ta irakurle euskaldunari"[23] (It is said that critics should respect the original writing; I, on the other hand, have to respect my conscience and the Basque reader).

In 1930 the first centenary of the birth of the Provençal writer and Nobel Prize winner Mistral was celebrated. In honor of the occasion, Orixe trans-lated *Mirèio*. This book was dedicated to the great French Romantic poet Lamartine, who had hailed Mistral as a great epic poet, "a true Homer." Mistral's poetry was born of Provençal inspiration and expressed his love for an idealized land, its people, and its language. His verse rose out of a people who were ashamed to speak their own tongue just because it was considered a mediocre patois.

Mirèio belongs to a post-Romantic period during which the ideals of early-nineteenth-century Romanticism (such as local color, regionalism, the search for new forms, the exalting of the imagination, nostalgia, and individual liberty) were still highly valued. The Romantic hero was in exile, a constant wanderer, the victim of his own emptiness, and a martyr to alienation. *Mirèio* is an epic poem written in verse. Orixe translated it into Nafarroa Beherean prose, although he did not put much effort into the work, as he himself admits on page vi: "Mirei poema nagusia. Euskeratzea etzait beste munduko izan lana, baño baditu bere oztopoak" (The great poem *Mirèio*. It was not a difficult task, but it had its problems).

Orixe's version is not a completely literal translation. As he related, he felt it necessary to avoid some of the Romantic excesses that were not in tune with the Basque language. On page vi he writes: "Nere ustezko geiegikeri bakar oriek euskarari ongi ez datozkiolako-ta . . . soildu egin ditut" (I have eliminated . . . only those excesses that in my opinion do not suit the Basque language).

In spite of these touch ups, Orixe was able to reflect the content of the Romantic poem with uncommon precision and skill. The brief fragment from page 21 that follows is an example of this skill:

> Estènt qu'an meme sa metien la fueio ensèn,
> Un cop li poulit det cherescle
> De la chatouno, dins l'arescle,
> Se devineròn entremescle
> Emé li det brulant, li det d'aquen Vincèn.
> Elo emai éu trefouliguéron,
> D'amour si gauto s'enflourèron,
> E toúti dous au cop, d'un fio noun couneigu
> Sentiguèron l'escandihado.

> Biek ostoa zakura sartzean, alako batean, nexkaren beatz meiak Bikendi gaixto zelako mutilaren beatz beroekin kakotu ziren. Dardar biek egin. Aien maitallak maite larrosaz gorritu ziren, eta biek batera su izkutu baten zirrara beroa senti zuten.[24]

> As they [Mirèio and Vicente] put the leaves in the same sack, suddenly the young woman's slender fingers entwined with Vicente's hot-blooded ones. Both were startled. Their cheeks reddened with the flower of love, and they felt the heat of a hidden fire.

The translation of *Mirèio* was well received, earning positive reviews and warm praise from critic Jesús María de Leizaola: "*Mirèio* has been translated into Basque, and with this work alone Orixe was, for me, the greatest Basque writer."[25]

Years later Orixe would regret having translated the work, because Mistral, instead of using the vernacular of Provence, had employed a beautiful language of his own creation: "Why did they [Aitzol, some members of Euskaltzaleak, for example, and Lizardi] put *Mirèio* before my eyes for translation? They caused me to have a respect for Mistral that I no longer have."[26]

During Orixe's stay in Bilbo, his first original book, *Santa Cruz apaiza* (The

Santa Cruz priest, 1929), was published. This work, written in Gipuzkoan, is truly a vernacular jewel. Its 141 pages are divided into 38 short chapters.

Orixe was very conscious of the political situation in the Basque Country brought about by the loss of the Basque *fueros* at the end of the nineteenth century. In this regard, he followed in the footsteps of other writers like Arrese Beitia (1841-1906). Orixe felt his people's pain very deeply, but he did not limit himself to complaining. Instead, he tried on page 8 in *Santa Cruz apaiza* to provide solutions to their problems: "Euskalerria ez da oso-tara il, baiño ba derama bide. Ilko ezpada, euskerak eutsi bear dio Euskale-rria'ri ta euskalduntasunari"[27] (The Basque Country is not completely dead, but it is on its deathbed. To keep it from dying, the Basque language and personality must be preserved).

The goal of *Santa Cruz apaiza* is pragmatic and pedagogical. The author thought he was performing a great service for the culture of the Basque Country and its simple people, as is illustrated on page 8: "Santa Cruz'en berri ematen dun liburua ikusi ezkero, erriak gogotik elduko diola nago, ta euskeraz irakurtzea zaila bada ere . . . oituko al dira euskaldunak irakur-tzen" (When they see this book that describes the life of the priest Santa Cruz, I hope that the Basque people will accept it good-naturedly, even though it is difficult for them to read in Basque . . . I hope they will grow accustomed to reading their own language).

To this end, Orixe tried to present his protagonist in *Santa Cruz apaiza,* the Basque priest from Ernialde, in a pleasing and likable form. Santa Cruz was a member of a group of guerrillas, but only because of the political situa-tion, a situation caused by General Maroto's treason after the First Carlist War. Orixe tried to justify the guerrilla priest's violence on page 10: "Eriotz asko eginarazi zula . . . bearra ere ba zegoan norbaitek ori egitekoa"[28] (He ordered many killed . . . someone had to do it).

In the face of liberal propaganda that characterized the figure of the cleri-cal guerrilla as an assassin and a criminal, Orixe tried to salvage the priest's reputation. *Santa Cruz apaiza* is an apologia in which the author takes a de-termined stand, a position he assumed before he even began to write.

The book is written in Gipuzkoan, Orixe's native dialect. His Basque is colloquial and easy to understand, as he believed the common people for whom the book was intended would require. Orixe did not attempt to cre-ate literature with this book, yet it is one of the most enjoyable Basque works of the twentieth century. He captivates his readers with his collo-quial Basque; reading the book requires no preparation on the part of the reader. It is sufficient to speak the Basque of the common man, and it is hard to put down once you have begun it. Orixe's prose is fresh, animated, and lively, attributable to his short, direct sentences. He occasionally employs dialogue to give his writing life and color, and he often uses the familiar forms of the Basque verb to re-create the colloquial speech of the unedu-cated people. His style never grows tiresome because of the musical rhythm of his sentences. He avoids baroque and ponderous sentences and imbues his work with mobility and flexibility. All these elements combine to demonstrate Orixe's mastery of the Basque language.[29]

OREXA, 1931-1936

In 1931 Orixe abandoned Bilbo and went to Orexa, where he remained until 1936. The poet moved from industrial Bilbo, where Spanish was the most commonly spoken language, to a small rural village where everyone spoke Basque. It was here that he was inspired to write two of his greatest works, *Euskaldunak* and *Barne-muinetan.* This period was very important because of his great friendship with Lizardi. It was also during this time that he lost his father.[30]

Euskaldunak. Los vascos

The Civil War and the prohibition against publishing in Basque delayed the publication of *Euskaldunak* until 1950, although it was written sixteen years earlier. The book describes a part of the prewar Basque world. Orixe, influenced perhaps by *Mirèio,* wanted to compose a Basque epic. On page 13 of the prologue he states specifically that he wants to represent "Erri baten arnasa" (The spirit of a people). For that reason, he chose the title. He was aware that the writing of this book was the highest goal of his life as a writer; he referred to the work as "nere bizi guziko lan aundia"[31] (the great work of my life).

Euskaldunak is deeply connected to Basque literary tradition. It follows in the footsteps of Juan Antonio Moguel (1745-1804) in *Peru Abarca* (1881) and Domingo Aguirre (1864-1920) in *Garoa* (1912) by representing the ancient farmstead as the heart of the Basque Country and the bastion of the Basque language. *Euskaldunak* is a long poem comprising 15 parts (11,800 lines) among which are sprinkled poems and popular songs such as "Txanton piperri," "Oi laborari gaixua," "Besta biharamuna," "Ardo gorri nafarra," and "Goizean goizik."[32] Some of its most important themes are labor, religion, sports, and family. The different parts of the work are laced together by the courting of a young couple, Mikel and Garazi, the main characters of the book, who first appear in the tenth line.

Euskaldunak takes place in Uitzi. The town's population of 250 comprised mostly laborers, shepherds, and charcoal makers. Orixe does not refer in general to the industrial sector, which was so evident in the Basque Country at the time. Nor does he say much about the life of the fishermen. On page 186 he writes: "Itsas-gizonak merezi badu nere kantetan tokia, . . . arrantzalea, gizagajoa, ez daukat aztuz utzia"[33] (If the man of the sea deserves a place in my songs . . . I have not forgotten the poor fisherman).

Orixe does dedicate an entire chapter to the regattas of Donostia, a chapter that brings to mind Virgil's descriptions. Orixe also dedicates several lines to celebrated Basque mariners such as Juan Sebastián Elcano, Antxieta, Legazpi, Urdaneta, Okendo, and Churruca.[34]

Euskaldunak is, without a doubt, the best example of Orixe's epic poetry. It was the topic of much discussion at the end of the 1950s. Most contemporary critics praised the book: "Badugu gure poema nagusia. Areago oraindik: non-naiko ta noiz-naiko, poema bikaiñenak bezin bikaiña" (We now have our great poem. More than that, it is as good as the best work of any time and place). For some, however, like the Basque writer and academic Juan San Martín, the book exudes an unrealistic idealism: "Mende onetako tajuratik urruti ibili zan 'Orixe.' Gure errian aspaldiko mendeetan loratu zen nekazaritzaren garaikoa. Ta ordurako ere idealizazio faltsuz beterik" (Orixe wandered far from the literary model of this century. His literature was related to a distant epoch when agriculture and sheepherding predominated in the Basque Country. Furthermore, his work is full of false idealization. Romantic [and] unrealistic dreams had a great influence on him).[35]

The work was also criticized for its stale romanticism and was accused of being reminiscent of the post-Romantic works of some Basque and French authors like Domingo Aguirre and Pierre Loti (1850–1923). I believe that Orixe was a more realistic writer than Loti. Both men visited the places frequented by the characters in their books (taverns, frontons, the Bidasoa River, etc.), but Orixe took care to think through how he described the Basque villager. Loti certainly became fond of the Basque Country and made an attempt to penetrate the secrets of the Basque soul, but he never managed to do so. In spite of the seven years he spent in Euskal Herria, his psychological studies of Basque characters suffer from a lack of realism. For example, the characters in *Ramuntxo* (1896), one of Loti's best novels, are sad. The protagonist is the son of a Parisian and is shown to be somber and melancholy. He is, more than anything, Loti's shadow, a solitary, wandering mariner. Another of his characters is the sacristan Itchoua, who, for a fistful of francs, does not hesitate to organize the kidnapping of a nun living in the convent. In reality, the Basque Country was for Loti a reflection of his own tormented soul. The game of pelota, as described by Loti and Orixe, is another clear example of the differences between the French writer and the Basque one.

Orixe is also more realistic than one of the best Basque *costumbrista* novelists, Domingo Aguirre, author of *Garoa*. Aguirre, a novelist from Ondarroa, describes a countryside that never really existed. Orixe, on the other hand, tells us about the experiences of his youth. He does not describe Basque life in its entirety, but what he relates is real, because it was part of his own existence. For him, the little village of Uitzi was like a musical score that he interpreted with his own voice through his narration. He was an epic storyteller.[36]

One can criticize the archaic and incomplete aspects of *Euskaldunak*, as well as the idealized love of the protagonists, Mikel and Garazi, but no one can deny that Orixe was a faithful observer of the rural world in which he lived. His work was not an exception, but rather an exposition of a strong Romantic current whose post-Romantic traces still linger in the Basque Country. It does not seem odd, then, that in the midst of the controversy that arose over the merits of *Euskaldunak*, there also appeared very favorable criticisms of the work.[37]

Three themes stand out among the many used by Orixe in *Euskaldunak*: patriotism, religion, and the Basque language. Orixe was both *euskaltzale* (a Bascophile) and *abertzale* (a nationalist), although he did not belong to any Basque political party. In spite of his respect and admiration for Arana y Goiri, founder of the Basque Nationalist Party, Orixe considered himself an independent in political matters: "Sabin zana gauza askotan Euskadi'k irakasle du ta izango. . . . Ni ez naiz Alderdiko, ez Euzko-Gaztedi'ko, ez iñongo politikako; baña bai euskalzale, bai abertzale ere" (The late Sabino is and will be master of many things in Euskadi. . . . I do not belong to the Basque Nationalist Party, nor to the Basque Youth Group or any other political party, but I am a Bascophile and a nationalist). His independent streak further manifested itself in the controversy over the spelling of the name of the Basque Country, Euskadi versus Euzkadi.[38]

Orixe clearly expressed his opinions on Basque nationalism in *Euskaldunak*. He never accepted the border that divided France and Spain, nor did he accept the division of Navarre between those two states. Like Xalbador, Orixe did not speak of the *seven* united Basque provinces (*zazpiak bat*) but of *six* provinces, including a unified Navarre:

> Naparroa bat ezagutzen dut
> gezur-mugaz an-emendi . . .
> mugaz angoa Espaiñi ez da,
> emengo au ere ez Prantzi. . . .
> Zergatik izan ez bear degu
> famili bakar osoa?[39]

> I recognize only one Navarre on either side of the border. . . .
> The Basque Country from here to the border is not Spain, nor
> is it France on the other side.

Orixe defended the Basque Country with his pen. He was especially interested in the Basque language, which he considered the essence of a Basque nation on its deathbed: "Azkenetan dagon Euskalerri ontaz"[40] (About this Basque Country that is on the verge of disappearing).

The second notable theme of *Euskaldunak* is religion. *Religious* is the word that best defines both Orixe and his literary work. The two loves of his life were God and the Basque language, which he loved so deeply he called it his "sweetheart": "Nere emaztegairik kutunena euskera izan da"[41] (Basque has been my dearest sweetheart). But he preferred to have it disappear than to see it filled with blasphemies and transformed into a weapon against God:

> Izkuntza au birauz loi bear balu,
> ez nuke nai Euskerarik.
> Ala balitza, ez dut bizitzan
> jetsi nai mendi ontatik;
> ez beintzat, gure mintzo ontan Jauna
> betiko jaso bagerik.[42]

> If our language were to be blemished with blasphemy, I would no longer love it. If this happened, I would not wish to descend from this mountain [Aralar] for the rest of my life, at least not if the name of the Lord is never glorified in our language.

All his work hinged on religion. It may seem incredible to some, but he returned to Euskadi from America not because he was homesick but so that he would be able to take daily Holy Communion. Prayer was his spiritual nourishment: "He returned from America solely to take communion every day. That land was much more pleasant and lovely to him than the Basque Country."[43]

In chapter 9 of *Euskaldunak,* Orixe presents his thoughts on God, the Basque Country, and his language. He begins by addressing the Basque people as if he were preaching to them: "Zillegi bekit gure Erriari // egi latz biren esate"[44] (Allow me to tell my people two bitter truths).

Orixe considered Mount San Miguel de Aralar in Navarre to be a kind of Mount Sinai where dwelled the Holy Trinity and the Archangel Michael, protector of the Basque Country. Aralar is opposite Zugarramurdi, where Basques once practiced pagan rites. According to Orixe, the Lamb of God ended the reign of goats, pagan gods, witches, the Basque deity Ortzi, and the *akelarreak* (witches' sabbath). Orixe thus found himself opposed to Baroja and Mirande, who felt that Judeo-Christian doctrine had damaged the Basque essence and that Basques should return to the pagan ways.[45]

For Orixe, God and the Basque language guaranteed the survival of the Basque people. He warned the Navarrese in *Euskaldunak* (227–28) that evil (represented by the serpent) walked among them through the Ribera, the *Koko-erri,* or land of the Spaniards. To remain faithful to their past, the Navarrese should follow the example of Saint Francis Xavier and Saint Ignatius of Loyola. Orixe seems to have been possessed by, and obsessed with, the idea of God. As we have seen, his having to leave the Jesuit order did not spring from any religious crisis or problem with the church, although he did disagree with a few of its official positions.[46]

As far as the stylistic aspects of *Euskaldunak* are concerned, Orixe employed over two hundred metaphors, similes, allegories, and comparisons, usually drawn from nature, especially animals. In this sense, he possessed a Franciscan soul. The first chapter begins with the comparison *Uitzi* (the partridges' nest), and the last chapter ends with another taken from the animal kingdom (p. 368):

> Zakurrak ala ogi-puskari
> erne erne begiratu oi.[47]

> The dog watches a piece of bread that way, attentively.

Orixe used traditional rhythms, often taken from the bertsolariak, although he did not generally favor popular rhythms of the type common to oral poetry, which was usually sung. He felt that such rhythms became boring and monotonous in written poetry. He did, however, employ them in *Euskaldunak,* because he was trying to write a popular epic, and many parts of the book were meant to be sung.

Barne-muinetan

During his stay in Orexa, Orixe wrote another book, *Barne-muinetan.* Each of its six chapters is made up of three parts, like a triptych, and each part contains twenty verses (950 lines). The main theme is God and His creation, humankind. Certain tenets of Christian theology are described in depth and with precision, such as the presence of God in children, in the Eucharist, and in humankind; Christian faith; the limitations of the human condition; the mystery of the Trinity; and the life of the Holy Family in Nazareth.[48]

Barne-muinetan is a mystic poem. At times it appears abstract and intellectual, and sometimes it is popular and intimate, but it is always deeply religious and very original. Estefanía describes it as follows: "Its most intimate and most penetrating aspect, that which lends it its own character . . . is the unbeatable fusion of intellectual light and emotional heat, of solid literary culture and popular simplicity and ingenuousness."[49]

This book is the expression of Orixe's most personal religious experiences and a declaration of his own faith. His favorite themes also appear here: God, Christ, the Church, mysticism, prayer, and Christian faith. Orixe begins the book by describing the presence of God with one of his most beautiful verses:

> Aitzin-gibel, ezker-eskuin
> gain ta barne
> neurtzen ari nauzun Begi,
> zure dirdaiz, argi berriz
> soil dakusat
> uts-ez, ogen-naizela ni.[50]

Eye that measures me front and back, left and right, top and bottom, with your brilliance, with new light, I see that I am nothing; no, I am sin.

The first part of the verse describes the immensity of the presence of God as the figure of an eye that takes in everything. In its divine light, humankind is conscious of its smallness and its sin. The second part of the verse reminds us of one of the basic ideas of the spiritual thought of the French writer Pascal, annihilation before God. God's presence possesses man completely, leaving no room for escape:

Begira daukat, begira nauka. . . .
Nagon ni Argan, bego neregan.[51]

It's looking at me; I'm looking at it. . . .
That I may dwell in Him, and He in me.

Christian faith is also very important in *Barne-muinetan*. Understanding is like a loyal brother, but faith supersedes understanding. This faith helped Orixe through many problematic times. Unlike Pascal's faith, which assumed anguish and unease, Orixe's entailed a constant, peaceful seeking. Nourished by prayer, his faith was the rock upon which the poet built his spiritual house.[52]

Orixe describes his faith as a woman with whom he had fused, like two pieces of iron:

Andre Sinismen, zure nauzu ta
lotu ditzagun esku ok
bi burni-mutur elkar urtuak
diran baino estuago.
Senide baino geiago zaitut,
ez al zakik aspertuko.[53]

Lady Faith, I am forever yours. Let us link hands more tightly than two pieces of forged iron. You are more than a sister to me. I hope you do not tire of me.

The fragility of the human being is evident in these verses, but God fills the vacuum. The Creator does not forget His creation. He tests it but does not abandon it. The final victory assumes a meeting between God and His creations:

Ba nator
Berriz uts garbia.
Ilun, utsarte, zulo,
ezer ez guzia.
Au nauzu, Zerbait, orde,
zurez, Jaun aundia.[54]

Once again I become pure nothing, darkness, emptiness, a pit: all of it nothing. Thus I am before Thee. But because of Thee, great Lord, I am something.

Barne-muinetan is dedicated to Orixe's friend Lizardi, who died the year before it was published:

> Nori dioket opa
> nik "Barne-muinetan"?
> iri, ik oroi baitidak
> "Biotz-begietan." [55]

> To whom will I dedicate *Barne-muinetan?* To you, who remembered me in your *Biotz-begietan.*

In Lizardi's opinion, Orixe's book was a deserving part of the overall anthology of Basque literature and elevated the level of the Basque language: "These poems have great strength and endurance and were born of a noble impulse of the heart. . . . [T]his is true literature, and it will truly elevate our poor language." [56]

In effect, *Barne-muinetan* proposed a new goal for both Orixe's poetry and Basque religious literature in general. From 1930 to 1935 written, cultured Basque poetry flowered, and with it a new poetic language came into being, as a result of the efforts of Lauaxeta, Lizardi, and Orixe.

PRISON, CONCENTRATION CAMP, EXILE, 1936–1950

The Spanish Civil War, which began on July 18, 1936, was a tragedy for Basque culture. Many writers went into exile. Others, like Lauaxeta and priests Aitzol and José Markiegi, were shot. Orixe did not belong to any political party, but loving the Basque language and being a nationalist were enough to cause his imprisonment. In 1936 he was arrested at his home in Orexa and taken to the infamous San Cristóbal prison in Iruñea. [57] Not everyone in Tolosa appreciated him; in fact, some wanted him dead.

With a touch of irony, Orixe described the spirit of the soldiers who came in the name of the Holy Crusade:

> Bego San Cristobal, otadia bego.
> Arrebak Tolosa'n izkutatu nindun.
> Agoan birago, Zure aldekoek?
> erria suntsitzen ari zitzaizkigun. [58]

Let San Cristóbal be, let the gorse thicket be. My sister hid
me in Tolosa. They blasphemed, were they Your supporters?
They were destroying our Basque nation.

Thanks to the diligent efforts of a relative in the priesthood, Orixe acquired
his freedom and avoided execution.[59]

Orixe spent 1937 in his sister's house in Tolosa. In 1938 he returned to
Orexa. When he was once again summoned by the authorities, he went into
hiding in Uitzi then into exile in France. He sought a peace that he could
not find in his own country, but he did not find it in France, either. In 1939
World War II broke out while he was in southern France. He was taken prisoner by the Germans and spent time in a Nazi concentration camp. "As he
himself said, he never worked so much as he did there."[60]

Freed by the Germans, he lived in various locations in Iparralde and
other parts of France: Donibane-Loitzun, Lourdes, Air-sur-L'Adour, and
Betharram.

Urte guziko meza-bezperak (Daily missal and book
of vespers)

After moving several times, Orixe settled down at
age sixty in Donibane-Loitzun, where he undertook the translation of Lefè-
vre's French version of the Roman missal, entitled in Basque *Urte guziko
meza-bezperak*. It is, without a doubt, his greatest contribution to Basque
liturgy and perhaps his greatest achievement as a translator. Orixe's translation is priceless in both form and content. From a literary point of view, the
most important parts are the hymns, sequences, and responsories. To some
extent, Orixe surpassed Raimundo Olabide's translation of the Bible with
a work that was cleaner and easier to understand.[61]

Orixe was very aware of the fact that the only place where Basque was
read publicly was in church; however, Basques did not yet have a complete
missal, and for that reason he decided to take on the task of providing one:
"In truth, it is a difficult job, I know this better than anyone."[62]

The difficulty is not only in the work itself but also in the style of Basque
he would need to use. He had to choose among three possibilities: the
Basque of the purists, that of the nonpurists, and a middle road. Orixe opted
for a dialectal combination of Gipuzkoan, Lapurdin, and Navarrese. Aware
that he could not please everyone, he chose a style of educated Basque that
has since been noted for the originality of its sentences, the beauty of its
syntax, and the appropriateness of its vocabulary: "Some advise me not to
use a patois of Spanish and Basque, and others say not to be too puristic.
As a result, I feel obligated to use language somewhere in the middle. . . . I
know beforehand that I will not please everyone. Evidently, not even my-

self. For whom is this book being written? Not for the common people, even though they will be its eventual destination."[63]

Orixe's version of the Roman missal received a warm welcome among Bascophiles, especially the clergy. Orixe possessed a musical ear, and in those parts where he combined words and Gregorian chant he was masterful, forcing neither lyric nor melody. Furthermore, the translation set the standard for young writers of religious and liturgical prose to follow. Orixe did not deceive himself when he foresaw that his book would be well accepted: "I have taken painstaking care with this book. . . . its contents will inflame the hearts of many Basques."[64]

From a literary point of view, the hymns and sequences are outstanding. It is not easy to choose a single best example, but "Lauda Sion," a sequence from the "Corpus Christi" Mass, is certainly exemplary. If the Basque translation is compared with the Latin, one can see that it faithfully renders the original.

LATIN AMERICA, 1950–1954

Late in life Orixe decided to go to America in search of peace and better health. At that time, there was practically no Basque literature in Hegoalde because of Franco's dictatorship. In Guatemala, however, Orixe's friend Zaitegi had just begun a journal publication, *Euzko-gogoa* (Basque soul).[65]

Orixe embarked from France and journeyed to Brazil, Argentina, Peru, Bolivia, Ecuador, El Salvador, and Guatemala. Rio de Janeiro impressed him deeply: "Donostia, Donibane-Loitzun, and Biarritz are very pretty, but Rio de Janeiro is beautiful. There is no city in the world like it."[66] His time in Argentina, Bolivia, El Salvador, and Guatemala was the most productive, however, for in those countries Orixe composed some of his best work.

From Brazil Orixe went to Argentina (specifically, Buenos Aires and Bahía Blanca). He lived there for a month with Basque friends Indart and Zuburu and wrote two of his most beautiful poems, "Berraondo'ko Meza" (The mass of Berraondo) and "J. S. Bach'i Elizan" (To J. S. Bach in the church).

In "Berraondo'ko Meza," Orixe continues one of his favorite themes, the presence of God. One morning he leaves the house very early and finds himself surrounded by total silence. There is no church, but nature serves as his temple. He feels himself to be the priest of this natural church, an empty church as round as the Eucharist. There is no sound, not the song of a bird, the murmur of a stream, or the sigh of wind in the trees. The only noise is the lowing of a cow, in which the poet hears the ringing of a bell inviting him to mass. In the midst of this profound silence, he prays to God, the center of all creation, where man holds a special place:

Ixiltasunik
ez nun osorik aditu. . . .
Ni niz apeza. . . .
Elizik gabe
Eliz hontan dut Jinkoa. . . .
Iruditzen zaut
Ororen erdi nizala.[67]

Such a complete silence had never been heard. . . . I am the
priest. . . . God dwells in this church. . . . It seems that I am
the center of everything.

Orixe also took advantage of his stay in Argentina to write "J. S. Bach'i
Elizan." In this poem, Bach's fugues are compared to the work of a weaver.
As soon as he hears a familiar fugue being played, the poet puts himself in
the presence of God through prayer. He then loses track of time and feels
imprisoned by eternity:

Geroen Batean
organuak soiñuz
Fuga bat asten du,
bai baitakit buruz . . .

Asi da, ari da
iruten, ariltzen
ekin eta jarrai
bilbatzen, eiotzen . . .

Azkenik, âztu zait
aldien aldia
eta betierak
nauka idukia.
Betikor senti naiz
Jainko-iduria.[68]

After a while, the organ plays a fugue that I know by heart.
It has begun, it weaves and reels and continues to warp and
plait. At last, I lose track of time, and eternity has taken me
prisoner. I feel eternal, like God.

Orixe continued his journey, traveling through Peru to the wide pla-
teaus of Bolivia. The breadth and light of Bolivia's blue sky gave a new perspective to his literature. He became the painter capable of portraying both
nature and the human spirit. He was surprised by the mountains, plains,
and sky of Bolivia, all different from and larger than those he had left behind in the Basque Country: "There you have meadows, tall mountains,
light, especially light . . . steeper and steeper, more and more snow, and
clear sky."[69]

He goes on to describe a Bolivian Indian. The painter of nature in *Eu-*

skaldunak now plumbed the depth of the human soul. The description of the Bolivian Indian would be appropriate in the best anthologies of Basque poetry:

> Eserita dago Indio beltxeran, an jaio ta bizi argiz aseago ni baiñon; ark are zerbait nai ikasi. Lepoa makurtuz galdez ari zaio bere kitarrari beti gauza bera, baiña beti berri. Biotza nai ase. Kitar-sabelean kuka du gordeki. ¿Zer du billatu nai? Nik nai nuken ua . . . ta berak ez daki.
>
> Agur, anai, biok, jakin ez jakin, batera goazi; kitarra joaz zu, neurtitzak onduz ni.[70]

> There is a dark Indian sitting there, on the spot he was born and where he has lived, more gorged on light than I; he also wishes to learn something. Head bowed, he asks his guitar a question that is always the same but always new.
>
> He yearns to satiate his heart. He hides it, in ambush, in the belly of his guitar. What is he looking for? For that one for whom I yearn . . . and he does not know it. Greetings, brother; whether you know it or not, we are traveling together, you strumming the guitar, and I composing verses.

Orixe was also surprised by the silence and solitude he experienced in Bolivia. He carries this silence over into his memory of his "grandmother," who taught him to pray: "Bolibi'ko zabaldia, ikusgarri dun; obeki esan neretzat, entzungarri. . . . Entzun berriz zer entzun? Ezer ez. Ez zugatzen abarrotsik, ez txorien txintakorik. . . . Yainkoaren ixiltasuna ta pakea. Indio beltxeran bat kitarra yotzen. . . . Olako otoi-lekurik ez dinat arkitu. . . . Amona Mari-Axuntziz oroitu nintzinan."[71] (You could hear nothing, not the rustle of branches, not the song of birds . . . only divine solitude and peace. A dark Indian playing the guitar. . . . I have never found a place more conducive to prayers. . . . I remember my "grandmother" Mari Axuntxi.)

Orixe also visited Lake Titicaca, Arequipa, and La Paz. Next, he went to Lima and from there travelled by plane to Guayaquil. The conversations he had there with his sister Dionisia, a nun, gave rise to a series of articles that later became a book, *Quito'n arrebarekin* (In Quito with my sister).

From Quito he went to Guatemala and after six months to El Salvador, where he stayed at Miramar with friends. He found it to be an oasis of tranquillity after his long years of wandering outside the Basque Country. His stay at Miramar was most valuable for his literary production. The poet felt he was living in paradise:

> DIONISIA: Zer diok San Salvador alde aietan?
> ORIXE: Ikusten naun; ezin obeki. . . . Emen Erdi-Amerika ontan igaliak eta eztia aski ditut.[72]

DIONISIA: What can you tell me about your stay in San Salvador?

ORIXE: I'm living proof. It couldn't be better. Honey and fruit abound in that part of Central America.

In "Miramar 1954," Orixe again remarks on the tranquillity he found in El Salvador:

Egonean jardun, jardunean egon,
eraginik gabe norbaitek naragi.[73]

I work in the quiet, and I'm quiet while I work; someone moves me without pushing me.

He stayed in El Salvador for three years (1951–1954), and during this time he wrote *Quito'n arrebarekin*. The work consists of twelve short prose articles originally published in the journal *Euzko-gogoa* between 1950 and 1954. Stylistically, *Quito'n arrebarekin* can be divided into two parts. The first is a dialogue between Orixe and his triplet sister Dionisia. At times, the prophet Elias takes part in the dialogue. This is the book in which Orixe uses the greatest number of familiar verb forms, especially when he is conversing only with his sister. When the prophet Elias enters the conversation, Orixe avoids the difficult familiar forms, and his Basque becomes easier to understand. In any case, his style is very personal and occasionally difficult because of its uniqueness and the unusual verb forms that he employs. His sentences are generally brief and concise, but he possesses a rich and varied vocabulary that is sometimes beyond the average reader. Orixe was a pioneer of neologisms, and his style varied greatly from one book to another and sometimes even within the same work, as is evidenced in *Quito'n arrebarekin edo argi-erri*.[74]

In *Quito'n arrebarekin edo argi-erri*'s first dialogue, Orixe describes his childhood, providing us with many autobiographical details: his upbringing in two homes; the special religious influence of his "grandmother," Mari Axuntxi; and the loneliness of a child whose loyalties were divided between two families. Neither his mother in Orexa nor his nurse in Uitzi could give him all the affection he craved:

Bi ama ta bat ere ez. . . . Ortatik gelditu zaidan beti biotzean ezin betezko utsa. . . . Nere bizi guziko utsaldia; bi ama ta amarik ez. . . . Biotz zekena dutala esan ziñadate; ez dutala biotzik. . . . Biotz bat arkitu nai nerearen atsedenerako, aurtzaroan eta gero ere, ta arkitzen ez. Nik ere aragiz egiña diñat eta amaren ordaiña billatzen ibilli arren, umezurtz gelditu naun. Amaren musu bat etzekiñak zer dan. Lagunartea etsai izan diñat oraintsu arte.[75]

I had two mothers, and I had none. . . . For that reason, I always felt an empty space in my heart . . . an emptiness that lasted all my life: to have two mothers and no mother. They tell me I have a selfish heart, that I have no heart at all. . . . In my childhood and afterward I wanted to find a heart where I could rest, and I never found it. Also, I was sensitive, and although I went looking for a substitute mother, I remained an orphan. I do not know what a mother's kiss is like. Until recently, society was my enemy.

The rest of the chapters, except for chapter 5, deal with religious themes: good and evil represented as light and dark; the *no* and the *yes;* the Church, or *argi-erri* (land of light), illuminated by Christ. Orixe presents the Church as the favored creation of God: "Prima omnium creaturarum, . . . sorkari guzietan lena dala Eliza"[76] (The first of all creations. . . . Among all creations, the church is the first).

The last stages of humankind also appear as themes, specifically, hell, purgatory, and heaven. Orixe was aware of the difficulties inherent in these themes, but he continued to use them, demonstrating his knowledge of mysticism and contemplative prayer: "Zailak bai; nerau ere bildur natxin, irakurleeri astunegi gertatu ote nakien"[77] (These themes are difficult, yes; even I was afraid that they would be too heavy for many readers).

In order to discuss these profound themes, the poet established himself in his "Tabor" and, in the company of the prophet Elias, listened to the word of God. Occasionally, Orixe expressed his theological knowledge of these religious themes through the words of the prophet. He demonstrated great familiarity with the Gospel according to John and the works of Saint Paul, Saint John of the Cross, Saint Teresa, Saint Bernard, and especially Saint Ignatius of Loyola. Orixe's fondness for Ignatius, the founder of the Jesuit order, was well known. He called him *maisuen maisu,* the teacher of teachers.[78]

The part of *Quito'n arrebarekin* devoted to purgatory is immensely interesting for the insight it provides into Orixe's ideas on creation, evolution, and the Bible. He received a traditional philosophy education, and he was also familiar with ancient philosophies. In *Quito'n* he sometimes cites Anaximenes and Plotinus. He cleaved very closely to his education and was not open to the philosophical currents of his time, which included existentialism. He never based his arguments on the authority of Martin Heidegger, Sartre, or Unamuno. He was educated at a time when creation was being explained without reference to the theory of evolution and the Bible was taken literally in many seminaries and religious houses. Orixe was a product of his age; he clung to it, and from it sprang his self-assured, closeminded personality.

The part of *Quito'n* that deals with purgatory also evokes the controversy that erupted in Iparralde after the Spanish Civil War. The controversy was born of a priest's lectures on like themes (the origin of man, the interpretation of the Bible, childbirth without pain, evolution, etc.). At one meeting,

Orixe rose up like a Quixote in defense of his Church against the lecturing priest. In his mediocre French he refused to accept the figurative meaning that the priest wanted to ascribe to the origin of the world and the creation of humankind. Orixe had such a hard time during those two weeks that he hardly slept, and he lost weight. He treated the lecturer more like an emissary from the devil than from God. His suspicious mind made him wonder if even the pope was agreeing with these new ideas.[79]

The fifth chapter of *Quito'n arrebarekin* has a religious-sounding title, "Hell," but in reality it deals with the Spanish Civil War. Orixe describes for us the hell on earth he experienced at the hands of the crusaders who came in the name of God and attempts to demonstrate the decency of the Basque people and their role in that war. The Basques, loyal to the idea of a democratic republic, opposed Franco in his bid for power. Because of their opposition, they were severely punished.

Orixe describes the cruelty and human misery of the war. He never approved of the crimes committed by the *reds,* but neither did he approve of the atrocities committed by the *nationals,* among whom were found the *good* bishops, nuns, and clerics, many Navarrese Christians, and soldiers who proclaimed their holy crusade and blasphemed at the same time. The details he provides serve only to corroborate the events of that sad war in which priests celebrated Mass with pistols tucked into their belts, soldiers fighting in the name of God used his name in vain, the bishop of Gasteiz performed funeral rites for executed priests of only one side, and the Benedictine monks of Silos, Spain, applauded the bombing of Gernika.[80]

The crushing of the Basque Country caused Orixe great sorrow, and he was also concerned about the future of religion and the Catholic Church itself. His words of lament hold a prophetic note: "Erlijio gaixoa! Nekez altxatuko din gurean. . . . Gure gazteria ezkerretara, gero ta geiago"[81] (Poor religion! With difficulty you raise your head among us [Basques]. . . . Our youth are moving ever closer to the left).

Orixe thought this work was one of his best, and in a biographical sense I agree because of the abundance of details in the book. But it was far from complete, because when he set about writing it he lacked the notes and material that he was forced to abandon in the Basque Country. There are noticeable repetitions and breaks in the narrative. The book begins as a biographical work and then becomes totally ideological and abstract resulting in an imbalance in the structure of the book.

Quito'n arrebarekin is, however, one of Orixe's noteworthy products because of the literary devices he employed: dialogue, symbols, narration and descriptions of places and people, and the use of different, complex verb forms. He narrates events with the freshness and liveliness of a novel. Orixe the author proves himself an exceptional narrator.

During his stay in El Salvador, Orixe did not restrict himself to writing prose. His poetic soul produced two of his best religious poems, "Getsemaní" and "Igan beti nire lelo" (My song is forever in thee). "Getsemaní" is a mystical and autobiographical poem. Using the Passion of Christ as a vehicle, Orixe narrates his own suffering. The poem is composed of ten smaller parts. In the first he narrates the passion of the Savior and in the second his own passion, using a concise literary style with little imagery.

In order to better represent the darkness of Gethsemane and the solitude of Christ, the poet closes his eyes while seated in a lovely garden:

> Baratz eder, bakar, ixil . . .
> Zer illun argi gabea![82]
>
> Beautiful, empty, silent garden . . . How sad the darkness!

While the apostles sleep, the poet follows the solitary figure of Christ, engages Him in a dialogue, and tells Him his troubles, especially his seven dark years in the Jesuit order:

> Zil bekit gogoratzea nere zenbait naigabe . . .
> zuk eta biok bakar dakigu
> Zazpi urte beltzen berri.[83]
>
> Allow me to recount for you my afflictions . . . you and I alone know of those seven dark years.

Orixe suffered many trials during his life: poverty, lack of affection, exile, prison, war, illness. As his nephew and confidant José Mari Aranalde indicates, "Orixe left this world for the next after suffering greatly."[84] But it was his time among the Jesuits, what he called the "seven dark years," filled with constant conflict, that caused him the greatest pain.

In "Getsemaní" the poet draws similarities between his suffering and that of Christ. Both went to pray before their final test. Orixe withdrew to the Collegiate Church of Burgos, Spain:

> Zazpi urte beltzak astera zoazin, zure bear nintzan gotor irauteko.[85]
>
> Those seven terrible years of my life were about to begin, and I needed you to keep up my strength.

Prayer, a form of communicating with the Father, was also for Orixe a way to recover strength:

> Indar berriak artzera ba zoaz otoitzera.[86]
>
> You go to pray to recover your strength.

His search for similarities continued. Both he and Christ were led away to prison in bondage. Orixe recalls the San Cristóbal jail. Furthermore, both were treated like madmen, Christ by Herod and Orixe by a Jesuit whose name he prefers not to mention:

Giltzapera nindôla esku lotuak burniz. . . .
Zoro Zu! Urliak billatuz aitzaki,
zoro-merikura nindun eramaki.[87]

While they led me off to prison in manacles. . . . You mad-
man! And what's-his-name, looking for the slightest reason,
carried me off to a psychiatrist.

As mentioned earlier, Orixe never revealed the names of those who put
him through his own "Getsemaní." He always used generic monikers for
them:

Ezin dut âztu Urliren bidez
erauntsi zenidan lorra;
ez Sandi Arek bide-erdian
ipini zidan zoztorra;
Gero, Berendi egin nun topo,
gogorrik bazan gogorra.[88]

I cannot forget the tribulation So-and-So caused me; nor the
problems that What's-His-Name put in my path; and later I
came up against another one, as cruel as the rest.

The Basque used in "Getsemaní" is rich, clear, and easy to understand.
Nevertheless, there are surprises. Occasionally, Orixe eliminates the main
verb from the sentence, leaving only the auxiliary one, as in the following:

Orixeko malkor lekarora nintzan.[89]

I went to the rocky desert of Orexa.

This sometimes creates comprehension problems. Several times he employs the circumflex accent, which is seldom found in Basque. He uses it to
lengthen a vowel, as in *âztu* (to forget) or *lên* (before), or to mark the omis-
sion of another vowel, as in *nindôla* instead of *nindoala* (going).

Orixe was a *porrokatua* (compulsive worker). Once he settled on a goal,
he had to reach it, no matter how many hours were required. His stay in El
Salvador was one of the most productive eras of his life, and it was there
that he composed another religious and autobiographical poem, "Igan beti
nire lelo"[90] (My song is forever in thee).

"Igan beti nire lelo" contains fourteen small poems and, along with
Barne-muinetan and "Getsemaní," it forms the trilogy of Orixe's best religious poetry. There are numerous autobiographical references in the poem.
Orixe talks about his childhood in Uitzi and his physical condition at that
time:

Gorputz gotorrean osasun makala:
beso, zango, gerri, ezueriz nagi.[91]

I had poor health in a robust body: arms, legs, and waist
indolent with gout.

Many times, as when he was in the Nazi concentration camp, sleep provided the only respite from his poor health:

Atseden, atseden! Otoitza ta loa
nere adiskide aundienak.[92]

Rest, rest! My best friends are prayer and sleep.

There was now only one thing left for Orixe to do during his trip to Latin America, and that was to keep his promise to visit his friend Jokin Zaitegi in Guatemala.[93]

The atmosphere of Basqueness and hard work that greeted Orixe in Guatemala filled him with delight:

Euskalerria baiñon Euskalerriago dirudin atzerri ontan.[94]

In this strange country that seems more Basque to me than
the Basque Country.

Unlike in the Basque Country, where nothing could be published in Basque because of the political situation, in Guatemala Orixe, as an exile, was allowed to think, live, and work in the Basque language. Exile not only made him homesick but also prodded him to work at maintaining his culture. Of all the people who collaborated with Zaitegi on his magazine *Euzko-gogoa,* Orixe was the most notable as a trailblazer and craftsman of Basque literature.

THE BASQUE COUNTRY AND DEATH, 1954–1961

When Orixe returned to the Basque Country after his lengthy pilgrimage to Latin America at the age of sixty-six, he had a long list of publications. People greeted him with demonstrations of admiration and affection. The cultural atmosphere under Franco continued to be dismal, but at least a few works were beginning to be published. Orixe kept working as hard as ever. He set about translating Saint Augustine's *Confessions* as *Aitorkizunak,* as he was inspired to do by a great friend of the Basque people, Clement Mathieu, the bishop of Dax: "Aturia'ko ta Akiza'ko Gotzai, Txit agurgarri Clement Mathieu, Jaunari. Jauna: Zuk eragin ninduzun emeki, obeki esan bultzatu ninduzun bortizki, Agustin Gurenaren Aitorkizunen liburua gure izkuntzara biurtu nezan"[95] (To His Excellency Clement Mathieu, bishop of Aturia and Dax. Sir: You gave me a gentle shove, or perhaps I should say a forceful push, toward the translation into our language of the *Confessions* of Saint Augustine).

Aitorkizunak, or the *Confessions* of the "eagle of Hippo," is one of the best examples of religious and psychological literature of all time. The humanism of the Renaissance had helped focus attention on Augustinian spirituality. Erasmus of Rotterdam turned to scripture and patristics, the writings of the fathers of the Christian Church, and specifically the works of Saint Augustine. The bishop of Hippo had a decisive influence on Christian thought. Catholics and Protestants alike have been inspired by him. Luther, Calvin, and Zwingli all interpreted Saint Paul in light of Saint Augustine's theories. From the Catholic perspective, Pascal also based his ideas on Saint Augustine, often preaching his doctrines with excessive severity.

Because of its philosophical and theological nature, *Confessions* does not lend itself easily to translation. But Orixe was prepared to carry the work to completion. For one thing, he wanted to demonstrate the potential of the Basque language. For another, religious and mystical themes suited him perfectly, as is illustrated by the celebrated Augustinian statement: "Fecisti nos ad Te et inquietum est cor nostrum, donec requiescat in Te," which Orixe translated as "Zuretzat egin gaituzu, ta eziñegonez daukagu biotza Zuregan atseden dezaño"[96] (You made us for Yourself and our hearts are uneasy until they rest in You).

The translation of this work was a great step forward for modern Basque prose. Orixe translated the difficult Latin of one of the best writers of the age with precision and elegance by using a combination of the Gipuzkoan and Navarrese dialects. His translation pleased even him, although he was very demanding where his own work was concerned. He felt that *Confessions* was a challenging work to attempt to translate: "Gaurkotik au geldtu diteke, Biblia leku, euskal-libururik bikaiñena"[97] (This could be the greatest Basque book from this day forward besides the Bible).

Orixe set the highest possible standards for the Basque he used in the book: "Zein duzu zure ustez, denetan onena? Euskerari begiratuta, *Aitorkizunak*"[98] (In your opinion, which is the best? Where the Basque language is concerned, *Aitorkizunak*).

Once this translation was finished, Orixe began to write what would be his last book. In 1954, while in El Salvador, he started working on *Jainkoaren billa* (In search of God). He finished it in the Basque Country in 1958, but it was not published until 1971. He intended it to be his masterpiece. It continues the religious themes he dealt with in *Quito'n arrebarekin,* because he wanted to produce not just translations but also an original book on a mystical theme: "Oraingo liburu ontan zakukoak atera nai nituke"[99] (In this book I would like to express my innermost thoughts).

He knew that he would struggle with difficult topics in the process, but that did not frighten him. There was a need for a Basque book on ascetic and mystical subjects, since not even the priests had tried to write one: "Zergatik ez dute egin apaiz oiek beroiek nik egin dedana? . . . Gauza zaillean sartu naiz berriro ere, gauza illunak eta izkutuak eta euskera errexez adierazi naiean"[100] (Why have those priests not done themselves what I have done? . . . I have turned toward a difficult topic, attempting to write on obscure and advanced themes in an easy-to-understand Basque).

Gipuzkoan is the predominant dialect in *Jainkoaren billa*. Orixe's Basque, once again, is elegant yet clear. He shows himself to be the master of modern Basque prose. The book was aimed at the common people: "Sartu dedilla liburu au baserriko sukalbaztarren batean ere, ta arta-sorora joateko gauza ez dan amonatxoak ere irakurri dezala, eltzeak gobernatzen ari dan bitartean"[101] (May this book enter even the kitchen of the Basque farmhouse, and may it be read even by the grandmother who can no longer work in the fields and so presides over the cooking pots).

The book's title announces its theme, the search for God through prayer. It is a treatise on spiritual theology divided into two parts. The first contains twenty-eight chapters and the second, fifteen. At the end of the book there are three brief appendices, the first two devoted to the Gospel and Christ and the third to the different schools of mystical prayer.

The first part of the book also deals with mystical prayer and expounds upon the doctrines of Saint John of the Cross. In the second part we can see the influence of Teresa of Ávila, as Orixe talks about the seven levels of prayer and Christ's prayer in the garden of Gethsemane. He also details his thoughts on the Incarnation, a mystery that caused him more than one doubt: "Sartu gaitezen fedezko misterio ontan. Au, bai, leize-zulo aundia edo tulunbioa!"[102] (Let us penetrate this mystery of faith. This is certainly a deep pit or abyss!).

Religious doubts and unfathomable pits did not frighten Orixe. As we have seen, his unshakable faith in Christ was the foundation on which he built his spiritual castle. It was also the solution to any spiritual problem he might have: "Segi Jesukristori. Bera degu bidea, ta bide bakarra aitak ala naita"[103] (Follow Christ. He is our only path because God wishes it).

Orixe chose the following simple, but meaningful, text from his poetry as the epitaph for his tombstone:

> Agur, fede, lurrean
> nuen itsu-mutil
> zuri esker leizean
> ez nun egin amil.[104]

> I salute you, faith, my guide on this Earth; thanks to you, I avoided the pit.

On a final stylistic note, in *Jainkoaren billa* Orixe occasionally uses uncommon, ambiguous, and even obscure words.

To complete the list of Orixe's works, I should mention three others: *El lenguaje vasco* (The Basque language), *Lati-izkuntzaren joskera* (Latin syntax), and the articles published in *Euskal Esnalea* as "Euskal-literatura'ren atze edo edezti laburra" (A short history or background of Basque literature). *El lenguaje vasco* is a grammar, *Lati-izkuntzaren joskera* is a booklet on the syntax of grammatical voices in Latin, and "Euskal-literatura'ren atze edo edezti laburra" deals with Basque literature.

Literary production as abundant as Orixe's could not go unrewarded. Not everything in his life was pain and sorrow. On November 22, 1959, he was elected as an "Euskaltzain osoa" (full member) of Euskaltzaindia. At a meeting attended by many friends, members, and lovers of Basque culture, Koldo Mitxelena praised Orixe highly, saying, among other things, "Euskaltzaindiak ez du Orixe goraltzen, bere barruan artzean, baizik Orixe berak Euskaltzaindia goratzen du bere barruan sartzeaz"[105] (Euskaltzaindia does not honor Orixe by naming him a member; on the contrary, Orixe honors the Academy by joining it).

In 1960 Orixe won first prize for poetry in the Olerti competition, organized by Onaindia and held in Zornotza. It was the first contest he had ever won. Shortly thereafter, he also won first prize in another literary competition in Tolosa. Unfortunately, these awards began arriving too late. After a long and painful bout with rheumatoid arthritis, Orixe died on August 9, 1961, leaving behind a great void in the field of Basque literature.

ORIXE'S USE OF LANGUAGE

As I indicated earlier, one of the harshest attacks against Orixe's work was prompted by its perceived lack of realism or excessive use of idealization. Txillardegi, among others, apostrophized him, saying, "Zuk opa duzun literatura ori ez litzake euskaldunen presunena izango, Euskalerriko tipismoarena baizik"[106] (The literature you propose would not be the product of Basque individuals but, rather, an example of Basque stereotyping).

Orixe's writing, especially his prose, was excellent. In my opinion, he is one of the greatest prose writers in the history of Basque literature. I do not mean to imply that all his works are perfect or that he is perfect in all his works. At times, he comes across as too abstract, cold, intellectual, and dry. When that happens, his literature appears to be intended for a select minority of readers and not for the Basque public in general. His conciseness, which suggests dominion over the language, can also make him difficult to understand and lessen the clarity of his writing, as is the case in certain passages of *Aitorkizunak*. He often shows an exaggerated tendency to suppress articles for the sake of poetic license and literary beauty.[107]

Nevertheless, Orixe took Basque prose to a new level. His writing is not as rhetorical as Axular's was, but it is more popular and, generally speaking, much more comprehensible. Modern Basque prose owes him a great deal, especially in the area of word creation. In his own way he was an aesthete of language who shaped his literary style by using short sentences, popular expressions, and new words, with all of nature as his inspiration.

Moreover, he knew how to infuse his Basque with a new musicality, a new purity, and a new freshness. As Koldo Mitxelena said, "Orixe-z geroztik doiñu berri batean ikasi du mintzatzen euskal prosak"[108] (Since Orixe, Basque prose has learned to express itself with a new musicality).

Orixe did not belong to any literary school, nor could one pinpoint in him the influence of any Basque or foreign writer.[109] He was, however, a great admirer of Sallust, Cicero, and Caesar for their excellent syntax. Still, he resisted the creation of a school that would follow his own style in spite of the fact that for several years he was admired by other writers.

Orixe did not limit himself to the local vocabulary of any dialect or people. In some of his works he employs many synthetic verbs but never as frequently as did Lauaxeta. We might also mention his scant use of conjunctions. Instead, he depended on the internal logic of his sentences to provide continuity. His style varies depending on the public for whom a work was intended, yet Orixe was a writer who at all times was consistent. His work is like a statue in that it cannot be understood without looking at the whole.

Orixe's stand concerning the unification of the Basque language was controversial. Many of his ideas were useful, but the unification of the language would have been difficult to achieve had his ideas been followed to the letter.

The modern age required Basques to create new words to fill the empty places in their vocabulary caused, according to some, by their savage or primitive nature.[110] The usefulness of concepts that had been important in the Middle Ages, such as essence and existence, became secondary to the need to create modern words like *television* and *computer.*

At first the majority of Basque writers agreed on the need for unification. The problem was how to implement it, since agreement on the concepts of modern culture and unification of the language was incomplete. The majority accepted the idea of unifying the language in the areas of spelling, declensions, and verb forms. But even here there was debate over how to go about the unification, and many fruitless arguments arose between two camps, one containing Koldo Mitxelena, Mirande, Txillardegi, Aresti, Villasante, Krutwig, and Intxausti, and the other composed of older writers.

Orixe stood against the purists who advocated a clean Basque, free of the contamination of words borrowed from other languages; however, he also attacked those who favored *mordoilokeria* (the unnecessary use of foreign words). His advice was first to exploit the possibilities available in the Basque language and, once these sources had been exhausted, to draw on foreign tongues. In this area he followed the wise advice of Txomin Aguirre: "Convenido que en vasco tomemos cuando no hay más remedio, raíces extranjeras, cuyo porcentaje es inferior a lo que se supone"[111] (Agreed that in Basque, when there is no alternative, we take words from foreign sources, and the percentage of them in the language is lower than you would think).

Orixe called himself a "moderate purist" who did not oppose all neologisms, because he felt that refined language needed a certain number of them. He believed that, at the moment of actually drawing from foreign sources, however, there existed the danger of accepting the opinions of foreign linguists as if they were law. This danger also extended to the excessive use of neologisms that would push Basque toward *mordoilokeria*.[112]

Orixe favored Urquijo's proposal to adopt the Lapurdin dialect: "Laphurdiko euskerara yotzen du berorrek. Ortan ere ez da izan lehengo. Lengo Euskal Zaindian ere ba-giñan ortara yotzen genunak; bañan Azkue Yaunak porrot eragin zigun 'Gipuzkera osotu' arekin"[113] (You mention the Lapurdin dialect as a solution. You are not the first to do so. In the previous Basque Academy several of us proposed this solution; however, Mr. Azkue won out with his idea of Gipuzkoan fortified by the other dialects).

Being a Gipuzkoan, Orixe could not oppose the use of his own dialect, which he considered ideal for preaching, but he preferred Lapurdin for literature. He did not consider himself to be against any dialect, but he proposed as a criterion that they should "reject all aspects of a dialect that set it apart from the others, and look with favor on that which is common to all." Furthermore, when it came time to apply rules, he asked that Basques go beyond their own dialect and enrich themselves by learning the others as well, at least up to a certain point: "Bakoitzak besteren euskalkiak ikasi ditzala, irakurtzeko lain beintzat, eta orra or Batasuna"[114] (Let each one study the other dialects, at least until they can read them; in that way, we will achieve unity).

Orixe defended the idea of a double language: educated Basque and popular Basque. He did not advocate unification for literature, for he felt that it would kill a writer's spontaneity, but he did want to preserve an educated Basque for literature. He feared that the use of *auntz-euskera* (low-quality Basque) would lead to the disappearance of the language, as happened in Greece with the advent of *demotiké*: "Zein errik izan du Grezia'k baño literatura oberik? . . . Oraingo grezitarrak lotsatzen dira beren izkera erritar edo demotiké'rekin. . . . Demotiké ori bezalako auntz-erdera zikin bat edo auntz-euskera zikin bat naiago al duzute? Nik ez, beintzat. Euskera orrenbesteraño itsusitze ezkero, iltzea berdintsu zaigu"[115] (What nation has had a literature as beautiful as that of Greece? . . . Today the Greeks are ashamed of their poor demotiké language. . . . Do you prefer a patois of Basque and Spanish, like the Greek *demotiké?* I do not. If Basque loses its beauty, then I could care less if it becomes extinct).

It is obvious that Orixe was worried about the purity of the language but was not about to abandon the problem of unification. Because of Basque, his "sweetheart," he lost out on the opportunity to teach other topics at the University of Bordeaux and the University of Guatemala. Regarding the question of the purity of Basque, he was always ready to attack his adversaries, like Quixote righting a wrong.

All the linguistic and philosophical discussions Orixe carried on reveal a character full of strong contrasts. On the one hand, there was Orixe of the childlike soul; on the other, there was a narrow-minded polemicist who was sometimes harsh toward others. At times he relied on the dictates of his conscience to justify his attacks on others. During his dispute with Txillardegi over the content of the latter's *Peru Leartza-ko*, Orixe wrote the following: "Barrenak ez dit agintzen ixillik egotea, liburu onek gaurko gaztejendearen artean egin dezaken kaltearengatik"[116] (My conscience will not let me remain silent, because of the damage that this book will do among today's youth).

The tone of his attacks was often quite strong. He called Unamuno a *sasijakintsu* (false intellectual), because of his attacks on the Basque language. He called the equally controversial academic Krutwig an ingrate: "Eskerbeltza da berori!" (You are ungrateful!). He referred to him indirectly on another occasion by talking about academics with "Falangist and German lineage." At times he felt himself to be so possessed by the truth that he even condemned ecclesiastics like Lafitte, whom he advised to study the theology of Saint Paul: "Lafitte'k ere ba'du teologiaren bearra, bereiziki S. Paulorena. . . . Egia au da, ta ez zuek diozutena"[117] (Lafitte also needs to learn theology, especially that of Saint Paul. . . . The truth is this, and not what you all say it is).

With his personality and manner of self-expression, Orixe was often in the midst of controversy. Unfortunately, when making any critical assessment of this author, it has not always been possible to transcend his religious prejudice. Nevertheless, the true measure of a poet's ability is not what he says but the manner in which he writes. A believing Christian should think the nihilist Mirande no less a poet because Mirande writes about prostitution, pederasty, and violence; the same tolerance should hold true for Orixe's readers. Unfortunately, critics have made him the standard-bearer for religion and a certain type of Basque language. In the last years of his life, this gave rise to a lack of critical objectivity.

There is no lack of critics who see Orixe as a great writer, however: "Aberik sendoenetariko bat galdu du euskerak"[118] (The Basque language has lost one of its most solid supporters). Even among those who did not share his religious temper, there are young writers who praise him, such as Gabriel Aresti:

> Zuek laurok,
> Lizardi,
> Orixe,
> Lauaxeta,
> Loramendi,
> nere barrenean kimacen zarazte
> are oraindik.[119]
>
> You four, Lizardi, Orixe, Lauaxeta, Loramendi, still flourish within me.

Orixe ends the prologue of one of his books with the following words: "El tiempo se encargará de decir lo que se debe a cada cual"[120] (Time alone will decide what each one deserves). I believe that in the years since his death, the exceptional quality of this controversial author, Nicolás Ormaetxea, known as Orixe, has been clearly demonstrated.

To conclude this chapter, I will cite Koldo Mitxelena, who sums up Orixe's life and work as follows: "Egiazko gizon, bere buruarekin borroka eta Jainkoaren bila, egiazko euskaldun eta euskaltzale, Euskal herriaren seme jator, ez hitzez eta oihuz, egunoroko lanaren lanez baizik"[121] (A real man, doing battle with himself and searching for God, a true Basque and Bascologist, a faithful son of the Basque Country, not only in word but in his daily deeds).

CHAPTER SEVEN

Jose Mari Agirre, Alias "Lizardi"

A Lyric Poet

From the mid-sixteenth to the mid-nineteenth century, Basque literature was dominated by religious themes and authors whose ultimate goals were essentially catechistic and apologetic, specifically, in defense of the Basque language. Around 1930 there appeared a group of poets who attempted to create a completely literary aesthetic.[1] For the first time in the history of Basque literature, a group of writers was consciously creating pure, that is, cultured, conceptual, and concise literature. It is appropriate, therefore, to place the beginning of modern Basque poetry between 1930 and 1934, with Lauaxeta's *Bide-barrijak* (New paths, 1931), Lizardi's *Biotz-begietan* (In the eyes of the heart, 1932), Orixe's *Barne-muinetan* (In the marrow, 1934), and some of Loramendi's poems.[2] Aitzol was the theorist and arbiter of the literary beauty of that cultural renaissance. The influence of this group, especially of Lizardi and Lauaxeta, is still evident in some postwar poets.[3] Jose Mari Agirre was not the most modern, but he was the most original and the most lyrical of this group—perhaps in all of Basque literature, even though he was self-taught in literature.[4]

Lizardi initiated a type of poetry very different from the traditional Basque romantic poetry of, for example, the Gipuzkoan Emeterio Arrese or from the wordy, sentimental poetry of the Bizkaian Arrese Beitia. Instead of a narrative epic, Lizardi gave us lyricism; instead of the popular stanzas of the bertsolariak, he gave us cultured poetry; and instead of the sensual verse of the Romantics, he gave us verse that was intellectual and conceptual.

Lizardi's style is very personal. He elevated the Basque language, transcending the popular language of the troubadours to reach the heights of a symbolic Euskara. The desire of the first Basque poet, Detxepare, to elevate the Basque language to a *gohien gradora* (higher level) is realized in Lizardi's poetry.[5] Aitzol reflects on this innovative aspect of Lizardi's language and poetic style: "The powerful intelligence and extremely pure aesthetic taste of Xabier de Lizardi has opened a new channel for the artistic future of the racial tongue. For that reason, he should be considered an innovator and the luckiest adapter of the Basque language to currents of modern thought. This has been his supreme aspiration."[6]

In spite of Lizardi's exceptional talent, his poetry was largely unknown to the general public. Laziness and ignorance of autochthonous values also contributed to the Basque people's limited and imperfect knowledge of his work. The high literary quality of that work, especially of his poetry, was, however, accepted uncritically.[7]

In this chapter I will give an overview of Lizardi's complete works, concentrating especially on the poetry collected in *Biotz-begietan*.[8] I will describe the historical context in which he lived, pointing out the influence of his family and that of Arana y Goiri in the literary, linguistic, and political areas of his life. I will analyze Lizardi's favorite themes, focusing on several of his most representative poems. Finally, I will study his poetic style.

HISTORICAL CONTEXT

Jose Mari Agirre was born in Zarautz, Gipuzkoa, on April 18, 1896. When he was ten years old his family moved to Tolosa, where Jose Mari received his secondary-level education. He pursued a career in law at the Universidad Central in Madrid, graduating in 1917. He managed the Perot metallurgical factory in Tolosa and in 1923 married Francisca Eizaguirre. He died in Tolosa on March 12, 1933, just short of his thirty-seventh birthday.

Lizardi's family was well-off. His father held a degree in mathematics and physical sciences and had monarchical political leanings.[9] The young poet was a cultured man who enjoyed the benefits of a comfortable social position that allowed him to pursue university studies, a rare thing for the great majority of Basques at that time. Lizardi did not become a Basque nationalist because of his father's ideas, however, but because of a meeting with the political idealist Arana y Goiri. Lizardi profoundly admired Arana y Goiri. He called him a "bomb of idealism." He later claimed that there was "a biography that, in my opinion, should be written without delay. That of Sabino de Arana y Goiri. . . . To erect this man as a model of fortitude, integrity, patriotism, and sacrifice to an ideal."[10]

Lizardi was born with a vocation for poetry, but Basque literature would never have known his lovely verses had he not come to know Arana y Goiri's political creed. Basque patriotism motivated him to become a poet. He dedicated "Gure mintzo" (Our language) to the founder of the Basque Nationalist Party, the man who "aberri ta mintzoz gu yantziarena"[11] (bestowed upon us our country and our language).

Lizardi's family did not favor his learning Basque, and by the time he finished his secondary education, he had almost completely forgotten what Basque he had learned in his childhood: "We had half-learned Basque in childhood, later we forgot three-fourths of that half."[12]

Years later, as a young man, Lizardi would reveal this unfavorable family atmosphere. On the fiftieth anniversary of Arana y Goiri's conversion to Basque nationalism, Lizardi recalled his own youth, an age of "lethargic and collegial" separation from the consciousness of his Basque identity and tradition:

> I remember that at eighteen, I considered myself a furious Spaniard. . . . As far as Basque was concerned, it did not deserve the least respect. I knew it, more or less, and by accident. My long stays in the kitchen of my childhood, and the obligatory, although superficial, contact with the boys of a school in a profoundly Basque town were responsible for the fact that my national language was not completely unknown to me, even though I never spoke it except with repugnance and without syntax.[13]

As a result of Arana y Goiri's teachings regarding the Basque nation and language, as well as his own efforts, Lizardi abandoned his lethargy and slowly mastered the language. While he was studying law, he implemented a serious study of Euskara, surrendering himself completely to the task. In 1916, at age twenty, he began to publish his first poems in Basque in the magazine *Euzko-gogoa*. In those poems we see the stammering of a young, immature writer who is still far from a mastery he will later demonstrate. This period of his production lasted a decade.[14] Lizardi did not publish most of these early works in *Biotz-begietan*, undoubtedly because he did not consider them good enough.

In the second decade of the twentieth century, both Basque nationalism and the literary arts experienced a great revival because of the efforts of Campión, Azkue, Etxegarai, Urkijo, Aguirre, Kirikiño, and Engracio de Aranzadi, alias "Kizkitza."

In 1919 the creation of Euskaltzaindia, the Academy of the Basque Language, filled many Basques with joy, because it foretold a hopeful future for Basque letters. That cultural flowering was cut off by the seven-year dictatorship of General Miguel Primo de Rivera (1923–1930), but the Basques were not cowed. In 1927, in the middle of de Rivera's dictatorship, a "Day of the Basque Language" was celebrated in Arrasate. Euskaltzaleak, the group responsible in large measure for the renaissance of Basque poetry, was born during that celebration.

In this historical context, Lizardi went public, using for the first time the pseudonym that made him famous, Xabier de Lizardi. He began giving lectures, writing articles in favor of Basque, and organizing literary celebrations, thus becoming one of the greatest defenders of the Basque cultural renaissance of his day.[15]

Because of his efforts, the Basque people, especially the Gipuzkoans, began to appreciate and respect him. He was named secretary of the *Gipuzkoako Buru Batzar,* or the Basque Nationalist Party of Gipuzkoa, but politics did not attract him. He was not a man with a political calling, but rather became involved in politics because of the specific historical context in which he lived. His passion was the Basque language that had been abandoned by the Basque bourgeoisie and attacked by Basque intellectuals like Unamuno.

Lizardi was a decent, principled man. Before criticizing other Basques for their lack of interest in their language, "a grandmother without grandchildren among the languages of the world," he plunged deeply into the study of the language until he had converted it into an instrument of literary beauty. As he tells us, he wanted to write, he wanted to sing, but he lacked the voice of a poet, even though he felt poetic inspiration at a very early age: "This desire to sing was born with me, and since childhood it has been one of my intimate desires. . . . I tried to sing, but in vain; I lacked the soothing voice required by my desire. . . . I owe the fact that a prisoner lived within me to his [Arana y Goiri's] teaching."[16]

After acquiring command of the Basque language, Lizardi began a critical analysis of its situation. He tried to make the use of Basque among Basques fashionable and fought against the intense racial dislike that many Basques felt toward their language. His main objective was the field of Basque literature, which, because of neglect, lacked indigenous monuments.

Lizardi began to attack Basques in general, especially those who proposed that the pelota and Basque berets were the essential traits of the Basque soul. Folkloric demonstrations were fine, but they were not enough.

He did not accept the attitude of the many Basques who said that their language was beautiful but spoke Spanish, nor did he accept the conduct of those who defended Basque but wrote only in Spanish, or the Unamuno-like position that Basque, unlike Spanish, was inadequate for expressing beauty or abstract concepts: "Gauzak ederki ta mamiz adierazten euskerak eztiola erderari batere zorrik"[17] (Basque is not inferior to Spanish for expressing things beautifully and profoundly).

Lizardi was especially aware of the upper class's abandonment of Basque. He was also aware of the profound influence that these social levels exercised over members of the lower classes, such as farmers, fishermen, and laborers. For that reason, Lizardi expresses his desire to see such a transformation become reality: "Euzko-aundiki guziek euskeraz ariko balira, euskera gaizkatua, salbatua, omen genduke . . . ta orren atzetik ari ere ditugu ainbat egiñal: gure aundikiei, euskera, biotzean ezezik ezpañetan ere, nondik itsatsiko"[18] (If all upper-class Basques spoke Basque, the language would be liberated and saved . . . we have made so many efforts to accomplish that: to place Basque not only in the hearts but on the lips of the Basque upper classes).

The memory of his old and wrinkled grandmother's funeral procession and burial was deeply engraved in Lizardi's mind, and he associated her death with the possible demise of ancient Basque: "Suddenly I suffered something like a hallucination, and I thought I was attending the funeral of the Basque language."[19]

At this point it would be fitting to specify what type of Basque our poet advocated. Lizardi knew that to save the language the different Basque dialects had to be combined into a unified, literary Basque language. He knew about the failed attempts to do this. He also knew that the Basques constituted a very small nation divided between two great states. Basque literature could not compete with the two great literatures of France and Spain, nor could Euskara compete with the languages of Cervantes and Rabelais. Modern life made it impossible for Basque to continue to exist in isolation, however. Nor did Lizardi forget that Basque had never been a vehicle for culture or the language of government or of the upper classes. Thus, there was an urgent need for a unified Basque, for a Gipuzkoan dialect enriched by the other dialects, and for a type of cultured poetry that would attract the attention of the Basque bourgeoisie:

> We cannot think today that Basque exists in isolation, or in the unchanging state in which it vegetated in the ancient past, when the future and imagined Spanish babbled its serious corruptions of Latin, and faced with the ever-narrowing paddock in which the languages of splendid literature and the glittering modern age have placed us, we must engage in open battle outside our ancient enclosure or perish; that is, we raise the Basque language to an honorable literary level, or it will die.[20]

With these well-defined objectives, Lizardi first began to take his poetic vocation seriously and to write cultured, conceptual, innovative poetry. In spite of his exhausting job as director of a company, he managed to combine his administrative tasks with his poetic mission. Like the French symbolists of the nineteenth century, Lizardi felt that he was charged with a special social mission: "The poet is a providential man in the revival and recovery of the people."[21]

Encouraged by his friend Orixe, Lizardi began to send his poetry to literary competitions. In 1930 he entered three poems—"Paris'ko txolarrea" (Sparrow from Paris), "Agur" (Good-bye), and "Otartxo utsa" (Small, empty basket)—in the First Day of Basque Poetry competition in Errenteria. Even though he did not win any prizes, he continued working intensely. It was during this period that he composed his best poems, "Urte giroak ene begian" (The seasons of the year in my eye), "Biotzean min dut" (My heart aches), and "Euzko-bidaztiarena" ([The poem] of the Basque traveler). The following year he presented the first of these poems at the Second Day of Basque Poetry and won first prize. This encouraged him in his creative efforts, and that same year he began to select twenty-one of his best poetic compositions to be polished and perfected before being published in *Biotz-begietan*.

Many critics attacked Lizardi's innovative verses, however. Like all pioneers, Lizardi had to suffer the consequences of criticism that was, occasionally, excessively rigorous and unfair.[22] Critics claimed that Lizardi's new poetry would serve only to eliminate the Basque language and to destroy other potential poets. One of the severest attacks came from Aitzol, the great theoretician and animating spirit of the literary renaissance, who underwent a drastic change of thinking with respect to modern poetry. As we saw in chapter 5, he believed early on that a political renaissance had to be preceded by a literary one, especially in the area of poetry. In the last years of his life, however, he opted for a popular type of poetry that was more accessible to the people. Aitzol's commentary on Orixe's *Barne-muinetan* and on Lizardi's posthumous poems and *Itz-lauz* demonstrate the change that was occurring in his literary thinking:

> In spite of their indisputable literary value, we can almost guarantee that they will not manage to strengthen and invigorate Euskara. They lack the essential ingredient: the freshness, the naturalness of an easy, intelligible, diluted Basque. The majority of their poems and articles are written according to linguistic formulas, and we note the absence of a feeling of simplicity and naturalness that is appropriate in a living, breathing language. In those poems and articles, there is a great wealth of study, work, decision-making, and even talent; but their artificial aspects dominate the art in them, research dominates their natural elements, and the twisted word dominates their spontaneity.[23]

Aitzol's attacks were not launched only against Lizardi but targeted Lauaxeta and, later, Orixe. Lizardi complained of the treatment he received, both on his own behalf and on behalf of the group: "Nik idazle errezzale, bakar bat ere ez det bere bidetik okertu nai izan. Bestalde, bere artan yarraitu dezaten alegiñak egiten dizkiet. . . . Guk badakigu idazle errezak, olerkari errezak 'publico' aundia dutena; gure bakartasunean otxan-otxan etsitzen degunezkero, ze dala-ta zuek guri arrika?"[24] (I did not want to throw any writer who is fond of an easy-to-read style off the track. On the contrary, I do whatever possible so that they will continue their work. . . . We know that easy-to-read writers, easy-to-read poets, have more readers than we do. Since we docilely resign ourselves to our solitude, why do you attack us?).

COMMON POETIC THEMES

The novelty of Lizardi's poetic art is not based on themes but, rather, on the form in which he treated them. His poetry usually deals with God, humankind, and nature. I will clarify these themes, concentrating on descriptions of the countryside, grief and death, the Basque language, and the caducity of life. Lizardi became intimately involved in transforming these themes with his powerful imagination through metaphors. Thus, natural phenomena appeared in his poetry with a force that they did not originally possess.

Nature

The countryside fascinated Lizardi and acquired a fundamental importance in his lyric poetry. The mountains were his inspiration, and botanical elements abound in his poems. Weary from his daily work, he liked to go alone into the forest or sit in a meadow to scrutinize the most insignificant details of a tree. In this way he composed "Urte giroak ene begian" (Landscape of the seasons), one of his best poems, which is divided into four parts that represent the seasons. Traveling through the foothills of Mount Urkizu or in the Muttitegi apple orchard, he carefully contemplated the changes in nature during the different seasons.

In winter he concentrated on the flower of the gorse thicket, the leafless bramble bush, the broken, empty nest, the oak trees thirsting for the light of spring. In springtime he was attracted by the different flowers, birds celebrating the season of love, the young orchard in blossom, strawberry patches in bloom, and the meadow covered in clover. In summer he observed the bees and the blackberry bushes in bloom. And, finally, in autumn he observed ivy in its prime, withering flowers, and butterflies. Furthermore, he contemplated the multicolored autumnal panorama of the Basque countryside, the copper-colored fern fields, like rust on the surface of the earth, in contrast with the green of the meadows. In spite of the fleeting nature of time and the sadness that invaded his soul at the approach of winter, the poet asked God to let him see once more the flowering of the gorse thicket.

Lizardi uses a lot of prosopopoeia—the personification of inanimate beings. The earth is a woman; the forest, a sweetheart; the sun, a husband.

He creates animated personifications, full of life, color, and movement and drawn from material elements such as the forest, a shadow, or the signs of spring. These inanimate elements stirred up in him a sense of living dialogue rather than physical emotions.

The contemplation of the countryside in Lizardi's poetry is very personal and intimate. He did not limit himself to describing nature and material objects in detail, as did realist writers, nor did he create the exuberant flora and fauna of the modernists or sentimentally describe the external aspects of reality, as did the Romantics. Lizardi, as a good lyricist, internalized what he saw and, by doing so, distanced himself from traditional Basque poetry, which gravitated toward a more epic and narrative emphasis. He knew how to turn his interior world over and express it through scenery, and he offered a new cultured, lyrical type of poetry to offset the sensual, verbose, easy-to-understand poetry of the Romantics.

Grief and Death

This double theme appears in Lizardi's poems "Xabiertxoren eriotza" (The death of little Xavier) and "Biotzean min dut" (My heart aches). The first is a sweet, heartfelt poem in which the author describes, with a touch of pathos, the death of his first child on Christmas Eve morning in 1925. It was written on December 24, 1926, to commemorate the first anniversary of Xavier's death.

In the poem, Lizardi's son, "the most intimate portion of two hearts," is already dead, but the parents do not want to believe it because of the smile that lingers on his face. The father rebels against the death, but it comes on relentlessly, and he is left with no consolation but his restrained tears. The parents' grief, especially the mother's, is very deep; her eyes are transformed into bottomless pits of sorrow.

But suffering did not make Lizardi sigh, as it did the Romantics. In his work, reason always dominates over sentiment. In the poem he states that his hopes regarding his firstborn were as fragile as butterflies or flowers. But it is Christmas Eve, and children come singing Christmas carols. The mother does not want to receive them, for it is a day of mourning, but she gives in at Lizardi's insistence. He turns to God, where life and death converge. His Christian sorrowful acceptance and the assurance that he will see his little angel in heaven ease his grief. Thousands of angels are not sufficient to adore the child of Bethlehem, so God the Father needs the presence of little Xavier to make the adoration complete:

> Gabon-egun-goizean
> seaskatxoan
> Xabiertxo gaxoa
> gaitzak ito-zorian
> zegoan.

Zer duk, eguzki orrek,
gure ederrena?
Nork min egin, esaidak,
biotz biren zatirik
maitena? . . .

Itxon! Ustez, arnasa
baretu zaio:
parre-antx gozo batek
ezpaintxoak argitu
dizkio . . .

Ene! Beldur! Ez il, ez
arren, txikia!
Ez yoan, gure poza,
ez, gure biziaren
argia!! . . .

Ene! Amen begien
negar-obiak
ondoa yo-eziñak
egin ete-ditu Yaun
aundiak? . . .

Eguzkiak inguma
bezin maitea;
ala maiteminduak,
maite-españek ukitu
lorea! . . .

Igan ipiñitako
amesak, baña,
auskorrak ete-ziran,
inguma ta loreak
ez aña? [25]

On Christmas Eve morning he was in his cradle, poor little Xavier, on the verge of suffocating from his illness.

What's wrong, our sun, our most beautiful, tell me who hurt you, most beloved of two hearts.

Wait! Your breathing seems to have quieted. A sweet smile illuminates your lips.

Ay! I'm afraid! Don't die! Please, little one, don't go, our happiness, no, light of our lives!

Oh! Has God perhaps created unfathomable pits of tears in those maternal eyes?

Beloved as much as the butterflies love the sun; or the lover loves the flower kissed by the lips of his beloved.

But were the illusions I placed in you more fragile than the butterflies and the flowers?

The second poem wherein we find the double theme of grief and death is "Biotzean min dut." This poem is an elegy full of art and feeling. Once again the type of restrained grief typical of the Basques appears in Lizardi's poetry:

> Biotzean min dut, min etsia
> negar ixilla darion miña.[26]

> My heart aches with resigned sorrow, the grief of one who weeps silently.

The poet and three of his cousins are carrying the coffin containing the body of their maternal grandmother, who passed away in her nineties. Lizardi feels the weight of the coffin more in his heart than in his arms. A refrain repeated eleven times in the poem represents the sound of the sad and measured footsteps of the mourners at the funeral, and that refrain imbues the entire poem with the rhythm of pathos:

> Ots!
> Ots!
> bizion oñok![27]

> The sound! The sound! Footsteps of the living!

While passing through streets where his grandmother ran as a child, empty today of children's voices, the grandson remembers the happiness of those past times, a happiness that contrasts sharply with the sad shadow of her death. In one verse, marvelous with contrasts, the poet wishes his grandmother eternal happiness represented by a bouquet of flowers. The contrasts between life and death are successfully achieved through the use of specific pairs of adjectives (old-new), verbs (go-come), adverbs (today-tomorrow), and nouns (happiness-sorrow, iron-silver):

> Egun zaarrak yoan ta
> berriak etorri,
> gaur poz biar oñaze,
> noiz burni noiz zillar,
> zenbaitek ondamendi
> baituten katea
> lore-sorta bekizu
> goi-muñoak zear![28]

> May this chain formed by old days and new days, days of sorrow and of happiness, days of iron and of silver; [may this chain that is the] ruin of so many be for you a bouquet of flowers through the celestial heights.

The poet enters the church in a state of mind beyond consciousness, pushed along by the crowd of mourners. After an hour, they leave the church, and as they head for the cemetery, once again we hear the rhythmic footsteps that had ceased during the funeral. Upon reaching the cemetery, everything changes, including the rhythm of the verses, which began with eight lines each and now have only six and four lines alternating. Life has ceased. For the last time, the poet can view the wrinkled, still-smiling face, and one silent tear appears on his cheek like a tiny star in the dark of night. At the end of the poem, his grief is transformed, and his heart, like a nesting place for hope, is filled with thoughts about his final encounter with his grandmother when his own life ends.

The Basque Language

Lizardi's most important poem dealing with the theme of Euskara is entitled "Eusko-Bidaztiarena" (Song of the Basque traveler). Unlike Arana y Goiri, who considered being Basque the first requirement for Basque patriotism, Lizardi identified a knowledge of the Basque language as the basis of Basque nationalism. In Orixe's opinion, Lizardi's cultivation of the Basque language reached a very high level: "Euskera erpineraiño landu digu"[29] (He has cultivated Basque to its apex for us).

"Eusko-Bidaztiarena" begins with a few introductory words of dedication to Unamuno: "To the illustrious Mr. Miguel de Unamuno, bestowing on him our contemptuous boldness."[30] It also contains a well-known quotation taken from *Linguae vasconum primitiae per Dominum Bernardum Detxepare Rectorem Sancti Michaelis Veteris* by Detxepare, in which he invites the Basque language to go out into the world:

> ¡Heuskera, ialgi adi kanpora!
> ¡Heuskera, habil mundu guzira![31]
>
> Basque, go forth!
> Basque, travel the world!

In a similar way, Lizardi wanted his "gogamenaren ezkon xuria" (white spouse of the intellect) to extend itself more and more broadly, thereby transforming itself into an adequate instrument of communication. In "Eusko-Bidaztiarena" he invites it to abandon its "campestre atavío" (peasant garments) and become a modern language capable of expressing any concept. Once again the poet uses contrasting pairs of words:

> Baña nik, izkuntza larrekoa,
> nai aunat ere noranaikoa:
> yakite-egoek igoa;
> soña zaar, berri gogoa;
> azal orizta, muin betirakoa.[32]

But I love you for every purpose, rural language: lifted up
on the wings of knowledge; old body, new spirit; yellowing
skin, eternal marrow.

Unlike Unamuno, who classified Basque as an intrinsically useless and
incapable language, in the poem Lizardi lobbies for a modern, scientific,
educated Basque language. Familiarity with Unamuno's ideas on this subject may help us understand the context in which Lizardi wrote this poem.

In 1901 Unamuno was invited to give a lecture on the occasion of the
Lore-jokoak in Bilbo. In that speech he announced the following, to the ex-
asperation of many Basques:

In the thousand years of the Basque language, there is no
room for modern thought. . . . Basque comes to us as a narrow
language; and since its fabric and its weave will not stretch,
let's break it. . . . Let's bury it in holy ground with a dignified funeral and embalm it with science; let us relegate this
interesting relic to research.[33]

Unamuno's attacks on the Basque language contrast sharply with his
unconditional support for Spanish. For him the only perfect and superior
language in Spain was Spanish. His main preoccupation was unerringly
centered on Spain and its official language. He mercilessly mistreated the
language of his ancestors.

Lizardi refused to bury his "white spouse," the Basque language. Basque
touched him in his "heart of hearts," just as Spanish did Unamuno, and for
that reason Lizardi the Gipuzkoan was able to do what Unamuno the Bizkaian was unable to do: He mastered the Basque language to the point of
transforming it into an instrument of literary beauty. He was not intimi-
dated by Unamuno's intellectual greatness, nor was he persuaded by that
writer's lovely words: "The thought that slept in a chrysalis in Axular's
Basque, imprisoned in the tangled cocoon of that venerable ancient language, will break out and bathe itself in light, its barely dried newly open
wings exposed to the sun, in the Spanish of tomorrow."[34]

Lizardi was worried about the survival of Basque. Thus, he proposed
a type of unified Basque, a common literary dialect composed essentially
of Gipuzkoan enriched by the dialects of Iparralde, preferably Lapurdin.
Some of the innovations he used were later accepted by Euskaltzaindia, for
example:

1. The ergative—using *ek* instead of the traditional Gipuzkoan *ak* as
   a plural subject marker for transitive verbs, as in: "Gizonek egin
   dute" (The men did it).

2. Suppressing the participial *i* and *tu* before verbal moods, such as the
   subjunctive, the imperative, and the potential, as in: *ikus(i) dezagun*
   (let's see it); *begira(tu) ezazu* (look).

3. Using words with different spellings, such as *erran* instead of *esan* and *itsaso* instead of *itxaso*.

4. Although Lizardi did not use the letter *h*, as is done in Euskara Batua today, he did respect the double letters, as in *zaar* (old), *leen* (first), and *aalmen* (power).

Lizardi was a very respectful man, a writer who did not want to impose his educated style or his Gipuzkoan dialect on others. He never looked down on the popular poetry of the bertsolariak nor on the other dialects. He succeeded in defending his opinions and his controversial cultured poetry without injuring those who did not share his ideas: "Gure baratzean mota guzietako landareak bear ditugu. Ez degu zapuztu-arazi bear ez bertsolari mordolloa, ez olerkari garbi-antxekoa, ez-eta ere berrizale biurria"[35] (We need all types of plants in our garden. We must not reject the crude bertsolari or the purist poet or the difficult-to-understand innovator. . . . Bizkaian, Gizpuzkoan, Lapurdin, they are all Basque and they are beautiful Basque. We need absolutely each and every one of them).

Caducity of Life

The fleeting quality of life is a theme that appears in Lizardi's poem "Bultzi-leiotik" (From the window of the train). From the window of a moving train, the poet sees how quickly the images of a farmer, the mountains, the trees, and the farmlands pass before him. He paints the Basque countryside impressionistically with colorful, verbal brush strokes, rhythmic exclamations, and the least possible number of verbs to slow the movement. It is transitory poetry. Human life does not have a stable consistency. It passes by like a speeding train. Humankind would like to stop the rhythm of life to capture and detain happiness, but cannot. Night inevitably follows day, and death follows life:

> Oi, lur, oi, lur!
> oi, ene lur nerea! . . .
> oi, goiz eme,
> parre gozoz ernea! . . .[36]

> Oh, land, oh, land!
> oh, land of mine! . . .
> oh, gentle morning,
> born with a sweet smile! . . .

STYLE

While analyzing Lizardi's poems, we have a glimpse of his style. I have described the poet as difficult to understand, even for natives, as cultured, innovative, and not a Romantic. I will now delve more deeply into his style.

Lizardi had his own personality, his own unmistakable art, and his own very definite individuality. As a result, he bequeathed a very personal and creative poetic heritage, a poetry that is intellectual, compact, concise, rhythmic, well constructed, and classical.

Well-Constructed Poetry

As an artist, Lizardi demanded a great deal of himself. The principal objective of his poetic production was always the search for perfection in language and form. He showed himself to be a painstaking craftsman who meticulously used the most precise and appropriate words to express his ideals and feelings. He was not a prolific poet, for he preferred to seek out perfection and precision. He never considered stylistic perfection to be dependent upon creative productivity. He avoided repetition and imitation, even of himself, and always sought original forms, unusual rhythms, and new ideas.

Lizardi demonstrated his artistic and perfectionist disposition in his criticism of other poets and of his own poetic production. In a letter to the then-young poet Jokin Zaitegi, he expressed himself as follows:

> Aolku bat eman nai dizut. Nere aburuz zure lantxo oietan neurtitz zabartxoak, ("prosaismos" esango nuke erderaz), arkitzen dira bear baño maizago . . . badirudi lanari ez diozula ekiten bear bezain astiro; biotzean darabilkizuna laisterregi jalki-bearrak, neurtitza aski lantzen galazi egiten dizula. . . . nere iritziz, lirikan beintzat, neurtitzak bitxia bezelakoa bear du izan, geldiro auznartua, gogoa ta belarria ase ez ditzan bitartean.[37]

> I want to give you some advice. In my opinion, in these works of yours there appear, more often than they should, what we would call in Spanish prosaic rhythms . . . it seems to me that you do not work for the required amount of time and that the need to tell what's in your heart keeps you from reworking your verse sufficiently. In my opinion, at least in lyrical poetry, the poem should be like a jewel worked very slowly and not accepted until the mind and the ear are satisfied.

Lyrical Poetry

Lizardi wanted to be an innovator, to end the populism of traditional and Romantic Basque poetry, and to create a written lyrical form destined specifically for select minority groups. He was able to bring his innovations to both lyrical poetry and the Basque language. He is, in fact, perhaps the best lyric poet in the history of Basque literature. His depth of thought and concentration did not eclipse the highly lyrical quality of his poetry. He knew how to make the best of brief sentences, compact language, and suggestive images, and he put them to use creating a type of lyric poetry that Basque literature had previously lacked. In the opinion of Koldo Mitxelena, "Gurean, beste nonnai bezala, eztira asko izan egiazko lirikoak. Lotsarik gabe aitor dezakegu. Eta norbait autatu bearrean, Lizardi autatuko genduke askok, iñori ezer kendu gabe, euskal-lirikaren ezaugarritzat"[38] (In ours [poetry], as in any other, there have not been many true lyrical writers. We must confess this without shame, and if we had to choose, we would choose Lizardi as the outstanding Basque lyric poet, and do so without slighting anyone else).

In his poetry, as well as in his critical writings, one of Lizardi's greatest concerns was that poetic creations not lack lyricism. Lizardi, a friend and great admirer of Lauaxeta, advised him on this point on more than one occasion:

> I would advise you, my friend, to make yourself all heart and eyes and leave almost nothing to your head, except for the caution I mentioned earlier, to link and give unity to the elements contributed by your heart and eyes . . . it seems evident to me that if lyric verse is to be superior in some way to prose, it will not be because of what every poem inevitably contains of the conventional, but, rather, because of that which helps extract the maximum expressiveness from the language . . . lyric poetry should aspire to concentrate within itself the greatest possible level of beauty.[39]

Concise and Difficult-to-Understand Poetry

Lizardi's poetry, like that of Góngora and Guillén, is difficult to understand, but the more you read it, the more you like it. It is difficult even for many Basque native speakers who are accustomed to Romantic verse or the popular poetry of the bertsolariak. Lizardi avoids verbosity and the monotony caused by the repetition of traditional rhythms. His conciseness, his lexicon, his use of synthetic verbs, and his use of elision contribute to the difficulty of his poetry.

Lizardi is a poet of detail and specificity. He does not ramble, nor is he prolific with words. Rather, he tends to be laconic in expression, sober in style, and brief of phrase. He pastes not only words together but sentences as well and eliminates verbs and certain words in the process.

The pureness of Lizardi's vocabulary is another reason that the reader may be slow to comprehend his poetry. We have noted his admiration for Arana y Goiri, whose reforms not just were political but also extended to poetic rules, to grammar, and to vocabulary. He created many neologisms, at times giving his Basque an artificial flavor. In the first stage of his literary creation, Lizardi employed some Arana y Goiri neologisms. Some of them, such as *olerki* (poetry) and *aberri* (country), have become part of modern Basque; others, such as *yaupaleme* (priestess) and *urrutizkin* (telephone), are merely memories of a more purist past.

Lizardi also used other techniques seldom employed in traditional Basque poetry, such as elision, caesura, dialogue, exclamations, question marks, clipped rhythms, and a variety of verses to break the monotony of traditional poetry and the bertsolari's use of syllables.

Profoundly Basque Poetry

Lizardi's poetry is Basque not only because it is written in Basque, but also because of its indigenous flavor. His goal was to create in accordance with the spirit of the Basque language and temperament. He created a type of autochthonous poetry that respected Basque characteristics and avoided the universalist label of verse that would be inexpressive and meaningless for his people. It seems strange, for example, that he was not influenced by the literary schools that were so important at the time, such as modernism in Spain and surrealism in France.[40] Our Gipuzkoan poet was not interested in the vanguard schools of the era, as was Lauaxeta. Lizardi's countryside is purely Basque, characteristic of and particular to a small nation with elements that set it apart from all others. His poetry is not as popular and ruralistic as Orixe's, but he uses native realities extracted from Basque life and the Basque countryside. It was always his intention to imprint his poetry with the idiosyncrasies of the Basque spirit: the sobriety of expression and constant use of opportunities offered him by the Basque language. He simplified his sentences by eliminating certain verb forms and enriched his lexicon by using compositional techniques and inventing new words. Expressions and speech patterns that were purely Basque also helped enhance the Basque flavor of his poetry.

Poetic Imagery

Lizardi's poetry is full of similes, comparisons, and metaphors. He surprises the reader with the beauty of his language and images. He uses many epithets and clashing colors and strives to shape his words into metaphors. His imagery is represented in a basically classical and traditional manner. He also attempts to give original personality to his artistic feelings by converting elements of nature into image and metaphor. For example, springtime is represented by a young woman dressed in blue, summer by a sea of fire, winter by an old man, the sun by a king, and the forest by a new bride. The day has blue eyes and night has black ones. In his poetry, Lizardi endowed nature with a unique and personal vigor.

In light of all this, we may conclude that Lizardi was an artist with words. He gave the Basque language a power and precision it had never known. He was undoubtedly the most lyrical poet of his time and the most creative voice in written poetry. Because he was self-taught in literature, he was also an isolated and unique case in Basque literature. Unfortunately, the briefness of his life prevented him from being better known, but what remains of his literary work is sufficient to define him as an exceptional writer.

CHAPTER EIGHT

Esteban Urkiaga, Alias "Lauaxeta" (1905-1937)

A Modern Poet of the Pre-Civil War Period

Never in all the past history of Basque literature has there been a trio of poets as important as Orixe, Lizardi, and Esteban Urkiaga, alias "Lauaxeta." Orixe's religious poems in *Barne-muinetan* (1934) and his epic poetry in *Euskaldunak* (first edition, 1950) reached heights that would be difficult to surpass. Lizardi became perhaps the best lyric poet in Basque literature with the intimate lyricism of *Biotz-begietan* (1932). Lauaxeta, thanks to the influence of foreign poets such as Baudelaire and Verlaine, was able to add *Bide-barrijak* (New paths) to Basque poetry.

Nevertheless, the Bizkaian Lauaxeta has remained somewhat forgotten and ignored for reasons that lie in the difficulties presented by his excessive use of synthetic verbs and archaic words and the secret flavor of his Bizkaian dialect. It is only in the last few years that the public has done Lauaxeta justice with the publication of several books and a doctoral thesis on the man and his work.[1]

Lauaxeta was the Basque poet most open to new literary currents from abroad, but his life was short. Falangists shot him on the morning of June 25, 1937, in the old cemetery of Gasteiz. Thus Basque literature lost one of the best poets of pre-Civil War Spain.

In the 1920s French literature experienced one of its periods of greatest splendor. Poetry, theater, and the novel were renewed because of such writers as Proust, Valéry, and Gide. In 1924 there also appeared the first "Manifesto of Surrealism," presented by Breton.

Lauaxeta knew how to take advantage of innovative trends, especially those initiated by the French because of his fondness for reading and his knowledge of languages. He read French, German, Italian, and Catalonian authors, not to mention Basque, Spanish, Latin, and Greek. We can deduce from citations in his works that he was greatly influenced by Baudelaire, Verlaine, Cocteau, and Apollinaire. Also evident in his poetry is the influence of the concise, conceptual, intellectual poetry of Juan Ramón Jiménez and Valéry, as well as that of certain members of the "Generation of '27," such as Federico García Lorca. But without a doubt the person who influenced him the most was Baudelaire. Lauaxeta even translated several of his poems into Basque.

LAUAXETA'S LIFE

Esteban Urkiaga was born on August 3, 1905, in Laukiniz, Bizkaia. Four years later, his family moved to Mungia, Bizkaia. At age eleven Esteban entered the Jesuit School in Durango, where he studied Latin and rhetoric. In 1921 he began his novitiate in Loiola, Gipuzkoa, and studied philosophy there and in Oña, Burgos.

The years spent as a novice studying philosophy (1921–1928) were decisive in Lauaxeta's formation because of the influence of his professors and friends. Father Ignacio Errandonea provided him with an excellent classical background in Latin and Greek. The future poet was able to familiarize himself with classical authors, including Cicero, Horace, Ovid, Virgil, Sophocles, and Demosthenes.

Father Estefanía, a professor of literature in Loiola, introduced Lauaxeta to European literature, especially the symbolist poetry of Baudelaire and Verlaine as well as the pure poetry of Valéry. The young student also became familiar with Spanish poetry (mostly the works of Luis de Granada, Luis de León, and Saint John of the Cross), English poetry (Keats), Italian poetry (Dante, Leopardi, Carducci), Portuguese poetry (Camões), German poetry (Goethe, Hölderlin, Heine), and Catalonian poetry (Joan Maragall).

While still in Loiola, around 1924, his friendship with Zaitegi opened up still another area for the young Lauaxeta, who was becoming conscious of his Basque identity that was evolving from a simple interest in the language to Basque patriotism and nationalism. Through Zaitegi he met others who later would be great writers, lexicographers, and Bascophiles, for example, Plácido Muxika and Andima Ibinagabeitia. This group published their poems and literary works in the Jesuit magazine *Jesus'en biotzaren deya* (The call of the heart of Jesus). Lauaxeta published his first short stories there, as well as some religious poetry and several translations of the works of Maragall. During this period, Lauaxeta used the pseudonym Basaraz.

From 1926 to 1928 Lauaxeta lived in the Jesuit convent at Oña. In 1928, for reasons still unknown, he left the Jesuit order.[2] He moved into his parents' house in Mungia, where he stayed until 1931. The interlude allowed him to rest, reflect, and at the same time dedicate himself to his literary production.

In 1928 he began to write sporadically in the daily newspaper *Euzkadi*, a publication with clear Basque nationalist tendencies. He published translations of poems as well as original poetry. During this period, he began using the pseudonym Lauaxeta.[3]

In 1931 Lauaxeta moved to Bilbo, where he combined work as a politician with that of a writer. As a militant member of the Basque Nationalist Party, he took an active part in all the meetings and propaganda events that the party assigned him. Diverse themes, such as the Basque language, the young, the role of the Basque woman in the nationalist movement, and unionism, showed up in his speeches. He lived Basque nationalism intensely and preferred being called a good patriot to being called a poet.[4] For him the simple fact that he wrote in Euskara was a political act.

From 1931 to the beginning of the Spanish Civil War Lauaxeta actively contributed to *Euzkadi*. Until 1933 he wrote a daily article for the section titled "Azalpenak" (Explanations).

When Orixe stepped down as director of the publication in 1931, Lauaxeta took over. His tasks were varied; he critiqued theatrical performances, translated plays, wrote small theatrical works, and, above all, took an interest in everything related to poetry as he dedicated himself intensely to the writing of it. As fruit of this intense labor, he won first prize in the premiere Day of Basque Poetry held in Errenteria in 1930. The prize-winning poem was entitled "Maitale kutuna" (The favorite lover).

Lauaxeta's victory shook the field of Basque letters, because the young poet was competing with the best writers of the time, such as Orixe and Lizardi. His polemic with the latter, as we shall see, dates from this period.

In 1931 Lauaxeta published his first book of poetry, *Bide-barrijak*. At first the book was well received by the critics, but before long it was attacked for its innovative exposition of themes and its break with traditional poetic language. In 1935 Lauaxeta published his second book, *Arrats-beran* (As evening approaches).

The year 1936 was important for him for two very different reasons: He made the acquaintance of García Lorca, and the Spanish Civil War began. Early in 1936 Lauaxeta became affiliated with the Asociación Libre de Ensayos Artísticos (Free Association of Artistic Essays, ALEA), where he met writers like Otero and Gerardo Diego.

On July 18, 1936, the Spanish Civil War broke out, surprising the young Basque poet in Bilbo. Shortly thereafter he was named quartermaster and also took charge of the formation and organization of the Basque militia. He managed to combine these tasks with his regular work as director of *Euz-kadi*.

On April 26, 1937, the German air force, with the consent of General Franco, bombed Gernika—a town sacred to the Basques. Three days later, Lauaxeta, who was interpreting for a French journalist, was taken prisoner there and was transferred to Gasteiz, to the convent of the Carmelite fathers, which had been converted into a temporary prison. In the remaining two months of his life he prepared for death by reading the poetry of Saint John of the Cross. What little information we have from that period is gleaned from letters, his will, and a few poems that the authorities forced him to write in Spanish. His last wishes, and the reason for his death, are reflected in his will: "I die as a Basque Nationalist, because I love this unfortunate people with a passion. I hope, in God's goodness, that some day this people will achieve that which this poor son longed to see in his lifetime."[5]

Lauaxeta was shot in the old cemetery of Gasteiz on the morning of June 25, 1937. A mind full of life and illusions was destroyed, and Basque literature lost one of its best representatives, just as Spanish literature had lost the great poet García Lorca ten months earlier.[6]

In the political arena, Lauaxeta was an admirer of the founder of Basque nationalism, Arana y Goiri. The latter's *Obras completas* was like a Bible for the young poet. He was always loyal to Arana y Goiri's political philosophy and to his party, although at times he differed from the founder's ideology on certain points.

Lauaxeta never molded his political philosophy into a concrete political program. Nevertheless, his principles regarding the Basque Country were very clear. His ultimate goal was independence, not an independence based on ethnic and racial premises, as was Arana y Goiri's, but, rather, one based on language and the old laws. It was a goal to be achieved through peaceful means, such as the spread of culture and the sharing of urban life.[7] Basque poetry was, according to Lauaxeta, the greatest weapon in the fight for independence. Basque nationalism and a lack of Basque culture were mutually exclusive. Euskara was the basis for the Basque nation and, in accord with the thinking of Aitzol, it would serve as a lever for obtaining what the independence movement wished to recover.[8]

LITERARY INFLUENCES

Lauaxeta was an educated man who busied himself learning languages and becoming familiar with the different European literary schools. This young, eclectic poet was influenced principally by French symbolism, Jiménez's *poesía pura*, and García Lorca's *poesía popular*.

Symbolism was a vague but pretentious literary phenomenon, a mixture of the mystical, the aesthetic, and the technical, a wisely organized disorder.

Baudelaire and Verlaine were two of the great symbolist poets. Baudelaire's *Les Fleurs du mal* (1857) is unanimously recognized as one of the sources of inspiration for the contemporary poetic movement. Verlaine, on the other hand, broke away from monotonous rhythms, giving poets more musical and sonorous alternatives. Both freed themselves from the overly strict rules regarding caesura, traditional hemistiches, the use of alliteration, enjambment, the mute French "e," and simple assonance to replace rich rhymes. Thus, Baudelaire and Verlaine attacked romanticism, realism (Balzac, Flaubert), naturalism (Zola), and Parnassianism (Leconte de Lisle).

Romantic writers were very fond of exotic locales, the Middle Ages, heroes, ruins, cemeteries, and churches. Against their eloquent rhetoric, verbosity, superficial pathos, and elegiac tones, the symbolists set nuance and suggestion to conceal the meaning of the words.

Symbolism establishes a conceptual relationship between two planes. When we see a symbol, we immediately think about its meaning—hence the correspondence between both planes—but the exact level of correspondence remains ambiguous, forcing us to seek it out and to develop hypotheses and conjecture, and filling us with doubt. According to the symbolists, more than anything else, poetry should be an obscure communication through which even the most literate reader must use the imagination to rediscover the hidden meaning of the words. Thus the reader becomes to a certain extent a miniactor.

Symbolism also stood opposed to the realism and the naturalism of the second half of the nineteenth century. Unlike those who defended the detailed observation of events, symbolists maintained that the poet should not copy reality, for nature is not outwardly beautiful. The naturalist school studied only trivial phenomena and did so superficially under the pretext of objectivity. It settled for the simple narration of empirical events. Symbolism, on the other hand, proposed that the poet's task was an interior and profoundly "mystical" one.

Lauaxeta was fascinated by this new poetic philosophy. Thus, it should not surprise us that he seems at times difficult to understand for poetic as well as linguistic reasons. The name Lauaxeta is inseparable from much of the research that links aesthetic art and concern with poetic technique. At first he was thought a mere iconoclast, a creator of idols with feet of clay. Some could not understand why he would adopt foreign styles when it was so easy to write poetry using traditional Basque meter. Unlike the traditional Basque poetry of Iparragirre and Arrese Beitia, Lauaxeta's work is not didactic, sculpted, descriptive, or declamatory.[9]

Iparragirre's "Ara nun diran" (There they are) does not fit within Lauaxeta's poetic creed.[10] Lauaxeta did not seek out emotions but instead limited himself to stimulating the imagination, the faculty that he felt should prevail over feelings. He was tired of the retrogression of Basque literature in the novel and poetry. The best novels of the beginning of the century, Aguirre's *Kresala* (1906) and *Garoa* (first edition, 1912), were excellent works of art but were only novels of manners. Lauaxeta pressed for a renewal of Basque literature. He was convinced that Basque poetry had lost its feeling for symbols and had reduced reason to pure logic and abstraction. He felt it necessary to open a window onto this new world in search of suggestive symbols.

The Parnassian poets were true adversaries of symbolism and not because the two schools had nothing in common. They both agreed that poetry should not be moralistic or didactic or a weapon for social or political change. Nor did they believe that poetry should philosophize, for the objective of literature was literature itself and not metaphysics. No goal was beautiful other than Beauty itself, and Beauty must never be the servant of Truth. Both schools also held romantic sensibility in low esteem and did not trust passion and inspiration.

The symbolists, however, believed that the Parnassian poets paid too much attention to rhymes and the stylistic aspects of poetry. Their basic principle of "Art for Art's sake" squelched imagination, in the symbolists' opinion.

The title of Lauaxeta's first book, *Bide-barrijak,* is very significant in this respect. The young poet wanted to insert new images and more musicality in his verses by means of analogy and metaphor. This was Baudelaire's point of departure.

Emanuel Swedenborg was the precursor of this new taste for symbolism. This "prophet of the North" maintained that everything in the world (form, movement, color, odor, etc.) had a corresponding and reciprocal meaning. The exterior world, including humankind, did not definitively exist but, rather, was a replica of the "world of ideas," proposed centuries ago by Plato. Plato argued that material reality was merely an image of a superior and transcendent reality.

Starting with these ideas, Baudelaire formulated his famous theory of "correspondences," which was essential to his literary thought. According to this theory, there is a correlation, a marvelous universal analogy, between exterior objects and the spiritual world. These correlations, or correspondences, are not merely a mind game but, instead, the most important fact in the universal order. Behind the concrete appearance of the realities of this world, there exists a spiritual and mystical reality that only the poet can perceive. Poetry is the only complete art form, and only the poet can decipher these analogies and correspondences.

As a result, Nature is not a reality that exists by and for itself, with its own entity, as the romantics wished. On the contrary, it is an immense depository of analogies and a stimulant for the imagination. All of creation is nothing but a collection of figures to decipher, like a forest of symbols that the human imagination must discover.

Some of Baudelaire's ideas were carried to the extreme by another great symbolist, Mallarmé. Mallarmé imagined poetry to be a sacred rite, a liturgy, the most sacred place in a temple where only the priest could enter.

The poet was the priest who refused entry to the lay majority and allowed only a select, predestined minority to come in.

Symbolism exerted a strong influence on Lauaxeta's poetic style. To those who criticized him for writing poetry that was difficult to understand, he repeated insistently that his poetic art contained a second meaning. For that reason, he recommended that his poems be read many times:

> Izkiño oneik ulertu gura dauzanak
> bein baño geyagotan irakurri begiz.
> Oraingo tankeran egiñak dira
> itzetan diñuena baño zerbait
> geyago atzaldu nayez.[11]

Let he who wishes to understand these little words read them more than once. They are written according to the modern canon. They wish to say more than what is said in words.

Lauaxeta felt suffocated by the rhythms of traditional Basque poetry, such as the *zortzikoak* (eight-line verses). He wanted to go beyond the monotony of the rhythms, the lack of enjambment, and the prosaic poetry based on the romantic expression of the "I."

Influenced to a great extent by the art of Verlaine, Lauaxeta tried to imitate that author's innovative ideas. In *Art poétique* Verlaine reveals himself as more of a musician than a painter. The sounds of his words, more than their meanings, were his means of expression. He attacked the traditional manner of getting inside a poem by seeing, reading, and understanding. Visual images, not impressions of sound, were produced by traditional lines of poetry. Verlaine used a different methodology: "De la musique avant toute chose." He was always looking for words that possessed a "halo," the power of suggestion over the power of expression.

In this way, Verlaine placed the very notion of poetry in the consciousness. For him, poetry was a vibration of the soul, like the impressionist painting that suggests a subjective and ephemeral impression without unveiling reality. For that reason, he varied the closed structure of his rhythms by means of enjambments.

Verlaine's influence on Lauaxeta is especially noticeable in *Arrats-beran* (1935). Lauaxeta went in search of originality and surprise by means of *poetic words*, rare and musical words, outrageous metaphors, and unexpected adjectives. The beauty of his themes was not important. Even the ugliest and most ignoble words were accepted by the symbolists if they were appropriately sonorous.

For Lauaxeta, the art of poetry had its roots in beautiful expression and in the grace of its sonorous forms, not in the semantics of its words. Thus, he did not hesitate to confront Orixe. The latter had criticized grammatical errors—the misuse of synthetic verbs, the confusion of the possessives *beren* and *aren,* and so on—in Lauaxeta's poem "Maitale kutuna" (The favorite lover). Lauaxeta accepted the corrections but did not lend them much importance. Of what consequence were syntactic strictness and grammatical precision to a symbolist poet? A word had value only to the extent that it suggested a hidden mystery. Orixe also criticized him for the excessive foreign influences in his poetry. Lauaxeta's prediction at the end of his first book, *Batzuk arrika egingo dauste* (Some will stone me), had come true.

The basis of the criticisms was not the grammatical errors that Orixe condemned in Lauaxeta's first book of poetry but, rather, the critics' concepts of poetry itself, the different vantage points from which each viewed classical poetry. For Orixe, classical poetry related only to writers of classic antiquity, those of the ancient Greco-Roman world, especially the ancient Romans, such as Virgil. His concept of the classical was based on the stability of eternal, unchanging rules: "There are eternal philosophical laws that are based on good sense, discipline, harmony, meter, and, above all, artistic unity."[12] As a result Orixe attacked Lauaxeta for writing excessively affected poetry, for being influenced by the French symbolists, and for returning to the heterodoxical themes of the past.

Lauaxeta defended the poetic philosophy of *Bide-barrijak*. He took an open and dynamic concept of the classical as his starting point. Instead of Orixe's eternal, unchanging rules, Lauaxeta offered a temporal concept of the classical, subject to time and space. Every century, every age and nation, has its specific way of creating classicism. For Lauaxeta, being a good classical poet implied expressing in one's poetry the concerns of one's age, the way of being and thinking in each epoch. These rules were valid, he felt, for all countries and times.

This does not imply a lack of respect for the ancients or for the Greco-Roman world. On the contrary, Lauaxeta was enamored of ancient Greece and its classical theater and considered Homer and Sophocles masters. His admiration for Greek literature and Greek tragedy was immense. He managed to link his modern poetry with ancient Greek poetry. He learned from the Greeks the meaning of beauty, liberty, and pathos or a tragic sense of life that he then incorporated into his own poetic work. As far as Lauaxeta was concerned, early poets such as Fray Luis de León, Fray Luis de Granada, and Saint John of the Cross were classicists just like the ancients, as were the modern classicists, French symbolist poets like Baudelaire, Valéry, and Mallarmé, and, generally speaking, all those who attempted to create a harmonious balance between form and content, thus creating literary beauty.

Furthermore, according to Lauaxeta, *classical* was not a concept that had any value in poetry. Poetry could be good without being classical. The concept of beauty as open, dynamic, temporal, and subjective prevailed over all aesthetic precepts, in Lauaxeta's view.

Lauaxeta's foremost concern, then, was the renovation of Basque poetry according to the canons of modern French verse. He intended to create a poetry that would be national and international. He wanted to be both Basque and cosmopolitan, to express poetic modernity, but in Basque. Thus, he was not a member of the surrealist movement because of that French literary school's highly international nature.

As a consequence of his political philosophy, Lauaxeta had to disagree with Orixe's ruling. In "Erantzuna" (Response) he defended his first book of poetry and urged the renewal of Basque poetry, but not with ancient formulas, no matter how good they were in their own time, because they were anachronistic and unusable for expressing modern reality.

Lauaxeta accepted Orixe's attacks as far as they related to affectation and the influence of the French symbolists. He did not consider "eclectic" a pejorative label. He felt that being eclectic was, in fact, the only way to compose modern poetry. Nor did Orixe's condemnation of his poetry as "heterodoxical" have any effect on him. Speaking as a practicing Christian, Lauaxeta argued that in the literary arts the criteria for beauty and morality did not have to coincide.

The Influence of Juan Ramón Jiménez

The Spanish poetry written after 1920 flowed in the same channels as did the poetry of Europe and was located on the poetic horizon illuminated by the lyricism of Baudelaire, Rimbaud, Verlaine, and Mallarmé and by the surrealism of Breton. Juan Ramón Jiménez and García Lorca were the most audible voices of this great chorus of Spanish poets. Both had a decisive influence on Lauaxeta's poetry. Jiménez's work was life transformed into poetry. This great poet of the pure poetry movement attempted to be both an Andalusian and a universal poet, and he succeeded.

The two Spanish poets found the groundwork already laid for their poetic creations. The modernism school, led by Nicaraguan Rubén Darío, and the French school of symbolism had come face-to-face with vulgarity. Darío broke away from declamatory music expressed in mediocre terms and restored the aesthetic and suggestive element of the language. Modernism meant overcoming the dull, commonplace style that had held sway by playing with meter and the musicality of words. Modernists also made use of exotic, archaic elements from classical paganism and medieval Christianity.

Symbolist influence was also important in Jiménez's poetic work. Although he does not quote Baudelaire, Jiménez was greatly influenced by lesser symbolists like Moreas and Jules Laforgue. Jiménez always felt himself to be the poet of select minorities, a writer for the immense minority. Like Mallarmé, he used poetic invention as if it were a type of alchemy, and that gave his words a power of suggestion that resulted in their transformation. This *poesía pura* contrasts with rhetorical poetry. It is pure because it is a counterpoint not to reality or life but to hollow, lifeless sound.

Like Jiménez, Lauaxeta also speaks of the select minorities for whom he wrote his poetry, and, in fact, a print run of a book of Basque poetry at the time did not exceed three hundred copies: "Erderaz 'minorías selectas.'

Onein gurtzaile nozu"[13] (I am an admirer of the poets included in the Spanish words "select minorities").

The innovations that Lauaxeta brought to Basque poetry were not as essential as those Jiménez introduced into Spanish poetry, but they were very important in the tradition of Basque literature, for Lauaxeta was one of the most cultured Basque poets of his time and certainly the most innovative. Jon Kortazar, a critic and Lauaxeta specialist, notes, "We will not give in to the temptation of calling Lauaxeta the Basque Juan Ramón, but we should not doubt that the author from Moguer [Jiménez] made the synthesis of modernity a reality for Spanish lyricism."[14]

Like Jiménez, Lauaxeta was a sensitive, daring, liberated poet. He felt the need to create in union with the best writers, to create for the immense minority and against the commonplace. His demanding perfectionism, however, alienated some more traditional writers.

For both Jiménez and Lauaxeta, the verbal instruments in their poetic creation had to be new, as if they were not composed of words from the common language. They wanted their words to divest themselves of the prosaic, to remove themselves from meanings created by common methods, and to separate themselves from the trivial mediocrity that looked down on symbols. Thus, it was necessary to dress up the new language with images, rhythms, metaphors, comparisons, and a select vocabulary. This language had to appear cut off from superfluous circumstances and events in order to create impressions, sensations, and auditory reflections that were difficult to narrate. This new language endeavored to capture the inherent charm of material objects in order to sublimate the matter itself.

According to Jiménez, this new poetry did not eliminate intelligence. Intelligence, he believed, should never be absent from the creative process, but neither should it be a substitute for inspiration, a muse to be meekly served. For that reason, Valéry's attempt to substitute intelligence for inspiration struck the Spanish poet as heresy. Jiménez purified, to the greatest extent possible, the veins of symbol, sensation, and intimacy.

For Jiménez, to live and to write poetry were the same thing. He was reproached for this tendency to convert his life into poetry, to think it through as if it were an evasion of reality. He did not flee from friendly conversation, but he lived like a monk, to the point of isolating himself in a cork-lined room so that he could work undisturbed by street noises: "I have Poetry hidden in my house, by its desire and mine, like a beautiful woman; and our relationship is that of impassioned lovers."[15] He sought out solitude so that he could live within his poetry, substituting for the outside world his personal realm, where symbol and suggestion were all that was retained of reality. For that reason, his poems cannot be explained. To do so would be to betray the author's intention. These poems must be felt and enjoyed individually on a personal level.

The Influence of Federico García Lorca

Federico García Lorca, a member of the Generation of '27, also profoundly influenced Lauaxeta, as is especially clear in certain poems from Lauaxeta's second book, *Arrats-beran*. In the opinion of Kortazar, García Lorca's work is "one of the most abundant sources in the work of the Basque author."[16]

In García Lorca's poetry, popular elements play a critical role. The romantics had already spoken of popular oral poetry as the expression of the soul of a people. His poetry represented the popular as a necessary point of departure for his creativity, but it was never the ultimate aesthetic ideal. Also, García Lorca considered himself a universal Andalusian who felt that popular poetry was gradually divesting itself of pure *costumbrismo*.

Lauaxeta was particularly interested in this aspect of the Spanish poet. Furthermore, there was no lack of voices in the Basque Country urging him to keep in mind traditional Basque poetry. Aitzol, a judge of the poetic beauty in existence in the pre–Spanish Civil War period, encouraged the young Lauaxeta in this vein. One had to pour the aged wine into new wineskins.

García Lorca's poetry captures the power of words in the people's spontaneous use of them, but the poet re-created the words, giving them a new, magical meaning. His fondness for popular authenticity gave rise to his interest in the common people, in the gypsies of Sacromonte, as seen in *Romancero gitano*. He was a poet with deep ties to his native land, but he later updated his language, re-creating his own instrument of expression. In his poetic art there is fantasy in the place of reality, fascination achieved by means of the magic of language, latent symbolism, lunar enchantment, and a fragmentary, chaotic world in opposition to the ordered one.

Violence and eroticism go hand in hand in the work of the two young poets, Lauaxeta and García Lorca. Eros, woman, the tension of love, and sorrow maintain the contrast in *Arrats-beran*. In the work of García Lorca, the river, the riverbank, bulrushes, and so on are converted into erotic symbols and images full of pagan sensuality. The harmful aspect of the moon, an obsession with blood, and irrational premonitions are often linked to erotic connotations.

García Lorca captured and assimilated the enchantment of the so-called poetry of the people without renouncing literary tradition or the most recent poetic innovations. The vanguard of the surrealist movement had left the door ajar for a type of poetry in which everything, even the irrational, was possible. García Lorca took advantage of these new elements. He drenched his poetry with fantasy and the irrational language of lullabies and nursery rhymes. This tendency is apparent in his intensive repetitions:

> Huye luna, luna, luna . . .
> el aire la vela, vela.[17]

Flee moon, moon, moon . . . the air your sail, sail.

and in his onomatopoeia and irrational phrases:

En la noche platinoche
noche, qué noche nochera[18]

In the night platinum night, what a nightlike night tonight.

LAUAXETA'S POETIC WORK, THEMES, AND STYLE

Lauaxeta did not live long enough to be prolific. Nevertheless, what he did write, especially his two books of poems, *Bide-barrijak* and *Arrats-beran,* is a good example of the quality of his poetic art.[19]

There is little originality in his choice of themes. Generally speaking, he limits himself to traditional ones and those popular in modern poetry: love, death, erotica, sorrow, eternity, the passing of time, the human condition, God, and so on. His personal contribution stems from his re-creation and reinterpretation of those traditional themes.

He did not settle for simply borrowing themes but reworked them into Basque themes and introduced his personal point of view. Consequently, Lauaxeta could say of his first poems: "Bide Barrijak jarri baderitxot ez da izkuntzagaitik geiagotik baiño. Orain arte erabilli ez diran gaiak diralako geure liburuan, izen ori jarri neban"[20] (If I have entitled this book *New Paths* it is not because of its language but for something else. I gave it this name, because it possesses themes unknown up to this point).

Bide-barrijak

Bide-barrijak (1931) is a collection of forty-one poems written during Lauaxeta's youth, from 1921 to 1931. They are incidental poems that contain no unifying factor. Lizardi considered Lauaxeta's first book a string of pearls whose thread was difficult to follow, the work of a beginner: "On occasion he fails to be intimate with the language, leaving the work suffering from 'expressive deficiency.' "[21]

Lauaxeta did not defend himself against this criticism, as he had done against Orixe's, because he liked Lizardi and respected him as an important poet. He simply accepted the criticism, for his work *was* the work of a young poet: "Gastaroko [*sic*] neurtitzok eztira sakonak, eztira gurenak gauza guren eta sakonik gastaruan [*sic*] eztalako egiten"[22] (These verses of my youth are not deep or transcendental, because in one's youth one is not aware of such things).

The influence of the different literary schools, styles, and themes is obvious in this first book. A steady evolution can be observed in the young poet. *Bide-barrijak* is full of religious and love poetry. In his religious work the influence of Saint John of the Cross and León is noticeable. Nature is the mirror of God. The influence of Saint Augustine and Unamuno can also be seen. In "Jaunagan Atsedena" (Rest in the Lord), the words of the Bishop of Hipona appear as an epigraph:

> Zeugan lotu arte,
> ene bijotza urduri dago.[23]

> My heart is uneasy until it rests in You.

Lauaxeta's religious poetry also bears some relationship to that of his compatriot Unamuno. The themes of God, faith, immortality, the human condition, and death occupy much of *Bide-barrijak*. Unamuno and Lauaxeta both felt the desire for immortality:

> Gixon-utz nazan arren, eztot deuseztu nai.[24]

> Although I am just a man, I do not wish to perish.

Both were men of faith, in their own way, who reacted with anguish and continuing belief. Lauaxeta's Christian belief, however, did not imply creation but was based on the theological faith that Unamuno detested. His last poems, written on the eve of his death, demonstrate the manner in which the young poet lived his Christian faith.[25]

Love is another often-repeated theme in *Bide-barrijak,* but it is still romantic love, appropriate to a young poet. It is wrapped in romantic images of white snow, a garden, roses and withering flowers, blue ocean waves, and the heart. It is described in perhaps the best poem of the book, "Maitale kutuna" (The favorite lover). There the poet is singing to a young woman whom he has never seen. There are none of the kisses and erotic images that we find in the second book. The young woman has an angelic face, and her "kisses are transformed into divine prayers." She is sister to the lilies of the field. The poet does not know her name, for he never sees her except in his dreams.

This romantic love appears consistently in all the love poems of the first book, as in the short poem "Bijotzean," which follows:

> Lorategiko edur zurian
> irarri zendun neure irudija
> Axia eldu ta egal otzez
> autsitu eban gustija [*sic*].

> Larrosa baten orri ganian
> idatzi zendun ixen maitia:
> udea eldu eta eguzkijak
> igartu eban lorea.

Neure gorputza esku miakaz
marreztu zendun are ganian:
etorri ziran olatu urdiñak
atzindu eban unian.

Beti-betiko iraun dagijan
badakixu non sakon irarri
Bijotz barruban, maite kutuna,
maitasun izkiz idatzi![26]

You pressed my image into the white snow in the garden. The
wind arrived and erased everything with its cold wings. You
wrote my beloved name on the petals of a rose! Summer came
and the sun withered the flower.

You drew the image of my body on the sand with a steady
hand. The blue waves of the sea came and erased it in an
instant.

Do you know, beloved, where you should impress my image
so that it will last forever? Write it into your heart with words
of love.

This book is characterized by a lack of maturity, which is to be expected
from a young poet. His mastery of the symbolist list of techniques was not
yet complete. One can still see the romantic influence of which Lauaxeta
had not yet rid himself: the use of the first person, the exteriorization of the
romantic *I* in a sentimental form, and the pessimistic tone. Lauaxeta's expression of unrequited love evokes the *mal du siècle* of the romantic poets of
the previous century, such as Lamartine, Hugo, and Musset.

In his first book Lauaxeta uses many more comparisons than he does in
his second. The comparative word *like* appears in its Basque variations *lako,
antzera,* and *baizen.* Metaphors, however, are scarce in the first book. Among
the most repeated similes are those referring to the forest, the garden, a star,
and the moon. Descriptions of sentimental images—such as the fountain,
the heart, snow, flowers, the rose, and the blue of the sea—abound.

Lauaxeta uses many synthetic verbs, archaic words, localisms, vocabulary items imposed on the purists by Arana y Goiri, and expressions from
other dialects, especially from Lapurdin. Occasionally, a dictionary is required to comprehend his Basque. All of this makes reading his work quite
difficult.

Arrats-beran

Lauaxeta's second book, *Arrats-beran* (1935), con-
tains forty poems. It is evident that during the four years after the publication of *Bide-barrijak* Lauaxeta made progress in his use of symbolist tech-

niques and improved the structure of his poems. He moved from romantic descriptions and declarations to symbolic suggestions. Also evident is the evolution of his language. His Basque is more flexible and avoids the exaggerated purism that is evident in his first book. He uses a cultured and refined Euskara in his second one.

In *Arrats-beran* Lauaxeta uses Basque lyricism and the Spanish *romance* as sources of inspiration. Within Basque lyricism, including the ballads and the oral tradition of the *kopla zaharrak* (old couplets), Lauaxeta was familiar with the collected folkloric material of oral texts compiled by Azkue, Manuel Lekuona, Padre Donostia, and Barandiarán.

The techniques used in the *kopla zaharrak* fostered Lauaxeta's poetic creativity. These couplets are short verses containing only two or three rhymes. They were traditionally improvised, sung, and accompanied by musical instruments. One curious note is their apparent lack of logic. They pass from a purely narrative level to a different, imaginative one with no logical connection between the two. There is a lack of coherence between the ideas and the imagery within each verse, yet we find an acoustic relationship between them on what might be called a prelogical level. Thus, in the old couplets we do not find the logical unity of a syllogism; however, there is a rapidity of movement, along with a chronological order and an apparently careless sort of logic in the succession of the diverse ideas in each strophe.

In the first verse of Bereterretxe's famous song, this technique is clearly apparent:

> Haltzak ez tü bihotzik
> ez gaztanberak ezürrik;
> enian uste erraiten ziela
> aitunen semek gezürrik.[27]

> The alder tree has no marrow, nor does cottage cheese have bones; I did not believe that noblemen would tell a lie.

There is no logical connection between the absence of marrow in the alder or the lack of bones in cottage cheese and the lack of truth in the words of a Basque man. But logic is part of philosophy, and the *kopla zaharrak,* in their turn, represent one of the techniques of poetry.

Lauaxeta was familiar with this technique of popular oral poetry, but for him the popular aspects of poetry were only a point of departure and never his ultimate aesthetic goal. For that reason, following the example set by García Lorca in *Romancero gitano,* the Basque poet was in the habit of purifying and transforming the folkloric material provided him by popular oral Basque poetry. A verse from "Burtzaña" (Cart driver) offers a significant parallel with Bereterretxe's song:

> Lerrdijak ez bijotzik,
> ezta arratsak samiñik
> Zeuri adi neskatxak

itxi dabe biarra.
Akulu orren puntan
dizdiz daukozu ixarra? [28]

The pine grove has no heart,
nor does the afternoon have pain.
Girls abandon their work
to stare at you.
Do you have a star glittering
on the end of a needle?

García Lorca's influence from *Romancero gitano* and the *Poema del cante jondo* (1921) is also evident in Lauaxeta's work, especially in certain poems near the end of *Arrats-beran*. Various motivations and images lifted from "Romance de la Guardia Civil española" and from "Prendimiento de Antoñito el Camborio en el camino de Sevilla" appear in this, the poet's second book. In the North the striking miner with the dark face who works in the red mines of Bizkaia is assassinated by the Civil Guard. In the South the gypsy woman Rosa de los Camborios slumps in a doorway, moaning, her breasts slashed by the Guardia Civil. Many lines are very similar to some we find in García Lorca and remind us of the Andalusian poet's strong influence on Lauaxeta's work:

LORCA [29]	LAUAXETA [30]
Apaga tus verdes luces que viene la benemérita . . . Tienen, por eso no lloran, de plomo las calaveras . . . La ciudad libre de miedo, multiplicaba sus puertas. Cuarenta guardias civiles entran a saco por ellas . . .	Cómo rebrillan en los senderos los tricornios de la guardia civil! Aspecto de matones el suyo, con largas escopetas sobre el hombro. En medio de cuatro guardias civiles baja el minero de rostro moreno . . .
Pero la Guardia Civil avanza sembrando hogueras	Las largas escopetas están en fuego —clamores de huelga en la ancha calle— Minero de rostro moreno, báñate en tu propia sangre!

The gypsy Antoñito the Camborio shames himself by giving up to the Civil Guard without a fight. His not confronting them, jackknife in hand, is interpreted as a betrayal of gypsy tradition. Lauaxeta, as well, berates the Basque miner for not having been brave:

Sendua ba'intz, etsai-odolez
bustiko eunkek pikotx zorrotzoi![31]

If you were brave you would wet the sharp tip of your pickax
with your enemy's blood.

Although the majority of Lauaxeta's poems maintain aesthetic goals according to the canons of pure, symbolic poetry, some can be considered compromised. For Lauaxeta, simply writing in Basque under the circumstances of his day already constituted a political act. "Amayur gaztelu baltza" (Black castle Amayur) is consistent with his political creed. At a time in history when the Navarrese, in spite of their Basque tradition, did not want to accept the Basque Statute (1931), Lauaxeta recorded the sacrifice of two hundred Navarrese soldiers who gave their lives defending Basque liberties against Spanish troops.[32] The end of this poem reflects the deception felt by many Basques because of the refusal of the Navarrese to associate with the rest of the Basque provinces. The following words, even today, preserve an echo of prophecy when one views the political reality in Navarre:

Ordutik ona,—zenbat laño—,
Naparruan ezta aberririk.[33]

Since then—how much fog—there has been no country in
Navarre.

In Lauaxeta's second book, the treatment of women varies a great deal from their image as presented in *Bide-barrijak*. In the latter, woman appears as a spiritual, idealized being. In contrast, in *Arrats-beran*, she is carnal, kisses with passion, kills and dies for love:

Soin onek mun-miña diño.[34]

My body speaks of the ardor of her kisses.

The myth of youth, making the most of the moment and enjoying it, the carpe diem of the ancient poets, is accompanied by the kisses of a woman. The young man tries to hold time still in order to live it fully, but the human condition imposes itself. Love, death, the passage of time, and the image of a man who yearns but cannot attain that which he yearns for—all these conditions create dissatisfaction and frustration in a person. These are the most common themes that create tension and contrast in *Arrats-beran*.

Lauaxeta's second book is more carefully crafted than his first. He makes excellent use of refrains, onomatopoeia, and colors. Several of his poems have the same beginning and ending. In this way, the refrain forces the poem to revolve around itself, as it does in "Ja-jai, goiz abil alai"[35] (You stroll happily in the morning). At other times, the refrain summarizes the essential content of a poem. Onomatopoeia is frequent: "Din-dan balendan, elixako atetan, gixon bat dilindan"[36] (Din-dan balendan, at the church doors, a man is hanging).

Red and black are everywhere. The former is linked to lips and blood and symbolizes sexual passion and violence; the latter is the symbol of death. Blue is the symbol of the sea and the sky, and green represents hope.

Lauaxeta was one of the most cultured poets of his era. His poetry was not modern if we compare it with French poetry, but literary genres in the Basque Country have habitually lagged twenty-five to fifty years behind the rest of the world. If, however, we compare Lauaxeta with the other Basque poets of his time, we must conclude that he was the most modern and most European of all.

CHAPTER NINE

Salbatore Mitxelena and Bitoriano Gandiaga

The Franciscan School

The Franciscan sanctuary of Arantzazu, Gipuzkoa, has been a center of Basque culture and spirituality for centuries. The Virgin of Arantzazu, patron saint of Gipuzkoa, attracts the devotion of many Basques who, as did Ignatius of Loyola, enter her sanctuary imbued with religious fervor. The high mountain location of the sanctuary and its Franciscan monastery provide an encounter with nature conducive to spiritual peace. Many preachers, theologians, missionaries, artists, musicians, and men dedicated to Basque culture have emerged from Arantzazu. During Franco's long dictatorship the sanctuary served as a spiritual refuge for Basques defeated in the Spanish Civil War who foresaw a gloomy future for their nation.

In this chapter I shall analyze the literary productions of two Franciscans from the Arantzazu sanctuary, Salbatore Mitxelena (1919-1965) and Bitoriano Gandiaga (1928-   ). Although very different in style, they are similar in many other respects: their love of the Basque language and the Franciscan order, their existentialist yearnings and concern for the future of Euskadi and the Basque language, and their love of nature and poetry. I shall present here summaries of their most important works, underlining their themes, their styles, and their similarities and differences.

Salbatore Mitxelena

Salbatore Mitxelena was born on the Etxebeltz farm in Zarautz, Gipuzkoa. He used several pseudonyms in his writings: Inurritza, Abendats, Egarin, and Talai, and, most often, Inurritza.[1] His mother died when he was very young, which affected his personality and his artistic production: "When you died, the farm lost a flower, and a beautiful star shone for us in the heavens."[2]

Mitxelena spent his first eleven years in Zarautz in an environment that would shape him for the rest of his life. His love for the Basque language was born there as well as his affection for Basque verse. He often listened to improvised verses his grandfather sang. Conversely, he also experienced there the budding aversion toward the Basque language common in schools during the dictatorship of Miguel Primo de Rivera. On more than one occasion he was not allowed to eat his lunch as punishment for using his mother's language, Euskara.

In 1930, at age eleven, he entered the school at Arantzazu. At fourteen he began to write poems, some of which appear in the first volume of *Idaz-lan guztiak* (Complete works) under the title *Olerki umezurtzak* (Orphaned poems). They were little more than the early words of an adolescent who liked to write poetry.

In 1936 he went to Olite, Navarre, to study philosophy. That same year the Spanish Civil War broke out. Mitxelena wanted to experience firsthand the fratricidal war he considered the source of all evil, so he enlisted in the army in Iruñea. He came to believe that the worst peace was preferable to the best war.

All of his poetry was inspired by the Spanish Civil War, and the majority of his work was conceived during its three years. His first booklet of poetry, *Aberriak min dit eta miñak olerki* (My country hurts and the pain prompts me to write poetry), contains several works composed during the war. Others were written in the years immediately following the conflict. The poet revealed himself to be a Basque nationalist by proclaiming JEL, the acronym for Arana's slogan, "Jaungoikoa eta Lagi Zarra" (God and the old law).

In these early poems, the things he loved most appear: God, his mother, the mortally wounded Basque Country, and his language, Euskara:

> Gurutzea daramat
> biotz-biotzean
> eta MAITE bat bere
> alde bakoitzean:
> goian JAUNGOIKOA ta
> AMA barrenean,
> eskubian EUZKADI,
> EUSKERA ezkerrean.[3]

> I carry a cross within my heart, surrounded on every side by a LOVE: GOD in front, mother behind, EUZKADI on the right, and EUSKERA on the left.

These early poems are not very good. At this point in his life, Mitxelena was still a long way from demonstrating the poetic mastery of his later years. He lacked the musicality that would appear in his subsequent works, and there is a purism reminiscent of Arana y Goiri in his vocabulary. In any case, his early poems clearly reflect the historical context of the moment.

The general feeling, even among the majority of Basque nationalists of that time, was that nothing could be done under Franco's ironfisted dictatorship. If the war had been lost, why keep fighting? The common people were either terrified by the executions, prison sentences, and forced labor of the postwar period or they were steeped in a profound lethargy.

In the midst of one of the worst periods in the history of the Basque Country, Mitxelena alone demanded the right to be Basque. As the voice of a gagged people, he became the interlocutor for a small nation on the verge of disappearing, the guide and inspiration of an oppressed and divided ethnic group, a faithful witness to his era, a preacher of passive resistance, and a cantor of the sorrow of the Basque people in defeat. In an environment in which the Basque language was censored and schoolchildren were punished for speaking it, Mitxelena offered himself as the troubadour of a suffering people, and he sang to them about the desire for immortality that coursed through his veins. From a pessimistic, realist viewpoint, he spoke of a tiny flame of hope flickering in the shadows, the hope that the Basque nation would survive.

Mitxelena was a writer forged by the tremendous crisis of war. He wanted to flee its wicked consequences as he would the chains of slavery, but he could not. He was one of the postwar writers who best reflected the pain suffered by his small ethnic minority. This sentiment, visible in the prewar period in the works of the great Lizardi, underlies all Mitxelena's works and, at the same time, is the source of his inspiration. The same feeling later appeared in many works by Gandiaga and José Luis Txillardegi:

> Zein ederra dan
> olerkaritza
> biotzak min duanean![4]

How beautiful poetry is when the heart is suffering!

Mitxelena was dedicated to the Basque nation, and he wrote for it. As he recalled, citing the formidable Spanish poet Aleixandre, "the writer who does not write for his people is suicidal."[5] Mitxelena occasionally scolded his people, particularly the nationalists who accepted the status quo of Franco's dictatorship and settled for being allowed a few purely folkloric or sportive demonstrations of Basqueness, such as Basque dances, stone-lifting contests, wood-chopping trials, or the right to wear the Basque beret, long tunics, and *albarcas* (Basque footwear). Mitxelena hated superficiality, and in his fiery, vindictive poetry he displayed his discontent by demanding respect for this minority ethnic group of barely three million members who still had not learned to unite against a common enemy.

In 1940 Mitxelena returned to Arantzazu, where he worked feverishly. In 1943 he was ordained a priest there. That same year, he wrote *Guruzbidea*, a ten-page work in which he describes the fourteen stations of the cross.

In 1949 he was named an associate member of Euskaltzaindia, and he published the first Basque-language work of the postwar period. *Arantzazu, euskal sinismenaren poema* (Arantzazu, poem of Basque faith) was a long spiritual poem that marked the beginning of the so-called *literatura de catacumbas* (literature of the catacombs).

Mitxelena was an untiring reader of Basque poetry. The poets who influenced him the most were Lizardi, Orixe, Lauaxeta, and Arrese. The young Bizkaian Lauaxeta, a martyr to Basque nationalism, is the theme of one of Mitxelena's poems.[6]

Mitxelena was convinced, however, that, as a means of knowing the life of the people, oral literature was better than written. For that reason, he became very interested in the Basque romance, in bertsolaritza, and in the *kopla zaharrak*.[7]

Two books had a powerful influence on him: Manuel Lekuona's *Literatura oral euskérika* (Basque oral literature) and José Adriano Lizarralde's *Historia de Arantzazu* (History of Arantzazu). From the former Mitxelena learned to write in a popular style and to fill his poetry with music. In the latter work he found much material, such as romances and old songs, that stimulated his imagination. Never a rigorous historian, he disliked doing research and preferred visiting oldsters on farms in the area to collect the songs, stories, legends, and romances associated with the sanctuary of Arantzazu. After the Civil War, Arantzazu appeared more than ever as a place of refuge. As the old song says:

> Zuk zer dezu Arantzazu!
> ames kabi, otoitz leku?[8]

> What do you have, Arantzazu! Nest of dreams, place of prayer?

Mitxelena turned to the Mother of God, the Virgin of Arantzazu, as the only hope for himself and the Basque Country. For five centuries the fortunes of Arantzazu had been so closely linked to those of the Basque Country that there existed a parallel between the two, according to our poet. The good times and the bad times, the sad historical events and the pleasant ones, occurred in and were shared by both places. The destruction of the Basque Country in the First Carlist War, for example, coincided with the Liberals' burning of Arantzazu.

Mitxelena spent the greater part of his youth in the Arantzazu monastery, and that enabled him to write two other books, *Ama-semeak Arantzazuko kon-*

dairan (Mothers and sons in the history of Arantzazu, 1951) and *Ogei kanta Arantzazuko* (Twenty songs from Arantzazu, 1954).

Arantzazu, euskal sinismenaren poema, a book of poems, contains three parts. Because of censorship, only the first two were published in 1949. The third part, "Bizi nai" (I desire to live), the most controversial because of its patriotic content, yet the most beautiful poetically, was published in 1955 in the Panamanian journal *Euzko gogoa,* edited by the Basque writer and priest Jokin Zaitegi.[9]

Mitxelena drew heavily upon tradition while writing *Arantzazu.* Good and evil, paganism and Christianity are personified in the Virgin of Arantzazu and Mari Gaizto. The latter was known among the Basques as the Lady of Anboto and the witch of Aizkorri.

According to legend, in 1469 the Virgin appeared to a young shepherd, Rodrigo Baltzategi, and asked him to build a hermitage in her honor on the slope of Mount Aloña. In the first part of the book one of the key ideas in Mitxelena's poetry appears, that of Arantzazu as a place of suffering:

> Ona Arantzazu, euskal-Golgota
> euskal-miñen Opal-maia![10]

> Here we have Arantzazu, the Basque Golgotha, the offering
> table of Basque sorrows!

In the second part of *Arantzazu,* two lines evoke the Arana y Goiri slogan "euskeldun-fededun" (Basque equals Christian). This idea of Basque nationalist Catholicism is argued from time to time in the works of our poet. Sentences like the following bring the concept to mind:

> Kristautasunik ez dunak euskal-
> tasunik ere ez anbat.[11]

> He who is not Christian is not very Basque.

Nevertheless, we should point out that the Basque nationalist Catholicism conceived by Mitxelena did not carry with it the triumphal character of the Spanish nationalist Catholicism of the Franco era, during which the church received economic aid in exchange for its silence and the government's exclusive right to present candidates for bishop before the Holy See.

The third section of *Arantzazu,* "Bizi nai," acquires a more dramatic tone; some consider it one of Mitxelena's best poetic creations among his epic poetry. Certain existentialist tendencies, expressed in his desire to continue being Basque and his inability to do so, are obvious in this part:

> Erdera gizentzen,
> euskera baztertzen,
> oiturak zabartzen,
> sinismena aitzen,
> genun dana galtzen. . . .
> Orra Euskalerria
> zertaratu den![12]

Spanish is spreading, Basque is confined to a corner, our customs are being corrupted, our faith is weakening, we are losing everything we possessed. . . . Here is what has happened to the Basque Country!

Using the metaphor of an apple that falls from the tree and rolls downhill, Mitxelena sees the Basque nation somersaulting downward, having lost its Basque roots and existing in a frivolous atmosphere: "Azalkerian, itxurakerian, itxurakeri ortan, jo bear dugu gure nai ta ezin'aren etsairik txarrena, ta gaurko gizadiaren minbizi zabalena"[13] (On the surface, at first glance, we must see the worst enemy of our desire and inability in this emptiness). This frivolity and these symptoms of superficiality are nothing but the "convulsions of a disappearing race."

Mitxelena wonders about the meaning of life in such a small country, where the wounds of the Civil War still have not healed: "Milla bider lasaiago biziko giñan: ez giñan ain aguro gaztezartuko; erriz-erri gabiltzala euskeraren atzerapenak aztertzean, ez genun naigabea naigabearen gain pillatuko"[14] (We had lived a thousand times better: we had not grown old while still young; we had not stored up so much suffering while verifying the retrogression of the Basque language in our perambulations from village to village).

According to Mitxelena, the Basque prototype was the *baserritarra* (the peasant), because he had been able to preserve the language better than anyone else. We see here the influence of Juan Antonio Moguel's *Peru abarca* (Peter farm shoe, 1881) as well as Aguirre's *Garoa* (Fern, 1912). For those authors, too, the Basque peasantry was the stronghold of the language. Nevertheless, when the Basque-speaking peasant descended from the mountains to the city streets into so-called Basque society and found himself scorned by shopkeepers and merchants, he rejected Euskara:

Izketa orrekin
zoaz zere basartera.[15]

Go back to the woods with that language.

Mitxelena adopted an unambiguous stance regarding the Basque language and the Basque Country's identity, an identity in danger of extinction. He loved Euskara and was a sincere Basque nationalist, of that there is no doubt. Nevertheless, he was not a politician, nor was he sympathetic to any specific political party, as were so many priests at that time. He wanted to participate in Basque politics only on behalf of Basque language and culture. In his cultural work, literature served as his weapon: "Euskalerri lenago, barruko edozein alderdi baiño"[16] (The Basque Country comes before any political party).

Because *Arantzazu* was a clearly religious book, it had to overcome many obstacles posed by the official censor. In 1950 Orixe's *Euskaldunak* (The Basques), intended to be the Basques' epic poem, was published. Its publication and Mitxelena's battles with the censors had a noticeable effect on his spirits and led to the writing of his second book, *Ama-semeak Arantzazuko kondairan* (Mothers and sons in the history of Arantzazu).

Although *Ama-semeak* does not lack details, dates, and descriptions of historical events such as the Carlist Wars, Mitxelena intended it to be more than a mere history. He attempted to show the Basque people what the Sanctuary of Arantzazu and the Virgin meant to the Basque Country. He once again availed himself of popular romances, at times respecting them totally and at others taking them as mere pretexts from which to create his own verses "elezarrak lagun"[17] (with the help of the old narratives).

A summary of *Ama-semeak*'s twelve chapters provides an idea of its contents: chapter 1—the Virgin appears to Rodrigo Baltzategi, a seventeen-year-old shepherd; chapter 2—the historical context of the year in which the apparition occurred (1469) is presented; chapter 3—the Sanctuary of Arantzazu is located in the center of the four southern Basque provinces and is one of Heaven's chosen places; chapter 4—the history of all the religious orders who inhabited Arantzazu before the Franciscans' arrival is related; chapter 5—the convents, hermitages, and churches that were housed in Arantzazu are listed, and the two fires of 1533 and 1622 are described; chapter 6—the sanctuary is revealed as a destination for pilgrimages; chapter 7—the sanctuary is revealed as a place of prayer and Christian faith, as demonstrated in the nocturnal vigils celebrated there; chapter 8—the miracles and favors obtained from the Virgin of Arantzazu are narrated; chapter 9—the spread of devotion to the Virgin of Arantzazu throughout the world (among Basques in America, the Philippines, China, and so on) is narrated; chapter 10—the antireligious spirit of the French Revolution, the presence of Joseph Bonaparte as king of Spain, and the anticlerical sentiments of the Liberals during the First Carlist War, which led to the sacking and burning of the convent and sanctuary in 1834, are described; chapter 11—in 1846 the image of the Virgin was placed once again in the Church of Arantzazu, and in 1886 Pope Leo XIII authorized the solemn coronation of the Virgin of Arantzazu, the first time this had ever happened in the Basque Country, and in 1918 she was declared patron saint of Gipuzkoa; chapter 12—the activities, publications, press, radio broadcasts, and buildings of Arantzazu are described, and the sanctuary is defined as "the holy mountain that the Basque Country has to ascend to heaven." In the epilogue, Mitxelena mentions the advantage of building a new sanctuary and the economic problems such a project would entail.

In the two works just discussed Mitxelena reveals himself to be both a poet and a writer of prose. In the two works to be dealt with next he demonstrates his talents as a dramatist and essayist. With two short dramatic works—*Erri bat guruzbidean* (A nation at the crossroads, 1940-1955-1958) and *Confixus* (1960-1962)—Mitxelena hoped to renew Basque theater, a genre that has never distinguished itself.

Confixus is a summary of *Erri bat guruzbidean*. The two represent the death throes of the Basque Country. These thoughts preoccupied Mitxelena throughout his life. The Basques suffered because, though their intentions were good, they lost four wars in one hundred years. Furthermore, the Catholic Church and the United Nations sacrificed the Basques. Euskal Herria found itself on Calvary, friendless and in pain, oppressed by Franco's dictatorship, forgotten by Rome and the democratic countries, scorned by the Spanish bishops, and misrepresented by the international media:

> obipean gauzkate
> Erroman ta Onun.[18]

> In Rome and the United Nations we are as good as dead.

The ideology of Basque nationalist Catholicism reached its zenith in these two theatrical works. The Cross of Christ and the Oak of Gernika form an inseparable unit. Christ, the Church, and Euskadi are united in spite of the Catholic Church's inability to understand the Basque problem. In his plays Mitxelena links religion with politics and the liturgy with the patriotic idea of the Tree of Gernika.

The existentialism that appears in these books, as well as in Mitxelena's work in general, has nothing to do with that of Sartre or with Camus's philosophy of the absurd. On the contrary, it is founded on Christian faith, on the Christ who died at Calvary and rose again, on the anguished but hopeful quest of Saint Augustine.

Mitxelena and his nationalist Catholicism should be judged in the historical context in which they existed. The majority of Basque nationalists accepted the postulate "euskaldun-fededun." Unlike Mirande, the great poet of Iparralde, who believed that one could not be a good Basque and be Christian, Mitxelena claimed that one could not be a good Basque without being Christian.

In the nineteenth century the Liberal general Baldomero Espartero had made promises he did not keep: "This sword that has fought against you will not be drawn again except in defense of your old laws." In the twentieth century came the lies and calumny of Franco, who blamed the Basques for the bombing of Gernika, their own city, by the Nazi air force: "Those who destroyed Gernika have no right to speak of Country." Mitxelena saw the *euskaldunak* as members of a ghetto, a minority group absorbed by the majority Spanish speakers, a dishonored race, like that of the Agotes.[19]

Mitxelena was a poet, a writer of prose, and a dramatist, but he was also an essayist, as is evidenced in *Unamuno ta abendats* (Unamuno and the spirit of the Basque race), his only volume in this genre. He wrote his last book in Montevideo in 1955, and it was published as an essay in Baiona in 1958. This book represents a notable advance in the meager genre of the essay in Basque literature of the time.

In his essays Mitxelena supports some of the ideas of Unamuno. Unamuno, a native of Bilbo, received no sympathy from the official religious and civil estates. Two of the most important works by this philosopher, *La agonía del cristianismo* (The agony of Christianity) and *Del sentimiento trágico de la vida en los pueblos* (Of the tragic sense of life in nations), were condemned by the Catholic Church and placed on the Index Expurgatorius, or List of Forbidden Books. Furthermore, many Basque nationalists were aggrieved and pained by Unamuno's obsessive opposition toward the Basque language. In his opinion, the Basque language was dying, and nothing could be done to save it. Its death was not due to external causes but, rather, to an intrinsic truth: it lacked the ability to evolve with the times. According to Unamuno, Basque was an obstacle to the spread of European culture, an inferior language; consequently, one should not waste time trying to promote it. He proposed that the Basques integrate themselves into Spanish culture and forget about their own language. By doing so, he claimed that they would lose nothing as Basques.

Mitxelena did not share Unamuno's attitude toward Euskara, but he defended Unamuno's philosophy because of the religious interest it aroused and because, deep down, Unamuno was very Basque. His was the tortured soul of the Basque people. In spite of the differences that existed between Mitxelena and Unamuno, they still had many things in common: a desire for immortality; a love of independent thinking; an aversion to closed structures; and a rebellion against the conflation of religion and politics.

Mitxelena defended independence and the importance of personal conscience as opposed to obedience to the laws of the Church. He believed the primary religious criterion, and not the Church, to be the gospel. Nor was he pleased with the way theology and Holy Scripture were taught in the seminaries, as defensive weapons against Rationalism. He did not like the negative posture assumed by the Church with respect to the modern world. Psychologically, both Mitxelena and Unamuno were sensitive, passionate, and restless; they both loved liberty and immortality. For those reasons, Mitxelena was very fond of Unamuno's philosophy: "Unamuno-tar Abendats nirea!"[20] (My Unamunian spirit of the race!).

If we go deeper into *Unamuno ta abendats,* we find many citations that substantiate these statements. With quotes from Lizardi and phrases from Shakespeare's plays, Mitxelena persisted in his yearning for immortality: "I do not want this day to turn to night" and "To be or not to be." The Basque people's desire to survive, their spirit of the race, resists the linguistic euthanasia of Euskara Unamuno proposed, for a people who maintain their roots do not deserve to die: "Ez eutanasirik Ama xarrari . . . 'Edozer gauza ori baño len!' "[21] (No euthanasia for the old mother tongue . . . 'Anything but that!').

Few Basque writers have demonstrated such a sincere appreciation for Unamuno or possess a soul as Unamuno-like. Nevertheless, in his essay Mitxelena scolds the philosopher from Bilbo for the mediocre quality of his Basque and claims that any schoolchild could write better verses than the knowledgeable rector of the University of Salamanca: "Euskera eztala gauza! Egi egia diñozu, Unamuno, lau itz oiei bosgarren bakar bat aurretik ipiñi ezkero. *Zure* euskera ez da gauza! Zurea ez. Ezta urre eman ere"[22] (Basque is not capable! You are right, Unamuno, if you place a qualifier before those four words. *Your* Basque is not useful. Yours, no. In no way).

According to Mitxelena, being born in the Basque nationalist family was a crime, a kind of "original sin." A greater crime was pretending to continue living as a Basque. This wanting to be Basque and being unable to because external forces would not allow it evoked the lines of another great poet, Lizardi:

> Biotzean min dut, min etsia,
> zotiñik-gabeko negar-miña.[23]

> My heart aches, a desperate ache, a silent weeping ache.

In 1944 Mitxelena published *Aboz abo: Arantzazuko kanta-zarrak* (From mouth to mouth: Old songs of Arantzazu). With this little book he hoped to demonstrate the past greatness of the sanctuary of the Virgin of Arantzazu, the Basque people's devotion to her, and the importance of popular Basque poetry. As Latin disappeared, the Romance languages were born, and from them sprang the romancero and the sung poetry of the people. For Mitxelena the existence of the Basque romancero, specifically, the romances related to the sanctuary of Arantzazu, reflected the history of that lovely little corner of the Basque world better than written historical chronicles did.

Ogei kanta Arantzazuko (Twenty songs from Arantzazu, 1954) is another minor work, this one begun in La Aguilera, Burgos, but never finished. These musical literary works are of interest to us, because they contain letters related to the sanctuary in some way and are proof of the devotion of the Basques to the Virgin of Arantzazu.

In 1955 Mitxelena published a minor book of poems written between his sixteenth and twenty-second years, *Arraun eta amets* (Oar and dream). The poems deal with his childhood, the farm where he was born, and the death of his mother. The work was finished in 1954, shortly before Mitxelena left for Latin America. The spirited temperament of the young priest had made him a sought-after preacher in many parishes but had also caused him a lot of trouble, and he was brought before the civil authorities.[24] For that reason, and against the advice of friends, he decided to leave the Basque Country. He went abroad with a heavy heart.

Mitxelena visited nine Latin American nations, spending four years (1955-1959) in Montevideo and two (1959-1961) in Havana, where he wound up in the middle of Castro's revolution. Upon his return to Europe, he worked as a chaplain for Spanish immigrants in Switzerland for three years (1962-1965). During the last few years of his life, he barely had time to write because of his pastoral duties. He died in 1965 in Switzerland at the age of forty-six, and his remains lie in the cemetery of the convent of Arantzazu, in the shadow of a statue of the Virgin whom he loved so much.

Bitoriano Gandiaga

Bitoriano Gandiaga was born on October 8, 1928, in the little village of Mendata, Bizkaia, very close to Gernika. He grew up on the Orbelaun farm, far from the heart of town. Even as a child his isolation and his union with nature and the mountains caused him to begin to closely observe even the smallest details, which he would later describe beautifully. While still very young he entered the Arantzazu school, where he had problems because he did not know Spanish and because of his love of freedom.

During his years as a student of philosophy in the convent of the Franciscan fathers of Olite, Navarre, he began to write poetry in both Spanish and Basque. But his first book of poems was not published until 1962. By that time, Mitxelena, approaching the end of his life, had stopped writing and was living in Switzerland. Nevertheless, his influence is very evident in Gandiaga's poetry.

The young student was an avid reader of Latin, French, and Spanish poets, and other factors prepared him to take up the pen as well: his readings of Basque writers (Lauaxeta, Lizardi, and, later, Mitxelena); his study of the poetry of certain Spanish authors (León, Saint John of the Cross, Jiménez, Antonio Machado, and Otero); his affinity for the French surrealists and symbolists (Paul Eluard and Charles Baudelaire); and, finally, his knowledge of Roman writers such as Horace and Virgil.

The publication of his first book, *Elorri,* brought Gandiaga considerable fame; it won the José Antonio Agirre prize in 1963 and would win other literary prizes. *Elorri* is divided into eight parts. It deals with the preoccupations and yearnings of human life, the struggle between the spirit and the flesh, the dual Basque Country (the one that really exists and the one that the poet would like to see), devotion to the Virgin of Arantzazu, and, finally, the Franciscan love of nature. *Elorri* means "thorn," and it is, in fact, a small bush that sprouts white flowers in the spring and in the fall becomes feeble and twisted, a symbol of the pleasures and pains of humankind.

This book does not recount the history of the appearance of the Virgin of Arantzazu or speak of her sanctuary, as does Mitxelena's *Arantzazu. Elorri* is an intimate book that springs from the collective history of a people. Gandiaga loves nature and humankind. He considers all people, the earth, heavens, air, and animals his brothers and sisters. In these tranquil poems he talks about human worry and suffering, uneasiness and serenity. The hope for spiritual renewal also lies hidden in these poems. The poet associates himself with the thorn alongside which he lives, hopes, and suffers. *Elorri* is a song for the spiritual Arantzazu, full of mystical emotion and Franciscan involvement in the countryside. Gandiaga does not associate suffering with Calvary, as did Mitxelena.

In *Elorri,* the history of the sanctuary of Arantzazu is not the central theme. It is, instead, a point of departure that leads the reader to the poetry of the Spanish mystics and the Generation of '27. The life of the author and the internal drama of his youth are also revealed in this book.

Elorri is full of tenderness and spirituality. It is the product of a jeweler who works words as if they were precious metal and who appreciates the tiniest detail, even that unnoticed by others, such as a leak in the monastery roof. Worldly objects, such as flowers, stones, water, the moon, and grass, are described as stylized realities that acquire new personality. Gandiaga feels free in the midst of nature, in fraternity with the Creator and the creatures of this world. *Elorri* is a book written with enthusiasm and hope, with sincerity and a feeling of liberation in an environment where the poet narrates his interior world without boundaries or restrictions. He clearly identifies with his work.

Generally speaking, these short poems search for beauty as the author describes the emotions that Arantzazu inspires in him. He longs for "arnas bat, zerak doi aitatzekoa, // berba mugarik bakoa"[25] (that breath in which beings are scarcely mentioned). In *Elorri* we see neither popular history nor epic based on old ballads, as we found in *Arantzazu*. Gandiaga's intention is much simpler:

> POEMATXUOK ba-doaz,
> zer nai daben jakin gabe,
> neure arima au bidez doan lez,
> arantz eta lore.[26]
>
> My LITTLE POEMS run on
> without knowing their own intention.
> Thus travels my soul, down paths
> with thorns and flowers.

Gandiaga is a postwar writer. At age nine he could hear the sound of Nazi bombs dropping nearby and see the ruins of Gernika, a town sacred to the Basques. He became a poet in a country where a fratricidal war had recently taken place and where many wounds were yet unhealed.

Throughout *Elorri* there is an underlying existentialism very similar to that of Mitxelena, one that has nothing to do with the existentialist philosophical doctrine but one that does affect human and ethical behavior. Gandiaga is interested in people, whom he sees as beings as small as thorns. He tells us that human life is like the life of the hawthorn plant, which sprouts with difficulty among the rocks during the four seasons of the year.

Although *Elorri* was well received by Basque literary critics, Gandiaga published nothing for twelve years after it came out. In the late 1960s only the poetry of social and political change, especially that of Aresti, the author of *Harri eta herri* (1964), was in fashion. Like Otero's, Aresti's pen was transformed into a hammer to fight against Franco's long dictatorship and to rebuild "my father's house."[27] In contrast, intimate religious poetry moved into the background, in spite of its considerable aesthetic value. Gandiaga threw away the poems he wrote during his twelve years of silence.[28]

When a controversial sculptor arrived at Arantzazu during construction of the new basilica, he encouraged the young poet to continue writing within the new historical context. Jorge de Oteiza succeeded in getting Gandiaga to mine the poetic vein that even he thought was still beautiful: "the best word still dwells within me."[29]

Gandiaga published a new book, *Hiru gizon bakarka* (Three men alone), in 1974. The image of the stylized statues of three men on its title page reflects Oteiza's influence and the artistic change that had taken place in Gandiaga. In this work, Gandiaga left behind the humid, isolated mountains of Arantzazu and went out into the world to face the cultural and sociopolitical reality of the Basque Country.

After a careful reading of Aresti's *Harri eta herri* and ongoing exchanges with Oteiza, Gandiaga began to reflect seriously on the soul of the Basque Country. He found Euskara to be central to its identity, and, as it had Mitxelena before him, the genocidal prohibition of the Basque language caused him anguish. From that point, he assumed a posture of poetic compromise. The desire to be and the inability to be—humanism and Christian existentialism—appear in a book that marks the end of the poet's internal crisis:

> Euskalerria Herri da.
> Herri nahi ta ezina.
> Nahi ta ezin honek ematen dio bizitza Euskalerriari . . .
> Izan nahi larri hori barik ez dago Euskalerririk.[30]

> The Basque Country is a nation. A nation that wants to be and cannot. This impotence gives birth to the Basque nation . . . Without this existential anguish, the Basque Country does not exist.

With the publication of *Elorri* and *Hiru gizon bakarka,* great ideological and literary changes took place. Thanks to the conclusions drawn by the Second Vatican Council and to an encyclical from Pope John XXIII, the defense of ethnic minorities at last found religious support.[31] In *Hiru gizon bakarka,* Gandiaga's words are transformed into very hard stone. It wasn't that he ceased to be inspired by religion. He continued to read the Bible, but now he did not speak of the Virgin of Nazareth, but, rather, of the Psalms and the prophets who defended the people of Israel.

Gandiaga was born in an out-of-the-way farmhouse and has spent his entire life in contact with nature, both in his village and in the sanctuary of Arantzazu. On one occasion he went to Madrid to attend a course on theological renewal. The capital of Spain produced such an impression on him that, instead of attending the course, he toured the city and contemplated its magnitude. As a result of his visit, in 1977 he published *Uda batez Madrilen* (During a summer in Madrid).

The social theme that appeared in *Hiru gizon bakarka* takes on a new aspect in Gandiaga's third book. In it he describes the dehumanization and compression of the masses caused by the great metropolis that crushes the human being. Some passages evoke comparisons with García Lorca's *Poeta en Nueva York* (1929-1930). Gandiaga also describes the places and common objects that only a poet would comment upon: the asphalt, the sidewalks, the huge buildings, the escalators, and the subways.

STYLE

Salbatore Mitxelena

Mitxelena was not an original thinker. He did not possess an innovative style, he did not use special techniques, and he was not a historian in the strict sense of the word. He did know how to apply a very personal poetic expression to the feelings shared by the nationalists of the postwar period, however, even though the tragic consequences of a lost civil war did not provide the most propitious moment for creating a new lyricism. His poetry contains neither Lizardi's carefully elaborated style nor the influence of French symbolist or surrealist poets, which we find, for example, in the works of Lauaxeta and Gandiaga. Mitxelena created his poetry using the patterns of ballads and the popular poetry of the bertsolariak. This explains why his rhymes are occasionally weak. He did not achieve the stylistic perfection of certain other Basque writers, but he captured readers with his lively, penetrating style and his depth of feeling. He knew how to say things directly and concisely and did so like an artist in a hurry to express his suffering.

Mitxelena's style is agile, popular yet elegant, easy to understand, and rich in syntax and vocabulary. His images, drawn from religion and the sorrow of the Basque people, were often dramatic. He was a romantic poet with a lyrical nature who opted for the epic poem, thanks to the popular songs that formed the basis of his poetic art.

He used his own Gipuzkoan dialect but borrowed words from others, especially Bizkaian. He spent several years in Bizkaia and preached in many parishes there. He also used some neologisms (*donoki, izparringi,* etc.) that were common at that time.

While other Basque writers such as Krutwig chose to create in classical Lapurdin Basque, Mitxelena used a simple and popular Gipuzkoan that had lost nothing of its elegant roots. One of Mitxelena's foremost objectives was to lighten Basque verse of the heavy load imposed upon it by its long rhythms. He managed to do this by means of his pure, concise Euskara, which was neither rhetorical nor baroque. His style cut to the marrow of the language.

I have said that his poetry is sometimes imperfect. In his poetry and in his prose he uses words oddly: *re* instead of *ere* (also); *lotsik* instead of *lotsarik* (shame); *apezpiku* to mean "priest" instead of "bishop"; *zere* in place of *zure* or *zeure* (your); *anbat* instead of *ainbat* or *hainbat* (so much). He also tends to repeat the meaning of certain words by providing a second word that will be more easily understood: "alogera edo jornala" (salary) and "egutegia edo kalendarioa" (calendar), for example.

In spite of what might be considered stylistic shortcomings, Mitxelena was an oasis in the desert, a pleasant voice in the dark night of Francoism. His message stimulated young Basques longing for a leader. Although a member of the long list of postwar poets who tried, without much success, to follow in the footsteps of Lizardi, Orixe, and Lauaxeta, Mitxelena offers us lively and very personal poetry.

Bitoriano Gandiaga

Gandiaga, unlike Mitxelena, is a modern poet and very current on European literary trends, especially French. Even similar themes, such as belief in the appearance of the Virgin of Arantzazu, and similar titles for their first books (both *Arantzazu* and *Elorri*) cannot obscure the significant stylistic differences of these two Franciscan authors.

Although Gandiaga constantly belittles his poems, we must admire his effort, his tenacity, and his perfectionism. He recoils from poetry that is rhetorical or too easy. He reworks his words, labors over them, looks for the *mot juste* to describe his ideas precisely. Eluard's surrealism presented Gandiaga with the techniques for renovating or re-creating words and for a return to the specific simplicity of language. Symbolists like Verlaine taught Gandiaga about the musicality to be found in the smallest of words. But much more important than all these influences are Gandiaga's laboriously outlined plan for his poetic work and his knack for sculpting words that is evident in the abbreviated rhythms of *Elorri*.

The sculpted, belabored words of Gandiaga's poetry are born of careful planning. He is a creator of popular images, an untiring seeker of symbols, an artist who trusts neither romantic imagination nor high-sounding words. His language is concise and carefully hewn, the product of a contemplative mind that applies the soul's vision to physical things. Gandiaga scorns the velvety sound of poorly created neologisms that have subsequently been rejected by learned circles, as well as bombastic phrases. He prefers to delve deeply into the interior of each word, creating a language full of both power and delicacy in its naked simplicity. The poetic art he created in *Elorri* is a far cry from the long verses employed by the bertsolariak.

One of *Elorri*'s greatest contributions is its metric innovation. In it we can discern an influence of modern experimental poetry that is absent in Mitxelena's work. Without abandoning traditional Basque rhythms, Gandiaga retouches them on occasion and, at other times, introduces new metric forms. Generally speaking, his lines of verse are short, consisting of six, seven, or eight syllables. He plays with words, looks for sonority, and employs many different rhythms. He uses brief strophes to give lightness to his verse, and he often relies on free verse to impose more variety on his rhyme scheme. Gandiaga knows how to give a very personal and distinct air to traditional tonal modulations, major and minor rhythms, and to the *kopla zaharrak,* as accompanied by the melody of the *trikitixa* (accordion) he feels inside himself.

Gandiaga's imagery, the beauty of his metaphors, his lifelike personifications of nature as re-created in his imagination, and the musicality of his lines of verse are also new. In a decade in which poetic images were generally traditional both because of the influence of the social poetry of Aresti, Lete, and other young poets and because of the Basque song of the 1960s, Gandiaga opted for modernity in this as well. He converted snow into "a newborn lamb," and the mountain Aizkorri and the Urbía region became "the hardworking mountain-men's sweetheart of the heights."[32]

Tastes change. Songs composed during a dictatorship are forgotten when it is overthrown. This has not happened with *Elorri,* however. Although some of its passages, such as the "Benedicta," (Children's song to the Virgin), appear childlike and meaningless in the lay world, the book is still an outstanding example of one of the best poetic works of Basque literature of the late Franco period.

The short poems of *Elorri* give way in *Hiru gizon bakarka* to long poems, and the Bizkaian dialect of the first book becomes Unified Basque in the second.[33] Through these dramatic poems, the reader reaches an understanding of the Basque Country's tragedy as well as the poet's interior anguish. His images are stark, hard, and expressive. Everyone understands his allegories. His alliteration emphasizes the strongest sounds of the Basque language.

The book begins with a comparison between the Basque Country and *txakoli* wine. This Basque wine, the vines for which are grown along the nearby Basque coastline, does not have the qualities of a good wine; it burns the mouth and the gut. In the same way, the Basque Country is a nation that wants to exist but cannot, because it is not allowed to. This situation brings with it the bitterness felt by many Basques: "Ardo pobrea da, ardo nahi lukeena, baina beste ardoen artean ardo ez dena, baina ardo dena halaz ere . . . Izan nahiak ematen dio izatea"[34] (It is a poor wine that wants to be true wine, but it cannot achieve that status when compared to others. Nevertheless, it is still wine . . . Its desire to be gives it existence).

In the third part of the book, there appear three solitary men who, like the bertsolariak, tell us about their problems. Later comes a part entitled "Alegiak eta beste" (Fables and other things) in which in poems dedicated to Otero Gandiaga expresses the truth as he feels it.

Gandiaga shines in his second book through the expressive force and perfection of his forms. His poetry both shocks and attracts because it is full of human life, a preoccupation with existentialism, and the shared human experience. He is convinced that poetry can be an instrument for transforming the world. For that reason, he abandons beauty that is merely formalistic, because he considers it separate from the anguished and pressing reality of the Basque Country during the Franco dictatorship. For him, poetry is a means of communication with other people, and that is why he joined the ranks of those who wrote the poetry of social realism. His interest has focused on the part of the world where he was born and where he lives. In his second book, Gandiaga feels the roots of his land and his race. For him, poetry is a constant requirement of sincerity:

> Gure egia
> ez dute ikusten
> edo ez dute nahi
> egiarik ikusi.

> Gure egia
> geure Herria da
> Herri bezala bizi nahi
> dugun egarria.[35]

> They do not see
> our truth
> nor do they want
> to see the truth.

> Our truth
> is our People,
> our thirst
> to live as a People.

Once again he proves himself to be a deep and detail-oriented poet who eschews baroque flourishes or unnecessary sentiment. He uses many word games in this book: puns, onomatopoeia, and repetitions that make words the true protagonist of the work:

> Egon gaude,
> baina egonean ez.
> Ez genuke egon nahi.
> Egon nahi'ezez gaude egon,
> egon nahi ezaren
> egon beharrezko nekez.[36]

> We are quiet, but not inactive. We do not want to exist without doing anything. We are quiet without wishing to be so, with the necessary tiredness of having to be quiet.

All that is new in a modern city is recounted in the old Basque language in Gandiaga's third book, *Uda batez Madrilen.* Gandiaga employs his usual devices, such as onomatopoeia, repetition, the echo of popular Basque couplets in the happy sound of the *trikitixa*, free verse, a lack of verbs in many lines, experimental poetry, and surrealistic images that give his poetry a certain modern quality within the history of Basque verse.

Gandiaga's fourth book is entitled *Denbora galdu alde* (While wasting time, 1985). It contains 160 pages, 109 of which are written in verse, 51 in prose. The title refers to the advice given Gandiaga by his psychiatrist to cure him of depression: to make time for leisure.

Denbora galdu alde is written in Unified Basque, the language he used throughout his literary production, with the exception of *Elorri*. The poetic sections of the fourth book are written in free verse. Gandiaga avoids the sonnet, which he considers inappropriate for the Basque language. Some of his poems are written with the rhythms of the bertsolariak.

As a counterpart to this peace, the poet reveals his sympathy for men who were assassinated by the violence created by economic interests and social injustice in our consumer society. He mentions the guerrilla fighter Camilo Torres, who was killed in Colombia, as well as Salvadoran archbishop Oscar Romero, who was assassinated while celebrating Mass. He also mentions Catalonian bishop Pedro Casaldáliga, defender of the poor in Brazil, and theologian of liberation Leonard Boff, punished repeatedly by Cardinal Ratzinger, who was in charge of the dicastery of the Vatican for the doctrine of the faith. Gandiaga is a man preoccupied by violence, liberation theology, and the underdevelopment of Latin America.

Gandiaga's sincerity in this book is impressive. The poet-confessor makes a public confession, using the pretext of a visit to the doctor. It is certainly the most autobiographical of his books. In it he expounds upon the most important epochs of his life: his childhood in the old, out-of-the-way farmhouse; the problems his bilingualism caused him during his years in the Arantzazu school; his long hours as a professor and confessor; his excessively rigid temperament and perfectionism ("zehatza, kezkatia"; very worried and worried a lot); and his tendency to be a nonconformist and an isolationist.

The themes present in *Denbora galdu alde* are largely the same as those in Gandiaga's earlier work. His religious concerns; his love of humanity; the importance of the Basque culture, especially the language; concern about the repression of the Basque Country; consumerism; and workaholism are recurring themes. Also mentioned are sociopolitical problems in El Salvador, Nicaragua, Chile, Poland, and Afghanistan as well as Soviet Marxism and U.S. capitalism.

Gandiaga's fifth book is entitled *Gabon dut anuntzio* (I have Christmas as a message, 1986). The title is a line from a verse in the book.[37] This is probably Gandiaga's book to which literary critics have paid the least attention. Its central theme is the peace of Christmas brought to us by the Babe of Bethlehem, "gabonak dut gaia."[38]

In *Gabon dut anuntzio* we find the poems that were sung on Christmas from 1970 to 1985. The book is dedicated to Gandiaga's parents as an affectionate remembrance of the sweet Christmases the poet spent with them in the old Orbelaun farmhouse during his childhood. It evokes the memory of the hearth on which the fire seemed like a sacrament of purification.

This book does not contribute anything new stylistically. Once again, Gandiaga's affinity for onomatopoeia and repetition is evident. He repeats the verb *etorri* (to come) eight times, *zorion* (happiness) six times, and Bethlehem four times in one verse.

Another Franciscan has set these poems to music. Gandiaga and the other brothers, along with the young members of the few families who live next to the sanctuary of Arantzazu, sing these songs at Christmas to the music of the accordion and a tambourine as they accompany the Olentzero, a mythological Basque character dating from pre-Christian times and a sort of Father Christmas for contemporary Basque children.

As mentioned earlier, Mitxelena and Gandiaga were both sons of the Franciscan Order, whose founder, Saint Francis of Assisi, called the animals his brothers. Nature plays a very important role in their works. Both men appear deeply rooted in a specific people, the Basques, and committed to Basque culture under an ironfisted dictatorship. Their union with the Basque people led them to use popular sources such as romances, old couplets, the popular melodies of the *trikitixa,* and the meter of the bertsolariak.

Nevertheless, their styles are very different. Mitxelena was a poet of the postwar era who drew on the literary tradition of the prewar one (Lizardi, Orixe, Lauaxeta, etc.). Gandiaga, on the other hand, does not forget those sources but connects with modern poetry, with the French movements of symbolism and surrealism. He reveals himself to be more of a perfectionist with regard to style and continues to be one of the best Basque poets of the second half of the twentieth century.

Despite their differences, both poets have managed to raise Basque poetry and the essay to a respectable level.

CHAPTER TEN

Jon Mirande

A Nonconformist Writer

It is not easy to describe the personality and works of the French Basque author Jon Mirande (1925–1972). In spite of being one of the best Basque poets of the twentieth century, few critics have dared to analyze him.[1] Mirande emerges as an exceptional case, an iconoclastic pioneer who broke *the* traditional Basque literary molds. He was a kind of *maudit,* or perverse poet, in the manner of French writers Verlaine and Rimbaud. His life was a paradox, a drama, and a scandal. He was attacked by the French and the Basque Left and Right. He was the first author to write against God and the Church in the Basque language. Moreover, he touched on themes such as pederasty, masturbation, lesbianism, sexual freedom, and impiety—themes that shocked the Basque sensibilities of the mid-twentieth century. His nonconformity extended to religion, politics, and culture, and he revealed himself to be anti-Christian, anti-Jewish, antidemocratic, anti-Marxist, antisocialist, and against both traditional Basque nationalism and French centralism. Furthermore, he declared himself a fascist, an advocate of violence, and a defender of paganism and minority cultures, especially the Basque and the Celtic. A bizarre death (probably a suicide) contributes to his complexity.[2]

In spite of everything, including his limited literary production, Mirande is considered a pioneer in the Basque poetry revival of the twentieth century.[3] The best critics view him as one of the most important figures in the history of Basque literature. His poetic prose, especially that showcased in the novel *Haur besoetakoa* (The godchild, 1970), attracts people sensitive to literary beauty.

Influenced by symbolism, Parnassianism, and surrealism, his intimate poetry, which differs greatly from the externalist poetry of late Romanticism that prevailed in the Basque Country at the end of the nineteenth and beginning of the twentieth centuries, changed the atmosphere of Basque literature. Moreover, through his poetry, Mirande is revealed as a polyglot and one of the great promoters of Unified Basque.

MIRANDE'S LIFE

Jon Mirande Aiphasorho was born in Paris on November 12, 1925, in the working-class neighborhood of the fourteenth *arrondissement*. His parents were natives of the little village of Sohuta in the Basque region of Zuberoa, in Iparralde. They both came from humble economic circumstances and moved to Paris in search of work. Poor Basques with little education worked in France as sacristans, servants, porters, and so on.

It is unclear whether Jon Mirande learned the Basque language from his parents or whether he should be considered an *euskaldunberri* (one who learned Basque as a second language). It is a matter of record that his parents spoke Basque better than they did French and that they always spoke Basque to each other. Nevertheless, with their children they spoke more often in French, given the necessity of building a new life in Paris. Thus, Mirande had to make a great effort to master not only his native dialect, Zuberoan, but also most of the other Basque dialects and Unified Basque.[4]

Mirande was self-taught to a great extent. His family's economic straits and World War II forced him to go to work at seventeen in the Finance Ministry, which prevented him from pursuing a university career.[5] In light of his lack of university studies, his facility with and dominion over the languages he knew are surprising. He spoke Basque (all the dialects), French, several Celtic languages—Breton, Welsh, Irish—Spanish, English, German, Dutch, Italian, Danish, Hebrew, Latin, and Greek. His favorite languages were Basque and the Celtic tongues.[6]

Mirande began to write in Basque at the age of twenty-two and continued to do so for about twenty years. During the last four years of his life he ceased writing. His study and use of Euskara can be divided into four stages.

Stage One (1949-1953)

During this stage of his career, Mirande was living in Paris and attending Basque classes given by a Bizkaian, Andima Ibinagabeitia. He studied the Gipuzkoan dialect with Peillen, and during this period he wrote only in this dialect. In his early writings, a certain purity of language is noticeable, a purity that springs from the influence of his teacher, Peillen, who was also his friend.[7] These are the years during which he began to write for the Basque magazine *Euzko-gogoa* (Basque spirit), which was first published in 1950 in Guatemala, because of the enormous effort of Zaitegi.

Stage Two (1953-1959)

In the writing that dates back to this period, Mirande used a Basque that was a mixture of the Gipuzkoan and Lapurdin dialects, a mixture that later served as a basis for the elaboration of Unified Basque. He continued to write for *Euzko-gogoa* during these years and also began to write for the magazine *Gernika*.

Stage Three (1959-1962)

Throughout this period, in Hegoalde, the intelligentsia was eagerly attempting to establish the basis of *Euskara Batua* (Unified Basque) or giving preference to the classic Lapurdin dialect employed by Axular.[8] The goal of the unification of the Basque language was quite clear in the minds of the reformers. Unification was absolutely necessary in order to ensure the survival of the language and to successfully adapt it to modern society.

During these years, Mirande received visits in Paris from Villasante and from Krutwig (in 1921), who lobbied in favor of the classical Lapurdin dialect, which the poet rarely used. Although the goal of unification was clear, Basque writers could not agree on how to achieve it or which dialects should prevail: Gipuzkoan, classical Lapurdin, or a combination? They chose the latter.[9]

Stage Four (1963-1968)

This is the period in which Mirande began to write for the short-lived magazine *Igela* (Frog) in a mixture of classical Lapurdin and Gipuzkoan.[10] Mirande saw in this particular dialectal combination the solution for the unification of Euskara.

During this period, Mirande also wrote in his native Zuberoan dialect, although not a great deal. At times he used vocabulary that was difficult for the majority of native Basque speakers to understand, including words such as *ekhia* (sun), *nehoiz* (never), *nihauk* (I myself), and *jin* (come). He even began to learn the Bizkaian dialect. Nevertheless, his principal concern was the achievement of a unified Basque language, a language that he describes in one of his poems as being fragmented into eight dialects and twenty-five subdialects.

In collaboration with Txomin Peillen, Mirande wrote a letter to Euskaltzaindia reflecting on the sad situation of the Basque tongue. They declared that only three languages had not achieved unification in Europe, and one of them was Basque. Although the Celtic tongues were minority languages, three of them had managed to unify. Gaelic, however, was disappearing because it had not been able to do so. Consequently, keeping in mind the desire for unification expressed at a meeting at Arantzazu in 1968, and the fact that previous attempts had not been successful,[11] Mirande and Peillen both lobbied for the unification plan. This plan would not be left in the hands of a single person but, rather, in the collective hands of Euskaltzaindia. They both accepted with pleasure the reforms carried out by Euskaltzaindia up to that point but felt that the biggest problem was the unification of the verb.

For Mirande their language characterized the Basque people. He preferred to speak in terms of Euskal Herria rather than *Euskadi* (a group of *euzkos,* that is, Basques related by blood). This concept of Euskadi, created by Arana y Goiri, seemed artificial to Mirande. In his opinion, the Basque language stood above other values in the fight for the survival of the Basque race. Folkloric elements, such as dances, the *txistu* (Basque flute), the Basque beret, and pelota, were nothing but empty symbols that French governors used to attract tourism to the Basque coast.[12] Only Euskara created a Basque consciousness that would be *gotor* (strong, robust) and not succumb to the many pressures of the majority cultures coexisting with the Basque culture.

Very clear in Mirande's writings is his nonconformist and iconoclastic character. The poet abhorred conformity and conventionalism as much as he did the humanism of persons considered "honorable." He occasionally used humor and bitingly satirical language, and in the battle for the survival of the Basque Country, the poet even advocated violence.[13]

It is difficult to pin down Mirande's paradoxical and apparently contradictory character. He revealed himself to be a pagan but spoke of the spirit. He was a spiritualist without God, an immoralist who preached a new morality, an antihumanist who was a great friend. He was a supporter of Nietzsche's superman, but he was also a lover of small towns and a champion of lost causes. He was a fascist but defended a free morality. He fought mightily on behalf of the Basque language but ceased to write in Basque during the last years of his life. He was an aesthete and a lover of beauty, but he supported the use of violence to resolve Basque political problems. He was a lover of all things Basque, but he was a critical patriot. He was a promoter and reformer of modern Basque poetry, but he was also a prophet of doom, like Unamuno who foretold the end of the Basque language. According to Mirande, "Euskera iltzera doa, eta ezerk ezin gaizkatu dezake nire ustez"[14] (Basque is going to die and in my opinion nothing can save it).

In spite of his nonconformist and iconoclastic personality, Mirande knew how to be a loyal friend. According to Jon Etxaide, Mirande had a good heart and was incapable of harming anyone: "Gizon ona zela, bihotz onekoa . . . inori kalterik egiteko kapaz ez zena"[15] (He was a good man with a good heart . . . he was incapable of harming anyone). His relationships with family members were always good, and he helped them economically: "Nire aita-amak zartuak lagundu bear ditut orain, eta zoritxarrez, familia oso txiroa gara"[16] (I must now help my old parents because unfortunately we are a very poor family).

Mirande never married, although he maintained stable relationships with three women. He did not believe in monogamy; he preferred free love. For him matrimony was nothing but a social contract, a hypocritical and boring convention, a kind of drug.

Much has been said about Mirande's love life. Txillardegi insinuates that the Basque poet preferred men: "Emakumeei muzin egin eta gizonezkoei eskaini zizkien bertso nabarmen batzuk"[17] (He disdained women and dedicated some daring verses to men). Peillen, one of the people who knew him best, asserted, however, that Mirande was not homosexual: "Hor azaltzen da Miranderi inguru mito bat, neska gabeko gizonarena"[18] (There arose a myth around Mirande, that of a man without women).

This controversy notwithstanding, Mirande was successful with women and attracted to young girls. Pedophilia, specifically an intimate relationship between a thirty-year-old man and an eleven-year-old child, Teresa, is, in fact, the plot of *Haur besoetakoa.*

Mirande had a weak constitution. He suffered from a nervous disorder and was hospitalized on several occasions. He was also an alcoholic, although he was sober for many years. After the death of his father he enjoyed solitude more than the company of others, and on various occasions he planned his suicide. He was extremely sensitive and inclined to pessimism and desperation. He died in Paris at the age of forty-seven.[19]

MIRANDE'S IDEOLOGY

Mirande's ideology was heavily influenced by the German philosophers Nietzsche and Spengler and by the Gipuzkoan writer Baroja. Because of these influences, he openly professed a kind of paganism. He had been educated in and practiced the Catholicism inherited from his parents: "ebili naiz, zure elizetan"[20] (I have frequented your churches), but around 1945 he lost his Christian faith and declared himself anti-Christian. In his youth he looked for answers in the Eastern religions, especially Buddhism. In a September 10, 1959, letter written to Etxaide he declared, "Ni ez naiz kristaua ez fedez ez moralaz"[21] (I am not Christian by faith or by morality). In his opinion, Christianity served no purpose, and Catholicism had damaged the Basque people. It was pointless to invoke God in moments of need, because He was far away: "Zeure zerutik deus ez duzu ihardetsi"[22] (You have answered nothing from your heaven).

In one of Mirande's harshest poems, entitled "Ohiko Jainkoari" (To an ancient god), he apostrophizes Jesus, the "Jew": "Gaur judu-seme, gutartera itzul bazinde gurutzifika zindezaket nik ostera"[23] (If you were to return to us, Jew, I would crucify you again).

He hated Christ because he hated the Jews, and Jesus was nothing to him except a Jewish man named "bar-Joseph" (son of Joseph) who brought to the Basques a message and a church that *irendu* (castrated) their primitive, pagan souls: "Euskaldun zaharren gogo basa, bortithz eta handia apaldu, ahuldu, hobeki erran irendu zuen haren doktrinak; otso ginelarik, bildots egin gaitu"[24] (Your doctrine weakened us, crushed the great and strong indomitable spirit of the ancient Basque; we were wolves, but you changed us into lambs).

The Church gathered the most intelligent young men in its seminaries, castrated them with its depressing ethics, and sent them out to preach for the greater glory of Rome. Mirande believed that if the Protestant Reformation, advocated by Jeanne d'Albret in Navarre, had prevailed, the situation of the Basque people would have been better. The Catholic Church restricted liberty and imposed servitude on the Basques. According to Mirande, the three greatest enemies of the Basques were Spain, France, and the Catholic Church.

Nietzsche's influence on Mirande is apparent. According to Nietzsche, Christianity brought hatred to life, beauty, and love by preaching pacifism and a transcending morality. Nietzsche tried to establish an equation of values in which the good were not those who suffered but those who were noble and strong. This new humanism and new morality held humankind to be the central and absolute value. Man was supplanted by God, but Nietzsche's superman demanded the death of God. God was dead, and man was his executioner. Churches were nothing but the tombs of God.

Basing his philosophy on these ideas, Mirande advocated a return to primitive Basque paganism as a solution to the survival of the Basque people, whereby Josu (Jesus) would be replaced by mythological beings and such Basque pagan divinities as Ortzi, Basajaun, the lamias and witches, and Mari of Anboto.[25] Mirande invoked Ortzi as a god several times: "Ortzi euskal jainkoari zuzendu galde othoitz bat"[26] (Direct your petition to the Basque god Ortzi). One of his letters is headed with the name Ortzi: "Ortziren izenean agur eta bake"[27] (Greetings and peace in the name of Ortzi).

More than anything, his paganism was aesthetic and sensual. A sumptuous table, sexual freedom, goddesses, and sirens—all had a place in his philosophy. Mirande was also very fond of the pagan rites of other cultures, especially those of the Celts. In one period of his life (1951), he would meet with Breton friends to celebrate the pagan rites of the Druids, and he would wear the ornaments of the *ovata* (pagan priest).

In Mirande's essay "Euskaldungoaren etsaiak"[28] (The enemies of the Basques), the influence of Baroja and his novel *La leyenda de Jaun de Alzate* (1922) is evident. The Basque god Ortzi Thor appears in that novel, whose basic premise is a defense of the Basque paganism that had been supplanted by Christianity. According to Baroja, Christianity had diminished the Basque spirit, making it more Roman, Latin, Italian, African, and Jewish.

Although Mirande did not agree completely with Baroja's view, he shared many of the ideas expressed in the novel and had great respect for the Gipuzkoan novelist. In a letter to Etxaide, he declared: "Baroja baita Euskaldun erdalidazleetan gauza zenbaitetan gogaide aurkitu dudan bakarra"[29] (Among all the Basques who have written in Spanish, Baroja is the only one with whom I agree on some things).

Spengler's influence was also decisive in the formation of Mirande's ideology. In *Der Untergang des Abendlandes* (1918), Spengler advocates force as the source of truth, justice, and morality. His philosophy was considered a precursor to Hitler's national-socialism, although the Nazis, who became his enemies, accused him of being a systematic pessimist. Spengler supported order and strong nations. He detested the ideologies and forms of government—such as Judaism, Christianity, Marxism, democracy, and parliamentarianism—that he felt had weakened Europe. For him, pacifism, egalitarianism, mutual respect, and the idea of universal brotherhood were symbols of a decadent ideology and of utopian qualities that had disappeared in battle. He was a supporter of nationalism and socialism in his homeland, Prussia.

Spengler's philosophy had a decisive influence on Mirande's value judgments about democracy, the Basque nationalism created by Arana y Goiri, and Christian humanism. Mirande consistently showed himself to be a nonconformist where the Basque nationalism of the time was concerned. For the many Basque nationalists who defended the Arana y Goiri slogan "euskaldun-fededun" (Basque equals Christian), Mirande was an antidemocratic pagan.

Mirande appeared isolated and paradoxical. He was not a conservative, but the Left branded him as a rightist and a Nazi. He was a fervent Basque patriot, yet many Basques dismissed him as a nonconformist and a leftist. For Mirande, Euskara, not the external representations of its folklore, was the soul of the Basque Country. He did not find what he wanted among the Basques who frequented the *Euskal Etxea* (Basque Center) in Paris, for the majority of them expressed themselves in French and were very French in their ideas.

In a letter to his friend Ibinagabeita, Mirande stated: "Ez didazu sinistuko, bainan ni urbildu ere ez naiz egiten emengo Centro Vasco ortara. Nazka ematen dit eta goragalea, erdera beste izkuntzarik entzuten ezten etxe ark"[30] (You won't believe me, but I do not go near the Euskal Etxea here. That house, where only French is heard, disgusts and repulses me). Mirande felt that France was a chauvinistic nation and that its chauvinism should be attacked. The *liberté* proclaimed by the French Revolution in 1789 offered no improvement for the Basque people but instead harbored cultural genocide.[31]

At the end of his life, Mirande become completely disillusioned with the Basques, the future of the Basque Country, and the language. This was due in large measure to the frigid welcome he and his literary work received from most Basques.[32] Mirande considered his profession to be the most serious thing in his life. Nevertheless, he quit writing in Basque in his final years because of the revulsion he felt: "Euskalerriarekin eta Euskal abertzaleekin aserik nago . . . 15 urte alperretan galdu dizkizut auentzat lan eginaz"[33] (I've had enough of the Basque Country and Basque nationalists . . . I have wasted 15 years working for them). In a letter to Peillen, the last he ever wrote, he speaks again of the same feelings of frustration. He was convalescing in Mauleon, Zuberoa, after having been in the hospital: "Asperturik nago zinez aldi huntan Euskal Herriaz"[34] (To tell the truth, right now I am bored with the Basque Country). It could be that these feelings were the result of the depression he felt in his final years, but there is no way to be certain. In a letter to Tauer written in 1955, Mirande had spoken of the Basques in the same way: "txapeldun, euskaldun eta fededun"[35] (wearers of berets, Basques and Christians). He scorned them for their materialism and their lack of interest in Basque culture.

The correspondence he maintained with this friend is very interesting because of Mirande's openness:

> Gainera itxaropen ta konfidantza oro galdu det Euskaldunen gain. Gezur andi bat baizik ez da aien delako "abertzaletasuna" eta funtsean, azaluts berekoi batzu dira abertzaleak. Amar urte galdu ditut aien alde lan eginaz, eta orain ez det geiago "Don Quijote" izateko asmorik. Bear bada, laguntzale ta jarraitzale zenbait aurkitu banitu, engoitik ere Don Quijote izango nintzan, ala ere, bainan ederki utzi naute nere aberkide maiteak (?) eta ordaindu gabe ez det aien alde ezer geiago egingo.[36]

> Furthermore, I have lost all confidence and hope in the Basques. The foundation of their nationalism is nothing but a big lie, and, in reality, Basque nationalists are egotists and hypocrites. I have wasted ten years working on their behalf and now I don't think I can continue playing the role of Don Quixote. Nevertheless, if I had found people who would have helped me and followed me, I would have continued being

Don Quixote, but my beloved (?) countrymen have abandoned me completely and I will no longer work for them unless they pay me.

Mirande saw little hope for the future of the Basque Country and the Basque language. In fact, he came across as very pessimistic. He believed that the degeneration of Basque was not due solely to Franco's dictatorship, but also to the negligence of the Basque people, for the same degeneration could be observed among the Basques of Iparralde: "Egia esan: ez dut itxaropen andirik Euzkadi-ren etorkizunari buruz; nire ustez Euskaldunak aberri eta enda bezala galtzen ari gara eta ori ez da bakarrik Francoren obenez, Frantziako Euskaldunak ere galtzori berean baitaude"[37] (To tell the truth, I do not hold much hope for the future of Euzkadi; I think that the Basque nation and race are in decline not just because of Franco, for the same degeneration is seen among the French-Basques).

In a letter written on August 15, 1971, to the editor of the Basque magazine *Anaitasuna* (Brotherhood), Mirande displayed his broken heart and his ideas about the future of the Basque Country. The letter was written in French, undoubtedly as a sign of his disdain. The poet's scornful nature is clearly revealed: "A few months ago I received the magazine *Anaitasuna,* which I never subscribed to and which I threw out without reading, for I am a fascist (although Basque) and I detest Christianity, or at least the democracy that is labeled Christian, which is in fact Jewish. And as far as I am concerned, the Basque language that I continue to speak with my Zuberoan family sounds strange to me as a language for politics and culture."[38]

This was not the first time that Mirande openly declared his sympathies for fascism, although his fascism was not Hitlerian and political but an attitude that he assumed in the face of life, according to his friend Peillen: "Bere fazismua sentitzeko manera bat zen, ez ideologia bat; etika bat zen, pagan kutsukoa, ez politika bat"[39] (His fascism was a form of feeling and not an ideology; it was an ethic flavored with paganism, not a political ideology).

Mirande's fascism and racism were selective. He had friends in France's ultra-right-wing Organisation Armée Secrète (Secret Armed Organization, OAS), and he despised Jews, blacks, and Asians. Nevertheless, his anti-Semitism was also very selective, as can be seen in the polemic he waged with Aginaga in the review *Egan*.[40] His aversion was not with Jews in general (some of his good friends were Jewish) but with those Semites who he believed abused their economic power. He affirmed in the *Anaitasuna* article that the French did not scorn the Jews because they were foreigners. There were Sephardic Jews who had lived in Bordeaux, Baiona, and other places for many centuries, and who had been well received by the French. The Gallic people abhorred only those Jews who, having arrived during the last few years from Central Europe, were taking economic and political control. According to Mirande, this French anti-Semitism was a popular movement, not a reactionary one, created by rich, intellectual fascists.

Mirande's nonmaterialistic paganism was also out of the ordinary. He detested Marxism. He believed in the everlasting spirit, although his concept was a long way from the Christian idea of God. In a letter addressed to Jon Etxaide, the poet speaks of the soul and the everlasting spirit: "Nik sinisten dut ispirituan, ariman, ots psykhismuan . . . askotan apaizekin gai orretaz mintzatu naiz . . . banan ezin sinistu dezaket . . . Euskalerriko jainkoek eta ez-jainkoek onespenez beteko al zaituzte 1959, urtean, bai eta urrengoetan ere" [41] (I believe in the spirit, the soul, that is, in the psyche . . . often I have discussed this with priests . . . but I cannot believe in the sense of having religious faith . . . May the gods of the Basque Country and God, who does not exist, bless you in this year 1959 and in all the years to follow). For Mirande, there was in every individual a part he called the psyche that was not a mere product of material existence, as the materialists claim. In a certain way, this soul of which Mirande spoke was the only reality.

In short, Mirande was essentially a paradox. He was a lover of Basque culture and an enemy of hypocrisy and falsehood. He was an aesthete and a perfectionist who lived in a dual world, that of Paris, with its days full of misery, and the ideal, unreal world of his dreams. This dichotomy filled his heart with pain and anguish: "Full of a surprising originality, his poems reveal a bitter rebellious soul, thirsting for violence, undoubtedly a reflection of a physically weak constitution, undermined by illness." [42]

Other Basques opted to continue fighting in spite of the adversity they faced as a result of belonging to a minority people divided between the two powerful states of France and Spain. But at the end of his life, as Unamuno did at eighteen, Mirande retired from the battlefield in favor of the survival of the Basque Country and its language. Unamuno's Spain ached; Mirande's beloved Basque Country bled. Neither one could see the dawning of Euskara, of thousands of children and adults learning the language of their ancestors. Only those who hoped and trusted in the great but tiny nation of Euskadi became believers.

LITERARY WORKS

Few Basque writers' ideas have been discussed as often as have Mirande's, nor has the literary value of many been as highly appreciated. This Basque poet was a misfit in both French and Basque society. Nevertheless, the beauty of his literary art had a tremendous impact, and not even his enemies would disparage his literary genius. According to Basque critic Antonio Arrue, Mirande was a "truly select spirit because of his authentic literary quality." [43]

Mirande brought a new vitality to Basque literature. He was an admirer of the poets who preceded him, such as Detxepare, Oihenart, Lizardi, Lauaxeta, Orixe, Zaitegi, Iratzeder, and Mitxelena, but he was also cognizant of the fact that his own contribution to poetry was original with regard to themes: "Nik nere olerkietan orain arte erabil ez diran poesi-ekaiak artu ditut"[44] (I have used subjects in my poetry that have not been used until now).

His artistic stature is even more surprising when we realize that he wrote little in Basque. His literary production in the language was limited to a short novel, several poems, short stories, brief essays, and articles spread among various Basque magazines. In addition to his original works, Mirande was an excellent translator, especially in French, English, and German.

His work is highly esteemed for its contribution to Basque literature, especially in the areas of poetry and black humor. With Mirande a new era of modern Basque poetry was born, and his was the first work in Basque to use black humor. The fruits of the seeds he sowed are evident in younger poets.[45]

Haur besoetakoa (The godchild)

Haur besoetakoa is considered by many Basque critics to be one of the best novels in the history of Basque literature. When it was published in 1970 its literary merit was obfuscated by the controversy that ensued over its sensuality and eroticism. The novel has a simple plot. A thirty-year-old man lives alone except for an old servant. He is about to marry his sweetheart, Isabela, but the relationship ends badly because she represents the hypocritical society the man abhors. He wants to flee from both society and Isabela and seeks a solution in the love he professes for his godchild (*haur besoetakoa*), Teresa, an eleven-year-old girl. His sexual relationship with the child separates him even further from society and his family, which are, of course, opposed to the affair. Only one friend, a painter, remains loyal to him. The protagonist seeks refuge in Teresa, but emotional problems arise because of his jealousy. At the end of the novel, Teresa and the main character drown.

Teresa is central to the novel. Mirande reveals many details about her— her age, health, orphaned state, modesty, appearance, and psychology. The male protagonist also plays a very important role. Even though we do not know his name, we learn many details about his family, economic situation, sexual desire for the child, violent character, hatred of society, and so on: "Etse on bateko seme zen"[46] (He was a son of a well-to-do family).

Upon the death of his parents, he remains living in their old house near the sea. He is a violent man. He once hit Isabela hard enough to draw blood. He also physically and verbally mistreats the old woman who has been his servant all his life. In the end, he throws her out. Up until then he lived according to the conventions imposed on him by society: "Besteen esanera gehiegi bizi izan zen orain artean"[47] (I lived until now mostly according to the rules of others), but alcohol becomes his best friend after Teresa's death.

None of the secondary characters are well defined. Isabela, the fiancée, is pretty, but the man is repulsed by her. She seems ridiculous to him, because she has little talent and is a slave to fashion. The action occurs mostly in the man's house, especially in his living room and bedroom. Time is linear. The narrator is omniscient but does not speak in first person. We are far from the modern techniques employed in the French *nouveau roman* or in the modern Latin American novel.[48]

Haur besoetakoa is divided into three parts. The first and the third are clearly defined: each plot lasts three days. The second part takes place over a period of a few months, from March until the beginning of summer. The first part of the novel begins on a day in March. During the first three days of the story, the author presents the most important principle: the sexual relationship between the man and the child. He also introduces the secondary characters, Isabela and the servant, and we witness the breaking off of the man's engagement to Isabela.

In the second part of the novel, we do not know exactly how many days pass: "Egunak eta asteak, eta hilabeteak, joan zitzaizkien"[49] (Days, weeks, and months passed). The author describes the child attending school, her new role as mistress of the house, the progressive development of the man's sexual relationship with her, their plans for summer, and the appearance of the man's friend, the painter.

In the third part of the novel, we are presented with the man's problems with his family (represented by a cousin), the expulsion of the old servant woman, and Teresa and the man's death.

Eroticism

Eroticism plays an important role in Mirande's prose and poetry. In this regard the influence of Baudelaire, Mallarmé, Verlaine, and Rimbaud is evident. *Haur besoetakoa* is an outstanding example of Mirande's erotic prose.

From the book's first pages, the man's sensual feelings are revealed. One cold afternoon in March, as he stands next to the stove, he feels a chill that excites him: "Gorputza ikara zedukala eta sutan gogoa, ez egurrezko su alaiaren garrez baina izaerazko suaz"[50] (His body trembled and his soul burned, not from the heat of the flames of the burning wood but with physical passion).

The godfather-godchild relationship is converted into sexual intimacy between the two main characters. The orphaned girl is taken in out of compassion, then displaces the old servant and the fiancée, Isabela, in the man's life: "maite haut! Beste gizonek beren emaztea maite duten bezala"[51] (I love you! As other men love their wives). The difference in their ages is not an obstacle for him.

The man's sensuality is transformed into eroticism as the book unfolds.

He becomes obsessed with the girl's body. Never in Basque literature has anyone written passages as erotic as those that appear in this book, even though the eroticism is veiled in similes:[52]

> Baina emakume batenaren eztitasuna zedukan haren larru esnetsuak eta haren iztarrak, mardul eta fresko zirenak, berotasun batez iraganak izaten ziren gizonaren eskuak heien gainean zabaltzen zirelarik eta barruko aldera eztiki oratzen zituztelarik. Urre ta marmorezko usain-ontzi bat zedukan hor eskuen artean eta, makurturik, ahoratzen zuen usain maite hori.[53]

> But her milky skin and her strong, vigorous thighs possessed all the sweetness of a woman. The man's hands encountered heat as he caressed them and touched their insides. He held in his hands a fragrant vessel of gold and marble and, bending over it, he tasted its intimate odor.

This intimacy is shared by the child in spite of her youth and the shame she feels: "Aita besoetakoen soak haragia erretzen zion gar bat izan balitz bezala"[54] (Her godfather's glance burned her body as if it were a flame). Certain similarities between the protagonist and Jon Mirande make us wonder if the man in the novel is not an incarnation of the author.

This eroticism evokes Baudelaire's poem "Lesbos" and appears also in Mirande's poetry and in his essays, although it is dressed in different raiment, as lesbianism, pederasty, prostitution, male homosexuality, and masturbation.

"Neskatxak" (Young girls) brings to mind Mallarmé's "l'après-midi d'un faune," but unlike the cryptic style of the great French poet, Mirande's is clear and understandable:

> Ahizpa gazte bi dantzari . . .
> alkharri muxuka, maitez
> bular zuriak ikara . . .
> erori ziran neskatxak
> elkarren besoetara.[55]

> Two young sisters were dancing . . . kissing each other tenderly, white breasts trembling . . . the girls fell into each other's arms.

Pedophilia is one of the most important themes in the novel *Haur besoetakoa,* where it is displayed with strong strokes of the literary brush. Pederasty also appears in some of Mirande's poems. In "Amsterdameko orhoitzapen bat" (Memories from Amsterdam, 1959) the poet evokes the memory of a little girl, Bessie, a tender flower who was loved in an unusual way:

> Baldin parketan bazen atsegin
> Hainbat loreren artean

Hêtan maitharzun ez-ohituek
ba zutelarik entseiu? . . .
Lore heietan, Bessie, gaur zutzaz
bertzerik orhoit duta nik? . . .

Blue-jean gorritan gorputxo bera
pereku-gose jadanik.[56]

She rested in the parks among so many flowers . . . among
them uncommon love had a feast . . . Among those flowers,
Bessie, today I remember only you? . . .

Still longing to caress that naked body in blue jeans.

Mirande describes prostitution more crudely in several poems. In
"Larunbat-arrats" (Saturday night), he depicts the hard life of the prostitutes of Paris in the midst of drunkards and "johns," and he likens the city
itself to an old whore:

Hoteletako
hirur ehun frankotako geletan
atsegin-neska nekhatuak . . .
zer bizitza . . .
Paris, puta zahar, lotara doa
. . . ni ere bai.[57]

In the three-hundred-franc rooms of the hotels, there are
worn-out prostitutes . . . what a life . . . Paris, the old whore,
is going to bed and so am I.

"Pigalle" (1951) is dedicated to the same theme. Mirande does not use
palliatives or euphemisms when describing the way of life on that famous
Paris street: "Puten sabelean arno beltza botz-kantuz"[58] (In the belly of the
prostitutes the red wine sings).

Similar ideas are repeated in "Oianone." The word *oianone* is not easy to
translate, but it could be a contraction of the Basque words *ohean* (in bed)
and *ona* (good), which in this case would reflect the idea the poet wanted to
express. This poem has an epigraph from one of Detxepare's most famous
poems:[59]

Oianone! Oianone!
Gau honetan zaitut ene;
larru legun eta zuri,
bulhar samur, sabel guri,
nire neska Oianone.[60]

Oianone, Oianone!
Tonight you belong to me, soft white skin, tender breasts,
plump belly, my girl Oianone.

The theme of male homosexuality is prominent in a brief essay entitled "Jainkozalea" (Lover of God). It deals with an act of love between a gentleman and a young traveler. The young man is looking for sexual pleasure, and the unknown gentleman offers it to him, saying, "Ni nauk maite dukana"⁶¹ (I am the person you love).

And finally, masturbation is treated in the poem "Eder bati" (To a beautiful young woman) where the poet substitutes the masturbating young man's hand for the female genitals:

> Zuretzat gehiago
> Ez dut maitasunik . . .
> Gaurgero, neska gazte
> Eskua dut emazte . . .
> Ez dizuket eskerrik,
> eskua dut aski . . .
> Zu joanik ere berdin
> Bai pozik naizela!
> Nerau neronen jabe.⁶²

> I don't love you anymore . . . from now on, young girl, my hand will take the place of a wife . . . I owe you nothing for my hand is enough . . . Even though you leave, I am happy because I own myself.

Mirande's poems may make him look hard and surly, yet those who dealt with him most often talk about his noble sentiments. Only when he took up a pen did he use the gruff tones we see in his poetry to reflect the world within him. His poems are an existential confession in the style of Unamuno. He wrote what he felt and made his feelings public. Social conventions did not exist for him: "Ezin nezakeon ene barneari uko egin"⁶³ (I could not say no to my conscience). With the exception of Detxepare, Mirande considered all Basque poets to be very shrewd, for they hid their most intimate feelings by drowning them inside.

Death

Death, generally accompanied by loneliness, also appears frequently as a theme in Mirande's work. The poet's personal isolation was not a peaceful withdrawing to allow creative concentration; it was a dark solitude. Not even his closest friends could save him from it.

The poem "Ohiko Jainkoari" (To an ancient god, 1951) is an example of Mirande's treatment of the themes of death and loneliness. His solitude was, first of all, the result of a break with God. As far as Mirande was concerned, Christ had abandoned him. The poem's epigraph is a biblical citation—the words Jesus directed at his Father on the afternoon of Good

Friday on Calvary: "Father, Father, why have you abandoned me?" The influence of Nietzsche is also evident in this poem:

> Josu bar-Joseph, ba dut othoi egin gauerdiz . . .
> eta zuk aldiz utzi nauzu . . .
> zeure munduan soilik nago edozein zakhur
> zoriontsurik bizi da ni bainoago . . .
> zeure zerutik deus ez duzu ihardetsi.[64]

> Jesus, son of Joseph, I have prayed to you at midnight . . .
> and you in exchange have abandoned me . . . I find myself
> alone in your world, where a dog lives a happier life than
> I . . . You have not answered me from your heaven.

When reading Mirande's work, one gets the impression that death is pursuing him. He does not fear it, nor is he obsessed by it, but it is constantly in his thoughts. According to Peillen, "Heriotza bere obra guzian dago"[65] (Death is in all his works).

In "Merry Christmas," which he wrote in French in 1947 and later translated into Basque, Mirande made public the repugnance and disgust he felt toward the Nativity. It was not mere coincidence that he chose this time of year to kill himself:

> Baina Eguberri eguna, besteak bezalako edo besteak baino
> txarrago denentzat? Eguberri on, nere lo gelan aspertzen
> naizen honentzat.[66]

> But is the night of the Nativity equal to or worse than all the
> others for everyone? Is it a Merry Christmas for this one who
> lies bored in his room?

Everything ends with death. The body decomposes and is good only for fertilizing the flowers in the cemetery:

> Illerrian bada lore
> euzki-lili krabelin
> zu zaituzte badut uste
> oingarritzat Kattalin.[67]

> In the cemetery there are flowers, sunflowers and carnations;
> it appears that they have you for fertilizer, Catherine.

In "Nil igitur mors est" (Everything is dead, 1952), faith in life after death is presented as useless; it does no good to hope for it. There is no need to fear death because "ez dena ezin diteke hil"[68] (that which does not exist cannot die). Nothingness and emptiness run neck and neck. The poem is one of Mirande's most difficult.

Mirande's nihilism reminds us of a poem by Krutwig, in which the latter affirms that the essence of things lies in nothingness and as a result nothing exists:

Gauzen izaitea' Ezerezean
dago; Nibbana da beren zentzua . . .
Ezer eztago, eztago Gogorik,
Spiritua ezta khimaira baizik.[69]

The nature of things stems from nothingness, its meaning is
Nirvana. Nothing exists, the soul does not exist, the spirit is a
mere chimera.

The idea of death appears several times tinted with black humor, and in
the tragic style of Edgar Allan Poe. In "Tzakur hil bati" (To a dead dog) the
poet shows us a dead dog adrift in the river and proceeds to pay homage
to it:

Nik soilik nire Ekklesian
dut ohoratzen hil anaia.[70]

Standing alone in my church, I pay homage to my brother the
dog.

Paganism

Another of Mirande's common themes is a type of
paganism that implies a negation of God. This paganism, in turn, leads
to belief in Basque pagan divinities. "Euskaldun laminei" (To the Basque
lamias, 1961) is dedicated to a category of goddesses or supernatural, mythological beings who, according to Mirande, have been supplanted by the
songs of the Catholic churches and by the Jewish god Baal:

Geroz zuen hatzak elas! dira galdu
ibai ta leizeetan, eta gure baitan;
Latinez otoituz zaituzte ohildu
Gizon beltzek elizetan.
Judaiar Baalen neu sinhestun ez naiz,
Jentilen odola niregan badabil
Asaben modura gur dagizuet . . .[71]

Later your tracks disappeared, alas! from our rivers, caves,
and consciences; men dressed in black in the churches forced
you to flee with their Latin prayers. I do not believe in the
Jewish god Baal, for pagan blood flows in me. I adore you, as
did my ancestors.

This return to pagan divinities also brings to mind pantheism. In *Haur besoetakoa,* when Teresa drowns, she marches off in the company of the sirens
to the world of children. The painter flings his ring at the sea god as an offering: "Urrezko zaldun-eraztun bat, itsasoko jainkoari oferenda"[72] (Offering
of a nobleman's gold ring to the god of the sea).

Patriotism

The fact that Mirande did not agree with tradi-
tional nationalism or with the ideas of Arana y Goiri does not imply that
he did not consider himself a Basque patriot. In fact, for many years he was
a radical, even a violent, patriot. Some parts of his writings shock us with
their violence. For example, in "Jeiki, Jeiki" (Rise up, rise up), when he
speaks of his enemies, he uses the verb *eho* (to grind up). The poem uses an
existing popular poem but changes some of the verses to make them more
violent:

> Jeiki, jeiki Üskaldünak . . .
> iratzarriko othe da
> lo den otso zaharra? . . .
> Aspaldian ginen bizi
> arrotzen esküpeko . . .
> sort-herriaren etsaiak
> denak eho ditzagün . . .[73]

> Rise up, rise up Basques . . . will the old sleeping wolf
> awaken? . . . We have lived a long time under the oppression
> of foreigners . . . Let us grind up the enemies of our country.

MIRANDE'S LITERARY STYLE

Mirande was a poet who broke traditional molds.
Although he was a member of a pragmatic nation that has traditionally used
its poetry for specific ends, Mirande was an innovator. Dispensing with the
apologetic, he tried to find beauty and sought out the aesthetic. His poetry
was not merely a protest, nor was it enough for him to just tell the truth.
Mirande was not a "socially involved" poet. For him poetry was a simple
word game in search of literary beauty.

He was aware of the uniqueness of his poetry. At times he discussed with
his friends the harshness of his surrealistic and symbolist style, but nothing could persuade him to move away from the aesthetics that marked the
beginning of his life as a poet. At age twenty-two he heard the voices of the
muses and followed them until his death.

Mirande created a new aesthetic. He could be called a virtuoso of the
written word. His elegant style imposes itself on the reader. His prose follows in the wake of his compatriots and J. Etchepare. One may or may not
agree with his ideas, but Mirande is surprising in his sincerity and attracts
readers with his elegant style. He is a writer of profound imagination and
great creative capacity. The beauty of his work is demonstrated in his metaphors and comparisons, in the variety and musicality of his rhythms, in the

richness of his rhymes, the audacity of his imagery, the large number of epithets, and the clarity of his expression.

Occasionally, his style—especially that of his prose—is baroque and excessively decorative. His artistry, however, does not imply secrecy in the style of Mallarmé, Góngora, or Guillén. Mirande's poetry is clear and comprehensible for the most part, because he avoided the purism that reigned at that time in Basque writing. He had no misgivings about borrowing words and used them whenever he needed them, although on certain occasions he felt obliged to change a word's orthography a bit. The only difficulty that many Basque readers will have when reading his works is in understanding his use of the various dialects, for he mastered most of them.

Mirande's Basque is linked to literary tradition, for he uses many words and expressions inspired by the classics. One must admire his mastery of the verb forms; he uses both the familiar and the formal with extraordinary facility. Following the example established by Lizardi, Mirande proved that Euskara was a poetic language. In this sense, he was an apologist on behalf of the language: "Euskera egin-egina da poesiarako. Nik, gaztea izan arren, zenbait izkuntza ikasi ditut, euskerari laguntzeko ain zuzen"[74] (Basque is a language created for poetry. Even though I was young, I studied many languages in order to help Basque).

In this regard, Mirande had a great advantage over other Basque writers. He lived in Paris, the cradle of the great literary trends. At that time the Pyrenees were like a giant zipper that closed Spain off from the influence of French and European ideas. Franco's Spain was more worried about saving the eternal values of the homeland than about becoming involved in the new literary movements of Europe. This was one reason that great Basque poets did not know what was happening in the literary world.

Such was not the case with Mirande. He was born, lived, and died in Paris. Except for a few brief stays in the Basque Country, he followed all the international literary innovations from his Parisian vantage point. Especially important influences were the works of Wilde, Poe, Baudelaire, Rimbaud, Pío Baroja, and Nietzsche. In his poetry, we can see the special influence exerted by Poe, Baudelaire, Verlaine, and Rimbaud. His black humor was inspired by Nerval and Poe. The musicality of his poetry had its origins with the symbolists. Some of his symbolist-inspired poems seem to have been written to be sung because of their brief rhythms, the repetition of key words, the use of certain consonants such as *tx, k,* and *n:*

> Etxe txiki txukun baten
> zure aitamekin
> zinan bizi, zintzo bizi
> ene maite Katalin.[75]

> My beloved Catherine, you lived decently with your parents in a small pretty house.

I have tried to describe the complex and contradictory personality of Jon Mirande. His personality reminds us a bit of his compatriot Unamuno; however, differences are apparent.

Unamuno wanted to be famous in his own land and could not. He competed for a Basque-language teaching position and did not acquire it. He tried to write Basque poetry but never transcended the mediocre.[76] He never even managed to speak Basque fluently. For that reason, he had to go to Salamanca, where he became famous throughout the world for his celebrated essays, novels, and poems.

Mirande could have achieved fame by writing in French in the city of lights, but he preferred to dedicate his energies to Basque. In spite of being an *euskaldunberri,* he managed to achieve what Lizardi had four decades earlier. He made Basque a language worthy of the most beautiful sentiments and capable of expressing them.

Unamuno foretold the end of the Basque language. Mirande preferred to dedicate the best years of his life to the language of his forefathers. He did not achieve a post as numerary member of Euskaltzaindia during his lifetime, but his name will be forever written in golden letters in the history of Basque literature. Time has already provided us with the perspective from which to better view his work and to evaluate his extraordinary contribution objectively. In spite of his limited production, this Basque poet is one of the few great writers of modern Basque poetry.

CHAPTER ELEVEN

Gabriel Aresti

The Poetry of a Fighter

Anxious to shatter the religious exclusivity of written Basque, in the mid-twentieth century a group of laymen began to write on nontraditional themes. Gabriel Aresti (1933–1975) was one of them. Aresti wrote poetry, plays, short stories, a novel, and many articles and letters. He received four first prizes for poetry and one for plays in various competitions. His literary production consists mainly of poetry; among the modern Basque poets, Aresti is one of the best. Both his themes and his forms are innovative, which give his art a personal and unique character.

His poetry follows the literary trends of the period after the Spanish Civil War. He was mainly concerned with the men who suffered war's consequences; hence, he wrote for a specific audience, the people of his own time. He used his poems to fight lies and injustice, and he dreamed about worldwide social change and an ideal world:

> Egun batean
> guztiok
> izanen gara
> zoriontsuak.[1]

One day we will all be happy.

Best known is his social poetry, much of which appears in *Harri eta herri* (Stone and people, 1964). The Spanish Civil War drove Spain's most celebrated authors into hiding. Other writers, advocates of the Franco regime, filled the vacuum. After the war there was a return to pseudoclassicism, a rebirth of the hendecasyllable, a return to the Garcilaso style of beautiful but noncommittal phrases, in short, the reappearance of empty preciosity and a repetitious, monotonous, passive poetry. Aresti's poetic ideology, though, was heavily laced with social concerns and eschewed the monotony of post–Spanish Civil War poetry.

After World War II social poetry came into its own. It focused on concrete, existential humankind, living in the here and now, shaped by historical circumstances, suffering the aftermath of war. No human topic was alien to this poetry. It endeavored to fight injustice, to "tell it like it was," and to change the world's collective conscience. This was not elitist poetry, and its authors were not interested in the pure poetics of Jiménez or in his "immense minority." Poetry was not an act of elaborate decoration, nor did it belong to the impenetrable world of the aesthetes, like Góngora and Mallarmé.

There were no specifically poetic objects for the social poets, and the traditional canons of aesthetic beauty did not interest them. Brothels were as often the targets of their pens as were sunsets. They used imagery as a function more of emotion than of ideas. Because of this, the poetry of Machado pleased them more than did that from Moguer. They had no use for dehumanized poetry. They used simple, direct, colloquial language that was clear, efficient, and at times even cutting. Their poetry was written more to be sung than read. It was not an end in itself but, rather, a means to an end.

This poetic sword would be pitted aggressively against the established sociopolitical structures. Many of these poets adopted a militant leftist stance, and they all felt themselves to be spokespeople for the collective conscience of the human community.

One of those in the Basque Country most heavily influenced by this poetry was Aresti. He arrived at social poetry at the same time as did his friend Otero, although they took different paths to get there. Aresti was a typical post–Civil War Basque from Bilbo. He was born in the dirty industrial city and capital of Bizkaia. During the nineteenth century it was characterized by the large number of Spanish immigrants and the little Basque that was heard in the streets. Aresti was born into a traditional Bilbo family whose roots were Basque but whose speech was not.

During the 1940s speaking Basque was officially discouraged and sometimes punished. Years later, Aresti complained about this situation:

> Herri horrek niri
> ez daut ezer eman . . .[2]
>
> This city has not given
> me anything . . .

At age twelve, Aresti began to study the Basque language, and he continued to do so throughout his life. When he later came in contact with the stevedores of the port of Bilbo, who were citizens of the valley of Arratia, Bizkaia, he improved his Basque while observing the social injustices created by capitalism: "Euskera Bilboko portuan ikasi dut"[3] (I learned Basque in the port of Bilbo).

Aresti and Otero were close friends. The young Aresti always demonstrated profound admiration for Otero's work, and his social poetry was heavily influenced by Otero, the author of *Pido la paz y la palabra* (I request peace and the word). In 1961 and 1962 Aresti translated several of Otero's poems into Basque and published them in the Basque review *Egan*.[4] In 1966, when Otero returned from Cuba, Aresti took him into his home, and Otero was even godfather to one of Aresti's daughters.

After Aresti's tragic death from cancer in 1975, Otero dedicated a heartfelt poem to him, the dedication of which follows:

> You defended the house down through the centuries for
> the centuries to come, our little country of grass and blood,
> brother and teacher . . . Gabriel, revolution of Basque poetry;
> be silent, be silent, next to his grave; someone is lurking,
> carrying the cross that you left; the house of our centuries will
> continue to live in your words, you will remain in our house.[5]

In this poem, we hear an echo of Aresti's famous poem "Nire aitaren etxea defendituko dut" (I will defend my father's house), in which he demonstrates his love for his Basque roots, for the Basque Country, and for the farms that traditionally gave Basques their names and provided the essence of their being.[6] In this vigorous and expressive poem, Aresti rises up as a gladiator to defend his ancestors' heritage. Like his friend Otero in the poem "En el principio" (In the beginning), Aresti may have no hands or lips left, but he will continue to speak with his pen, using the written word as a last resort in his effort to defend his father's house:

> Nire aitaren etxea
> defendituko dut.
> Otsoen kontra,
> sikatearen kontra,
> lukurreariaren kontra,
> justiziaren kontra . . .
> Galduko ditut
> aziendak
> soloak
> pinudiak;
> galduko ditut
> korrituak,
> errentak,

interesak,
baina nire aitaren etxea defendituko dut.
Harmak kenduko dizkidate,
eta eskuarekin defendituko dut
nire aitaren etxea;
eskuak ebakiko dizkidate,
eta besoarekin defendituko dut
nire aitaren etxea;
besorik gabe,
bularrik gabe,
utziko naute,
eta arimarekin defendituko dut
nire aitaren etxea.
Ni hilen naiz
nire arima galduko da,
nire askazia galduko da,
baina nire aitaren etxeak
iraunen du zutik.[7]

I will defend my father's house against wolves, against
droughts, against usury and the courts. I will lose cattle, gar-
dens, and properties; I will lose pine seedlings, rents, and
interest, but I will defend my father's house. They will take
away my guns and with my hand I will defend my father's
house. They will cut off my hands, and with my arms I will
defend my father's house. They will leave me armless and
chestless, and with my soul I will defend my father's house.
I will die, my soul will be lost, my progeny will be lost, but
my father's house will still be standing.

Aresti's social poetry marked a noticeable change and a distinct break
with the past. In the Basque Country during the 1950s, writers were still
using themes and styles that dated from before the Civil War. Authors like
Orixe; Etxaniz; Juan Ignacio Goikoetxea, alias "Gaztelu"; Zaitegi; Monzón;
and Onaindia continued to contribute to the world of traditional poetry.
Aresti's break with tradition was inspired by two motives: his desire to create a new poetic language for a highly industrialized Basque society and his
friendship with the Marxist Otero. Little by little he moved away from his
family's Christian faith and aligned himself closer to the Communist Left:

Nire bihotza
ezkerrean dago
eta bertako odola
gorria
da.[8]

My heart is on the left and its blood is red.

This blood, reminiscent of that which appeared twelve times in Otero's "Crecida" (Grown) is the blood of humankind suffering from social evil. And in Aresti's opinion, that social evil came from the Right and was a result of the unjust socioeconomic conditions created by capitalism:

> Dirurik eztagoen egunean
> ezta
> gizonik
> erosiko.[9]

> Humankind will no longer be exploited on the day when there is no money.

The influence of biblical texts is noticeable in Aresti's work, an influence that is also obvious in his poetry. A list of the biblical phrases used in his work would be quite extensive, because whenever it came time to formulate something he felt was important, he used introductory expressions taken from the Gospel or from other parts of the Bible, such as "Benebenetan diozuet" (Verily I say unto you), "hau diot" (I say this), and "ni naiz naizena" (I am the one).

His new Marxist faith did not completely erase the traditional Christian faith he had inherited from his parents. Having converted his pen into a sword, Aresti assumed an aggressive posture and lashed out as both prophet and preacher. In this way, his poetry became more expressive. He considered himself to be the voice of a suffering people. In spite of confessing to having "neither hope, nor faith, nor charity," he adopted a biblical tone. The number of biblical quotations spread throughout his books is surprising. He felt like a prophet damned to suffer persecution in the modern world. Aresti was heavily criticized during his lifetime for his nonconformist personality. He became aware of the fact that a poet, like any pioneer, could be persecuted, if not with weapons then with lies and slander, because the audience to whom he preached neither listened to nor understood him. Occasionally he would personify himself as Christ:

> Ni naiz
> gizona,
> gizonaren semea,
> gurutze batean behin il
> zena,
> golgota haretan
> akabatu zena,
> ni naiz Kristo
> urdina,
> eta
> ez besterik.[10]

I am the man, the son of the man, he who died on a cross, the
one whose life ended on Golgotha. I am the blue Christ and
nothing more.

Also evident in various passages are scatological allusions to the Messiah
and references to the end of the world, as seen in the following text in which
he affirms that during the Final Judgment the leftists will be at the right
hand of the eternal judge:

Orduan
azkenak
izanen dira
lehenak,
eta haren eskuman
jarriko dira
ezkerrekoak.[11]

Then the last shall be the first, and those on the left shall be
placed at his right side.

As we have seen, Otero's influence on Aresti's poetry was enormous.
Aresti knew how to take advantage of biblical sources, but he also impressed on his creative work a very personal and characteristic stamp. One
of the differences between him and his friend Otero was that Aresti considered it a poetic obligation to write in the Basque language.[12] Furthermore, some of the social changes that he proposed were linguistic. The
Basque language was denied official status, and it suffered considerably in
its struggle as a minority language against Spanish. Aresti came to its defense and protested this situation by repeatedly using the same sentence:
"Ez nago konforme" (I don't agree). He felt that the two things he held most
dear, humankind and truth—or, in this case, the Basque people and their
language—were suffering unjustly:

Entzun nahi didanari . . . esan behar diot eznagoela konforme . . . nire protesta presentatu behar dudala, gizonaren
alde nagoela, behin Zorrotzako portuan prometitu nuen bezala . . . Egia gurekin baldin badago, eztadukagu zergatik
gezurrikan asma. Hala da, ni egiaren alde nago, gizona eta
egia batera doazalako. Gizona egiatik aldaratzen denean, nik
eztakit zer den. Eta inork entzun nahi ezpadit, berdin dit,
esanen diot hiriari, izarrari, zeruari.[13]

To whoever wants to listen to me . . . I should tell you that
I do not agree . . . that I must present my protest, that I am
on the side of humankind as I promised once on the dock in
Zorrotza . . . If the truth is with us, we have no reason to invent lies. And so it is, I am for the truth, because truth and
humankind are one. When a man distances himself from the

truth, I do not know what he is. And if no one wants to listen to me, it makes no difference, I will say what I have to say to the city, the stars, the heavens.

Aresti considered the truth to be so important that he included it in his definition of poetry. According to him, a poet is one who loves humankind's truth, one who explains it with his words and sings about it. This idea of truth, and the desire to proclaim it, became an obsession in Aresti's social poetry. He felt that the truth could not be spoken by the wealthy. In a world where money dominated everything and, in Aresti's opinion, bankers were held in high esteem, Aresti felt that his truth was worth as much as that of a banker, in that he believed that truth was inseparable from human worth.

Aresti worried about all humankind, not just Basques. He believed that humankind had no single name. In the expressive poem "Egia bat esateagatik" (For telling a truth), he proclaims his unswaying decision to speak the truth. In the same way that Otero was left without life or voice in "En el principio" (In the beginning), so Aresti left himself without children, wife, house, hand, language, or name in "Egia bat esateagatik." But even though he had none of those things, he would always speak the truth. The deprivation, exclusion, and negativity in this poem are quite powerful:

Egia bat esateagatik
alabak
hil behar bazaizkit
andrea
bortxatu behar badidate,
etxea
lurrarekin
berdindu behar bazait;
Egia bat esateagatik,
ebaki behar badidate
nik eskribitzen
dudan
eskua,
nik kantatzen
dudan
mihina;
Egia bat esateagatik,
nire izena
kenduko badute
euskal literaturaren
urrezko
orrietatik,
inoiz,
inola,

inun
eznaiz
isilduko.[14]

If for telling the truth they would kill my daughters, violate
my wife, tear down the house where I live; If for telling the
truth they would cut off the hand I write with, the tongue I
sing with; If for telling the truth they would erase my name
from the golden pages of Basque literature; at no time, in no
way, in no place will I be quiet.

Nor did Aresti accept the idea of country as many Basque nationalists
currently understand it. Although he respected the father of Basque nationalism, Arana y Goiri, he seems to have had an aversion to some Sabinians
who had degenerated into chauvinist racism. Aresti, the clerical worker,
never forgot the economic privations he suffered at the hands of Basque
capitalists. He saw little merit in Arana y Goiri's Basque nationalism, but
he limited himself to verbally lashing out against the racism he believed it
promoted. He did go so far as to call the nationalists crazy ("Euskotar aber-
tzaleen erotasuna"):

Kromosoma eriak
jene kiratsak
hazi ustela
odol kutsatua!
Madarikatua izan bedi
unibertsal-negatibotasun
hau,
eta hura sublimatu nahi
duten
ero
etoiak.[15]

Sick chromosomes, fetid genes, rotten seed, contaminated
blood! Be damned this universal negativity and the unfeeling
crazy people who want to exalt it.

Aresti's friend Mirande influenced Aresti's attacks against the Basque nationalism of Arana y Goiri, just as he influenced Aresti's style in *Maldan
behera* (The downward slope, 1959).

The influence of Mirande's elegant symbolist style, as well as that of the
classical Lapurdin dialect, is visible in Aresti's first book, *Maldan behera,* a
long poem of 1,916 lines divided into 21 parts and 222 stanzas. It is, without a doubt, his best work. It is a symbolist poem written in admirable
language, but it is difficult to understand, even for many native Basque
speakers. His stylistic secretiveness in this poem has caused it to be mis-
interpreted and overshadowed by his social poetry.

Nietzsche's *Also sprach Zarathustra* was very influential in Mirande's ideology, and that influence was also noticeable in Aresti's *Maldan behera,* although it was more thematic than stylistic. The German writer's footprints are found here and there throughout the book in characters such as the eagle, the serpent, and the monkey, in the stages of ancient civilizations (pastoral, agricultural, and urban), and in the idea of Nietzsche's superman, disguised by Aresti as a Messiah-like character. Whereas Christ asked for forgiveness, however, Zarathustra, Mirande, and Aresti asked for vengeance and revolution.

Maldan behera won a prize the year it was published. One of the work's many merits, in the opinion of Koldo Mitxelena, was that it served to a great extent as a role model for Unified Basque, the foundation of which would be established several years later: "En el aspecto lingüístico, en esta obra toma cuerpo, como en una profecía, la síntesis que diez años después propondría la Academia de la Lengua Vasca como modelo del vascuence escrito, el cual descansa en un equilibrio entre la lengua viva actual y la tradición clásica de nuestra literatura."[16]

Shortly afterward, always alert to change and in contact with the common people, Aresti wrote several poems in his native Bizkaian. The poems of *Bizkaitarrak* (The Bizkaians, 1959)[17] initiate a new stage in his poetic composition. This is poetry of the people, very similar to the *bertsoak* (oral verses) of the Basque troubadours. Its verb forms and certain words, such as *enbra* (woman), reflect a Basque that may contain words borrowed from Spanish but that is nevertheless popular in the area of Bermeo, Bizkaia.

Aresti showed himself to be knowledgeable about Basque literary classics. Authors like Detxepare, Leizarraga, and Axular were well known to him. The reforms Aresti advocated in the areas of literature and unification of the language were not the product of a snobbish mentality but the result of an arduous inner struggle.

Aresti also had a profound knowledge of oral literature and had great respect for the Basque bards, among whom Txirrita is an outstanding example.

Classic Greco-Roman culture did not influence Aresti's poetry; however, he was very interested in foreign literature. He valued the Spanish-language authors Alberti, García Lorca, Neruda, Vallejo, M. Hernández, Gabriel Celaya, Otero, and Tomás de Meabe as well as the French writers Rabelais, Baudelaire, Verlaine, Aragon, Eluard, and Sartre. He also had respect for the Italian Boccaccio, part of whose *Decameron* he translated, and for writers in the English language such as Eliot and Whitman. In addition, he held the poetry of the Turkish revolutionary Nazim Hikmet in great esteem.[18]

Aresti wanted his poetry to be so clear that anyone could understand it. For the sake of this clear, direct style, he sometimes sacrificed the purity of the language for clarity by using Spanish words that were often chosen by

Basque people over seldom-used Basque ones. This obsession with clarity and his desire to be understood by everyone made him choose free verse for much of his work. In this respect, Aresti's poetry is a long way from the rhythmic beauty of Otero's sonnets. At times, he falls prey to the same facile device that he accused the bertsolariak of using, specifically, the avoidance of difficult rhymes, but he always managed to write expressively. Still, his language is often Neruda-like in its crudity, and slang and sexual expressions are frequent:

> Nire poesia oso merkea da,
> herriaren ahotik hartu nuen
> debalde,
> eta debalde ematen diot
> herriaren belarriari.[19]

> My poetry is very cheap. I took it freely from the mouths of the people and freely I return it to their ears.

Poetry was a weapon, a hammer, and as such it had to be accessible to the people. They had to be able to glean the entire meaning of the poem, and its language had to be clear, direct, and simple so that everyone could understand it. Aresti avoided hypocrisy at all costs, and his social poetry reveals him to be a sincere, authentic, unswayable man:

> Gauza zelaiak,
> errezak
> edonork konprenitzekoak,
> esan behar ditut
> azalduko naiz
> Bizkaiko
> gizonik
> tontoena.[20]

> I have to say simple, easy-to-understand things, so that anyone can comprehend them; I will look like the biggest fool in Bizkaia.

Many of Aresti's poems were written to be sung rather than read, and as such they appear closely related to oral poetry. These simple lines, excerpted from one of his social poems, are an example:

> Apur dezagun katea
> kanta dezagun batea
> hau da fandango
> biba Berango.[21]

> Let's break the chain, let's sing together, this is a fandango, viva Berango.

In the opinion of Koldo Mitxelena ("Miscelánea filológica vasca"), "Aresti's meter, like his lexicon, his grammar, his poetry, and his work in general has a complexity and implies a knowledge that we are far from determining, that we have not yet totally fathomed. Aresti was an intuitive person who possessed acute intelligence."[22]

I believe that Aresti tried to fulfill a moral obligation required of him by the circumstances in which he lived, for he was a child of his time. He committed himself to the Basque language when such a commitment was dangerous. His poetry marked a boundary between hackneyed tradition and the modernization of Basque literature in the twentieth century. He was born in the industrial city of Bilbo, and he died there. His place of birth and the sociopolitical environment in which he lived shaped his poetry to a significant extent. His social poetry was full of nonpoetic elements. He liked to change, to be original, and his was a changing world. As a result, he tried to create a poetic language appropriate to the modern environment. Gabriel Aresti must be considered one of the most creative minds of modern poetry. He never rejected his duty to the public. He lived for his poetry, and it sustained him throughout his life.

CHAPTER TWELVE

Juan Mari Lekuona

A Bridge Between Cultured Poetry and Popular Literature

Juan Mari Lekuona's work is vast and diverse. Among his most important accomplishments are six books, thirty-six articles, and sixteen prologues, almost all of them dealing with Basque literary themes.[1] His translations of biblical texts and episcopal pastorales into Basque have made a noteworthy contribution to Basque religious culture.

He taught in the Seminaries of Saturraran (1960-1963) and Donostia (1963-1978) as well as at the University of Deusto (1978-1996). He has presented innumerable lectures, has served as judge and expert in the bertsolaritza competitions and as a member of Euskaltzaindia since 1962, and performed the many tasks associated with the office of vice president of Euskaltzaindia from 1989 to 1996.

THE INFLUENCE OF FAMILY

On a Basque television program entitled "Ispiluan" (In the mirror, aired in 1994), Lekuona confessed that he owed his fondness for verse to his mother and his love of song to his father. If we delve more deeply into possible family influences, we find the figure of his uncle—Manuel Lekuona, one of the great pioneers of oral Basque literature, especially in the area of definition of the characteristics of oral expression.

Five families appear closely involved with the history of Basque literature. In Bizkaia there is the Moguel family: Juan Antonio (1745-1854); his nephew, Juan José (1781-1849); and his niece, Vicenta (1782-1854). Also in Bizkaia are the bertsolariak of the Enbeitia family, famous for at least three generations: Urretxindor (1878-1942); Balendin (1906-1986); and Jon (b. 1950). In Gipuzkoa we find the family of bertsolari José Elizegui, alias "Pello Errota" (1840-1919), from Asteasu; his siblings Juan Cruz (1851-?) and Sabina (1842-1932); as well as his daughter Mikela (1869-1967); and a niece. Also in Gipuzkoa, we find the Otaño family of Zizurkil, who produced Pedro Mari, alias "Katarro" (1857-1910); his grandfather "Errekalde Zaharra"; his uncle, Jose Bernardo (1842-1912); and a niece. Finally we have a family containing three generations of writers: Miguel Antonio Iñarra (1864-1898), Manuel Lekuona (1894-1987), and Juan Mari Lekuona.[2]

In Juan Mari Lekuona's "Manuel Lekuonaren literatur kreazioa" (Manuel Lekuona's literary production) dedicated to the literary creation of his uncle Manuel, there is a note of great interest to those who wish to understand something about these three generations. Juan Mari gives us details about Iñarra (Manuel's uncle), who won first prize in the 1891 Euskal-Festak in Donostia for his poetry in competition against, among others, Txomin Aguirre. When the young priest Iñarra died, he left his library to his nephew. That library was a key element in Manuel Lekuona's fondness for literature, and it would in turn leave its mark on the literary leanings of Manuel's nephew.

Juan Mari also describes Manuel's literary production. If we examine the twelve volumes of Manuel's complete works (*Lekuona'tar Manuel. Idaz-lan Guztiak*), we observe a shift in methodology between the academic works (1918-1936) prior to the Spanish Civil War and the research works carried out after the war. During the first stage, Manuel wrote several notable works in Basque, especially in the areas of children's literature, narrative poetry, and the essay. We run the risk of always identifying "Lekuona the Elder" with oral literature and, as a result, remaining ignorant of his written contributions. Fortunately, Juan Mari Lekuona sums them up for us clearly in his article.

Manuel Lekuona appears in the handbooks of Basque literature as a writer who cultivated poetry, theater, and prose. His nephew begins by affirming that his uncle was an atypical poet if we compare his literary style and technique to those used during both the prewar and the postwar era by such writers as Lizardi, Orixe, Salbatore Mitxelena, and Gaztelu. Lekuona describes only his uncle's *Iesu Aurraren Bizitza* (The life of the Child Jesus), *Txuri eta gorri eta Kikirriki* (White and red cockledoodledoo), *Gerrateko nere amabi kantak* (My twelve songs of wartime), *Erti-izti, Eun dukat* (One hundred ducats), and *Zigor* (Punishment)—all published in *Lekuona'tar Manuel. Idaz-lan Guztiak*.

THE CHRONOLOGICAL STAGES OF
JUAN MARI LEKUONA'S WORK

Phase One

"Libro blanco del euskara" *(The white book of Euskara)*

Juan Mari Lekuona spent more than forty years writing Basque poetry and has written much about oral literature, especially about bertsolaritza. In 1977 the Academy of the Basque Language asked him to write an article on Basque literature, a request that forced him to give serious thought and form to many ideas that he had been fond of for years. The Academy suddenly found itself preoccupied with the situation of the Basque language and urgently wanting to mark certain achievements while determining its goals. In the opinion of the Academy, it was a matter of "endowing the new democratic institutions that will be born at this time when, finally, the normalization of Euskara among its people will be viable, with a minimum valid level of knowledge."[3]

Juan Mari Lekuona's article "Ahozko euskal literatura" is limited, as the title indicates, to oral Basque literature. The author offers a general summary that reflects the problems inherent in the theme. He focuses especially on poetry (partisan songs, improvised verses and those that circulate on published flyers, and the *kopla zaharrak,* or petitionary verses and serenades); theater (pastorales, mascaradas, tragicomedies) and different types of *xaribaris;* the narrative (stories, novels, etc.); and, finally, the world of proverbs and idioms.

Lekuona's article proposes the classification of popular Basque literature into various genres, offers a vision of unity, and signals chapter by chapter what each genre entails. Following the tradition of Vinson, Azkue, and Manuel Lekuona, Juan Mari Lekuona condenses his knowledge of oral Basque literature into a coherent synthesis.

Cultura vasca *(Basque culture)*

Throughout the 1970s Juan Mari Lekuona was widely known for his poetic work, his participation in bertsolari competitions, and his courses at the Seminary of Donostia. During the 1975-1976 and 1976-1977 academic years, the Escuela Universitaria Técnica de Guipúzcoa (Technical University School of Guipúzcoa, E.U.T.G.) of the University of Deusto invited him to lecture at conferences held on their Donosti campus. Those lectures were published in 1978 in two volumes entitled *Cultura vasca.* The book includes Lekuona's "Literatura oral vasca" (Basque oral literature). This work, unlike *Libro blanco de euskara,* was not intended to study the problem of the Basque language, but, rather, Basque literature as a component of the autochthonous culture.

Lekuona starts from the lack of manuals and didactic material in the field of oral literature. He mentions that the two best-known histories of Basque literature (by Villasante and Sarasola) do not deal directly with oral literature. To fill this void, Lekuona dedicates a chapter to bertsolaritza. If this theme was treated in only thirty-three lines in "Ahozko euskal literatura," in this one he uses ten pages to describe bertsolaritza, point out its origins, and summarize its history. Lekuona demonstrates his knowledge when classifying and organizing data and preparing outlines and contents useful for university teaching. He classifies the abundant data on the life and art of the most important bertsolariak, submits those data to rigorous examination, and analyzes them within objective parameters of artistic beauty.

Lekuona also confirms here that his ability as a researcher was growing. He set high objectives for himself and tried to enhance communication between the teacher and the student at the level of oral expression. He is not a theoretical researcher lost in the ancient documents and files but prefers a path that requires great effort and long hours of work.

Ahozko euskal literatura *(Basque oral literature)*

As Juan Mari Lekuona was gradually becoming known as a professor of oral literature, he was also becoming more committed to research on this topic. UZEI (Unibertsitate Zerbitzuetarako Euskal Ikastetxea), a group dedicated to the publication of specialized dictionaries in Basque, asked him to write an article about oral literature for one of their dictionaries, but, unfortunately, the dictionary was never published. Instead, "Ahozko literaturen osagaiak" (Components of oral literature) became the first chapter in *Ahozko euskal literatura,* published in 1982.

This chapter deals with much that was previously published in two earlier articles, but it contributes a number of new elements:

1. General aspects of oral literature: notions about oral literature, popular literature, components of oral literature;

2. Sociocultural aspects: the audience as traditional depository, the task of the artist, improvisation, exceptional memory;

3. Literary aspects: mobility of images and ideas, rhythmic techniques, nonclassical techniques, modifications of text; and

4. Historicocultural perspective: prehistoric reminiscences, medieval texts.

Ahozko euskal literatura is dedicated to Manuel Lekuona. Its fifteen chapters cover several themes related to oral literature: decorative poetry, the *kopla zaharrak,* the Basque romancero, bertsolaritza (history; models of verses;

Indalecio Bizkarrondo, alias "Bilintx"; Iparraguirre; Txirrita; and Basarri), popular theater, the narrative, and old sayings and figures of speech. With its publication Lekuona ended the first stage of his literary production and moved on to the second.

Phase Two

"Ahozko literaturaren historiaz" (Concerning Basque oral literature)

In *Libro blanco del euskara* and *Cultura vasca* (volume 2) Juan Mari Lekuona proffers certain points that later appear in "Ahozko literaturaren historiaz" (pp. 127–222). In those earlier works, however, he does not offer an exhaustive historical and ordered summary of popular literature. Studies by other authors also do not present an overall view. Thus, I think that Lekuona's greatest contribution is his panoramic overview of popular literature, which allows the reader to comprehend the different expressions of popular Basque literature with relative ease. The author's different points of view on poetry, the theater, the narrative, and the study of proverbs through the centuries mark the general currents in popular Basque literature.

"Ahozko literaturaren historiaz" begins with the first Basque literary fragments from the anonymous songs of the fourteenth and fifteenth centuries and is accompanied by a brief analysis. Next comes a section dedicated to the renaissance in poetry, theater, and proverbs in the sixteenth century. Lekuona discusses certain notable changes attributable to the disappearance of the fighting medieval clans, the establishment of relative peace accompanied by a certain economic well-being, and especially the appearance of the printing press. While popular theater was disappearing in the great cities of France and Italy, in the northern Basque Country the pastorales survived and flourished, especially in the province of Zuberoa. In the field of poetry we see the appearance and development of apocryphal songs such as the "Leloren Kantua" (Song of Lelo). Finally, the most notable popular proverbs are from Esteban Garibay who gathered and created a list of Basque refrains of enormous linguistic and literary value. These three genres defended Euskara and moralized with no observable literary consciousness.

In the seventeenth century, the influence of the Counter Reformation on Basque literature was prominent, and just as evident were the efforts of Oihenart as historian, poet, and collector of proverbs. In general, the continental zone of the Basque Country during the seventeenth century was a huge depository of information on popular Basque literature, while the peninsular zone saw the gradual replacement of love ballads by religious and moral themes. Thus, for example, paroemiology, or the study of proverbs, was vigorously maintained, as Julio de Urquijo's (Julio Urkijo) studies demonstrate.

The eighteenth century is of great importance for Basque literature because of two genres that appeared concurrently with lyric songs: the carnavalesque plays of Iparralde and the religious theater of Hegoalde. The neoclassicism that reigned during this century conditioned poetic technique, as metrical requirements were stricter, and the role of rhetoric became more and more important. Poets tended toward more careful and elaborate construction of verses and leaned markedly toward major meters as well as toward rhyme patterns that required greater technical skill.

The old drama forms, like other popular expressions such as the mascaradas, pastorales, xaribaris, serenatas, and so on, acquired considerable importance, especially in the provinces of Zuberoa and Nafarroa Beherea. Among the tragicomedies, three stand out for characters that represent abstract ideas: "Bacchus," "Pansart," and "Ihauteen epaiketa eta kondenazioa" (Trial and condemnation of carnivals).

In the Century of Light, the creation of Real Sociedad Vascongada de los Amigos del País (the Royal Basque Society of Friends of the Country) was important for its influence on popular theater, both that of the Christmas season as well as that of Holy Week.

The nineteenth century is significant for two genres: bertsolaritza and popular theater as represented by the pastorales. While there was a noticeable decline in other literary genres, these two expressions acquired major importance. Thanks to the *bertso-paperak*,[4] the technique of bertsolaritza was improving, enriching Euskara and invigorating the bertsolari tradition. The names of some of the bertsolariak of the nineteenth century, such as Xenpelar, Bilintx, Iparragirre, and Etxahun, who are accepted as some of the best Basque poets of the nineteenth century, appear on the list. The bertsolari competitions as well as the Basque festivals (where there was always a bertsolari competition) became very popular in the Basque Country during this century. Although the bertsolari competitions disappeared after the Second Carlist War, they served as a point of reference for similar competitions, such as the *txapelketak,* which became so successful in the twentieth century.

It is evident that "all the rural theater (of France and Italy) disappeared at almost the same time, around the middle of the nineteenth century. The only one that has lasted until today is the Basque theater."[5] As time passed, the religious themes of the pastorales were disappearing, giving way to biographical themes in plays such as *Bereterretxe, Etxahun, Iparragirre.*

The twentieth century is characterized by the boom in bertsolaritza and the pastorales, because both knew how to adapt themselves to the sociological and cultural changes of the Basque Country. Unlike the bertso-paperak, which lost the importance they had in the nineteenth century, the *bapateko bertsoak* (improvised verses) are gaining a prominent place in the history of the phenomenon. Thanks to men like Juan José Makazaga,

Manuel Lekuona, and Aitzol and to bertsolariak like Basarri and Manuel Olaizola, alias "Uztapide," bertsolaritza experienced a tremendous boom before the Spanish Civil War. Postwar interest in this literary phenomenon grew in large part to the *txapelketak*. This artistic expression thus became an indispensable part of festivals in many Basque villages, primarily because of the importance given it in the media.

The same can be said for the popularity garnered by the pastorales. Changes were introduced to cater to modern tastes: performances were shortened, themes were updated, new techniques were used, and awareness of this literary phenomenon spread throughout the Basque Country.

"Literatura oral del País Vasco" (Oral literature of the Basque Country)

In the spring of 1985 UNESCO solicited an article from Lekuona about the existing relations between written and oral literature in the Basque Country. He prepared his contribution in Basque but was asked to shorten it and translate it into Spanish. His study, entitled "Literatura oral del País Vasco," was published in UNESCO's magazine *El Correo* (August 1985). In spite of its brevity, it is notable for the prestige of the organization that requested it and the number of people who read it (the magazine is distributed in thirty-two languages). In addition, the fact that Lekuona was one of the very few Basque writers asked to contribute is proof of the esteem in which he is held.

In "Literatura oral del País Vasco" Lekuona echoes an important postulate: Basque literature comprises two traditions, the oral and the written, intimately linked through the centuries. Written literature arrived relatively late, yet it is testimony to the survival of Euskara. Oral literature, for its part, is as rich as that of any country and, furthermore, serves as a faithful expression of the most deeply rooted Basque cultural values.

Euskaldunak. Euskal etnia

"Usariozko euskal olerkigintza," translated into Spanish as "Poesía y oralidad" and published by ETOR, consists of ninety-five pages liberally illustrated with black-and-white and color photographs. The author and publisher worked carefully together to produce this splendid work, which surpasses the expectations of the most demanding reader.

In *Euskaldunak. Euskal etnia* Lekuona concentrates exclusively on one genre of Basque oral literature: oral poetry. His university affiliation allowed him to constantly renew his knowledge of the genre. He polished his imagery, clarified ideas presented in his first three articles, and contributed valuable facts to our knowledge of oral poetry, for example, the *Procedimientos lúdico-corales*—annotations made about each bertsolari, and the new classification of oral literature. Concerning the *Procedimientos lúdico-corales,* Lekuona says the following:

> The contribution of decorative poetry is considerable within Basque oral literature: It becomes a poetic genre that cannot be omitted and about which many competent studies have been done. And it seems to us that these ditties and songs have incalculable value for understanding ancient poetry and for experimenting with vanguardist forms in modern poetry. They bring us a genre that is based on the sonorous effect of words, on song and dance, and bring to mind stylized images, colors, and content that make us think of modern art. And, what is more, it [decorative poetry] connects us with our most ancient verbal roots, perhaps with roots that come to us from prehistory.[6]

"La lírica popular vasca en el siglo XVIII"

At the Second International Basque Congress, Lekuona talked about popular Basque poetry in the eighteenth century.[7] He discussed the creation of Basque poetry in accordance with the precepts of oral style and the composition of nonextemporaneous verses dealing with lyric themes that catered to eighteenth-century tastes and techniques. In Lekuona's opinion, we find ourselves faced with a literary phenomenon with peculiar characteristics, one that requires special treatment as a result. He begins with a theoretical presentation, expounding on the precepts of those popular poems or songs (since oral poetry is sung to traditional tunes). "Popular lyricism," a poetic genre, reached its peak in the eighteenth century. It encompassed a collection of poems that require study because they are special and different. Unfortunately, there are not many examples of this poetry left in the Basque Country.

The stylistic differences between lyric songs and the ballads and bertsolaritza are obvious. The same can be said for the *koplas* or *trikiti* (a shorter *kopla* accompanied by the accordion and the tambourine) and verses of a comical nature. The epic and dramatic genres are excluded from this lyric poetry of the eighteenth century, thus omitting historical citations and third-person narrations. Prominent in this lyric poetry are themes of love, feelings expressed in the first person, singing, and dialogues that play a special role. Love is practically the only theme in this type of poetry, where young couples defend their attitudes using the first person and a dialectic in which the subjective, mental state of the characters is prevalent.

Long, well-developed verses are used for this purpose. If we compare them with the verses of ballads, we see that the lyric poetry verses are more self-contained, possess a richer rhythm, and produce broader acoustic effects.

"Erdi-ahozkatasunaren literatur estiloaz" (Literary style in Basque semiorality)

On July 30, 1988, Lekuona became a full member of Euskaltzaindia. This solemn investiture took place in the town hall of his native village of Oiartzun and coincided with an exposition in honor of his uncle, Manuel Lekuona. The importance of the occasion called for the writing of a special article.

Lekuona focused his talk (later published as an article) on the concept of semiorality in Basque literary style. The concept of orality, or orally transmitted literature, attracted many specialists beginning in the 1920s. Following the division established by Jousse in *Le style oral* (1925; see chapter 13 here), in "Erdi-ahozkatasunaren literatur estiloaz" Lekuona distinguishes three literary styles: the mimetic or gestural style, the oral, and the written. He claims that until 1925 no one could describe the differences between oral and written style, because we live in a civilization in which the influence of the written word is overwhelming.

In the first part of the article that came from the lecture (pp. 20-25) Lekuona points out examples of semiorality in personal texts, family texts, guild texts, and the surprising case of the bertsolari Udarregi, who invented his own writing system in order to record his compositions. Since he could neither read nor write, he needed his friend José Txiki to transcribe his compositions. Udarregi, a native of Usurbil, had kept track of the number of verses by marking lines on the walls of his farmhouse attic. Lekuona also presents examples of other published texts that belong to this semioral genre: flyers containing verses or bertso-paperak, magazines, and small books.

In the second part (pp. 25-32), he deals with the phenomenology of semiorality while keeping in mind the textual incarnations, the author's personality, laws of consumerism, and the transmission of the texts.

In the third part (pp. 32-39), Lekuona analyzes the stylistics of semiorality by gathering examples of the different styles: ballads, religious writing, theater, and popular magazines. He also points out changes in literary precepts, the structure of the pieces, the influence of writing, the use of poetic sources, and the dimension of narrative.

"Kontapoesiaren modulu metrikoak Hegoaldeko usarioan" (The metrical structure of ballads in the tradition of Hegoalde)

Lekuona believes that much progress has been made in the field of Basque popular narrative poetry. It is one of the best-studied fields of popular Basque literature; nevertheless, there remains much to look at. Thus, in "Kontapoesiaren modulu metrikoak Hegoaldeko usarioan," Lekuona studies verse structure in Basque ballads. He uses volume 2 of *Euskal baladak,* because he considers it to be one of the best works on the subject.

He was well aware of the difficulties presented by an in-depth study of the meter of ballads, having observed the lack of agreement among critics because of the existence of two distinct traditions: that of Iparralde and that of Hegoalde. Lekuona chose to follow the guidelines he established in *Ahozko euskal literatura* (pp. 139–69) and classify verses according to the bertsolaritza tradition of Hegoalde.

Lekuona claims that the verse is not the only Basque metrical unit (although it is the one used most often), because the percentage of verses whose psychodynamic effects (repetitions, free forms, etc.) are not found within traditional versification is rather high. In general, units are shorter than those traditionally used by bertsolariak, although, because of the important presence of the savage ballads, the *zortziko txikia* is prevalent.[8]

Unlike Spanish meter, the metrical pattern in Basque poetry is different in every poem, and each one has a distinct melody. Thus, the "golden rule" in Basque music calls for using one melody in each poem, as can be seen and appreciated in the Basque ballads.

"Basarriren bertsolari proiektua" (Basarri's bertsolari project)

Lekuona has always demonstrated appreciation of all bertsolariak, because each of them has enriched the treasure-house of Basque literature. His appreciation of Basarri is particularly strong because the latter's contribution represents a notable change in the history of bertsolaritza after the 1935 championship. Lekuona also studied Bilintx, Txirrita, Uztapide, Xalbador, Manuel Lasarte, and even Basarri himself, but he wrote this article on the occasion of a tribute to Basarri held in Zarautz.

It is commonly accepted that before the Spanish Civil War bertsolaritza was not highly esteemed, and the Basque bard was regarded as a buffoon and a clown who was limited to entertaining in cider shops and taverns and making the audience laugh. Basarri, however, managed to move bertsolari performances into theaters, movie theaters, and frontons. He also proposed a profound set of changes that affected subject matter, duration, versification, rhythms, rhymes, music, language, and the cultural level of the Basque bard.

Among the numerous qualities that came together in this great bertsolari champion, Lekuona points out Basarri's exceptional ability to perform as part of a team in the competitions without severing his partner's dialectic thread. In this way, teamed with his dear friend and another excellent bertsolari, Uztapide, he was able to maintain and renew the flame of traditional bertsolaritza for more than twenty years while traversing much of the Basque Country during the difficult Franco years.

The Prologues

Lekuona is not an inaccessible artist who loses himself in the difficult labyrinths of cultured poetry. Rather, he knows how to descend from those heights to appreciate the beauty in even the simplest works discussing Basque literature. Given his knowledge, many of his friends ask him to write prologues to their books.

I shall use two of those prologues as examples of secondary work that aids in the understanding of Basque oral literature.[9] In 1974 Lekuona wrote the prologue to *Lengo egunak gogoan,* the only prose work Uztapide ever wrote.

Lekuona depicts Uztapide as the guardian of an inexhaustible deposit of oral Basque literature, someone who expounds on a rural society on the road to extinction. Following in the tradition of Sebastian Salaberri, José Ramón Zubillaga, Martín Ugarte, Antonio Zavala, and others, Uztapide surprises us with an agile, popular, lively, and rich prose about his life and the environment in which he lived in the Basque Country.

Lekuona's prologue for this book was his first. As of this writing, his latest ("Hitzaurrea") is dedicated to the phenomenon of contemporary bertsolaritza. Lekuona begins his prologue by situating the issue of the journal in which it is published on a long list of important works that have been published in the last decade in the field of popular Basque literature. At the end of his prologue, Lekuona emphasizes the importance of three landmarks in the history of the phenomenon: Xenpelar in the nineteenth century; the changes introduced by Basarri after the championship of 1935; and the grammatical changes contributed by Xabier Amuriza since the 1980 championship.

In this third part Lekuona claims that the seven contributors to the issue belong to a new generation and are witnesses to the changes that have occurred in today's bertsolaritza.

LEKUONA'S CULTURED POETRY

Lekuona's poetic beginnings date from his sixteenth year. His first creations were published in the magazine *Egan* in 1950; from 1954 to 1956 he published in the Guatemalan periodical *Euzko-gogoa.* His poem "Izadi abestia" (Nature song) won first prize for obligatorily themed works in the literary competitions organized by "Educación y descanso" (Rest and education, a political society that existed in Franco's time to regulate this type of competition) in Donostia in 1950, and he won the same prize with his poem "Ama" (Mother) in 1951.

In 1966 he published a small book of poetry entitled *Mindura gaur* (Suffering today). Its fifteen poems would later form the second of three parts of his second book, *Muga beroak* (Warm borders), published in 1973.

The first part of *Muga beroak* is called "Herenegun" (Day before yester-day) and consists of seven poems. Throughout these poems we can see the influence of Basque poets of the pre-Spanish Civil War era, especially Lauaxeta and his *Arrats-berran* (As evening falls, in *Olerki guztiak*, 1935), Lizardi, and Orixe. In the first three poems, "Izadi abestia" (Nature song), "Ama," and "Begi Beltxaran" (Dark eyes), there are also suggestions of Romanticism. In "Goiz Argi" (Dawn) and "Ubel" (Purple), colors, de-scribed in an impressionistic manner, play a prominent role. The poet paints nature for us without fixating on objective reality; rather, he focuses on his personal, subjective impression and uses stylized language.

The second part of the book, "Atzo. 1966. Mindura gaur" (Yesterday. 1966. Suffering today; originally published as *Mindura gaur* in 1966), repre-sents a great change in Lekuona's poetry. After abandoning intimate, Ro-mantic poetry, he offers here a poetry more in tune with the taste of the 1960s. This part of the book comprises four triptychs, three of which con-tain three poems; the third contains four poems. The theme of each of the poems is related to existentialism, although the point of departure for each is very different.

The third part represents a qualitative leap in theme and style. He moves into earthly symbolism and interprets humankind by means of fundamen-tal archetypes but without remarking on their differences. Without focus-ing on a specific ideology, as he does in his social poetry, Lekuona presents us with a poetry of the cosmos: earth, fire, water, and air, described with lovely images that bring to mind the religious background of Unamuno's "El Cristo de Velázquez" (Velázquez's Christ) and the doctrine of the French paleontologist Pierre Teilhard de Chardin.

Ilargiaren eskolan (In the school of the moon)

Lekuona has spent more than forty-five years pur-suing the precepts of poetic aesthetics. One result of that research is his third book, *Ilargiaren eskolan*. Its first part, "Oihu ilunak espiralean" (Dark cries in the spiral), presents a type of difficult-to-understand cultured poetry full of analogies and surrealist metaphors. In the second part, "Libu-ruen karroxak" (*Xarivari* of books), however, Lekuona offers poetry created according to the guidelines of popular poetry. It is satirical, critical, and popular theater, and the language is easy to understand.

After a six-year break (1973-1979), Lekuona moved from a poetry of ideological and earthly roots to a more personal and reticent poetry. He took as his inspiration Ingmar Bergman's *Cries and Whispers*. The poem found in the first part of "Oihu ilunak espiralean" is based on the four female pro-tagonists of that film and emphasizes the personal appearance and style of dress of each one of them as representative of ways of being and communi-cating.

The five parts of the theme—*bizileku* (dwelling), *esku* (hand), *ile-adats* (hairstyle), *haragizko estatua* (state of the flesh), and *begitarte* (face)—are interwoven by means of a darkly surrealist metaphor that makes for slow reading. Each part consists of a realist poem, a symbolist poem, and a surrealist poem. Lekuona's aesthetic analysis starts from objective descriptions captured by the senses in order to develop them more fully and finally to synthesize it all by stylizing as a spiral ("Oihu ilunak espiralean"). Thus, for example, the "hand" ceases to be a physical member and becomes a suggestively symbolic sculpture.

An exception to this classification scheme is the popular, or folk, form used in the part dedicated to the hand. Here, some lines, because of their rhythm and popular semantics, remind us of children's songs and of lyric decorative poetry.

The second part of the book, "Liburuen karroxa," is completely different from the first. The word *karroxa* (popular theater from Zuberoa, where satire is abundant) warns us from the start that we are in a place where humor, satire, and irony play very important roles, far from the abstraction and profound thoughts reflected in the first part. Five critical and humorous books represent different literary and cultural groups in existence during the last Franco years: "Liburu horia" (Yellow book) or *Don Kixote Mantxako* is an ironic interpretation of Berrondo's translation of Cervantes's book; "Liburu gorria" (Red book) or the *Obra Guztiak* of Aresti; "Liburu urdina" (Blue book) or *Euskal idazleak, gaur* by Torrealday; "Liburu berdea" (Green book) or *Odolaren Mintzoa* by Xalbador; and "Liburu zuria" (White book) or *Euskararen liburu zuria*, a work prepared by various authors one of whom was Lekuona himself.

Mimodramak eta ikonoak (Gestures and icons)

Lekuona is an innovative seeker of poetic language. After eleven years of silence, from 1979 to 1990, during which he was forging a type of poetry very different from his previous work, he published a surprising collection of poems outstanding for their wealth of vocabulary and abundance of metaphors. He transforms images into concepts, but without losing the gamut of metaphors.

Mimodramak eta ikonoak is dedicated to two persons who have influenced Lekuona's poetic career: anthropologist Barandiarán and sculptor Oteiza. Lekuona also dedicates to Barandiarán the last poem in the book, which, in addition to being a warm tribute, is also the best example of structure in the whole collection. The six-sided angelic vision of Saint Bonaventure is presented to us.

The book is divided into two parts: "Gruteskoak" (Grotesqueries) and "Planeten adar biran" (In the orbit of the planets). Each part further subdivides into three sections, which in turn comprise six poems each. The first part is related to the world of caveman and atavistic memories inherited from that life. Using the genesis of terror as a starting point, we hear the roar of earthquakes, explosions, and howls, which conclude in the reality of death.

The backdrop of terror disappears in the second part, and the reader begins a journey through the astral bodies and seasons of the year. The reader feels the light-filled planetary heartbeat, which allows us a glimpse of the anthropological and cultural history of the Basque Country.

The book's thirty-six poems are presented in a symmetrical structure. In contrast, the poetic discourse of each poem is irregular, written according to the aesthetic guidelines of free verse. Lekuona uses a wide range of poetic registers, such as alliteration, repetition, parallelism, enjambment, and metaphors. We could in fact say that the whole book is a continuous metaphor.

The lexicon is elaborate, which may cause comprehension problems for many readers. Lekuona's rich Basque, acquired with great effort, is the Unified dialect he so strongly defends.

Lekuona's cultured poetic work is very personal, albeit researched as if he were an architect preparing plans for a great building. He carves out his words, looks for the most appropriate and unexpected similes, finds unexpected metaphors, submerges himself in the roots of the Basque identity, and offers a cultured poetry of great beauty that makes his reputation as one of the best Basque poets of the second half of the twentieth century.

Prologues

Lekuona wrote ten prologues for books about cultured written literature. Two of them were written for important poetry collections by Gandiaga, the second edition of *Elorri* (1989) and *Uda batez Madrilen* (One summer in Madrid, 1977).

The latter book is Gandiaga's third, a product of his stay in the Spanish capital. His first two books, *Elorri* and *Hiru gizon bakarka* (Three men alone, 1974), were written at the monastery in Arantzazu and without abandoning his beloved Basque Country. During his stay in Madrid, he separated himself from the intimate poetry of his first book and from the social poetry of *Hiru gizon bakarka* to create poetry inspired by the great city. Gandiaga was surprised by and marveled at the architecture and the routine life of the depersonalized masses of the Spanish metropolis.

The word, with its different sides and faces, is the protagonist in Gandiaga's poetry. This word takes the form of poetry loaded with social expressionism and describes the space/human relationship as the new vision of modern humankind.

Lekuona's prologue points out three qualities in Gandiaga's poetry in *Uda batez Madrilen:* the structure of the *trikiti* symbolized by the tambourine;

the influence of decorative poetry; and the symbolic significance of spatial poetry. Lekuona claims that these qualities contribute new forms of poetic expression as the poet strolls through surrealism and popular literature. He also points out the plasticity of Gandiaga's poetry and describes the movement the poet suggests from external to internal planes. Gandiaga's careful conceptualization of sensory perceptions based on concrete reality and the use of different prisms of a word according to its semantics are some of the aspects of Gandiaga's literary art that Lekuona treats in his prologue.

Lekuona's second prologue analyzes *Elorri,* which is considered the best of Gandiaga's five books of poetry. Lekuona begins by emphasizing Gandiaga's tremendous importance in the postwar period. Once again, the word is the centerpiece of Gandiaga's poetic creation; he uses it to dress the images born of vision that invite the reader to sing. Gandiaga reveals himself in *Elorri* as a very sensitive person at one with his homeland and submerged in an existentialism that uses tiny creations like the hawthorn plant to lead us to the Creator.

The influence of popular literature is evident in this book in the short traditional rhythms of the *koplak* and *trikitiak.* Nevertheless, it is not Gandiaga's intent to describe the epic or to narrate the history of the sanctuary of the Virgin of Arantzazu. Rather, he fixes his attention on simpler, subtler objects, such as the hawthorn, the leak in a cloister, a stone, water, and grass, as stylized realities that take on a new personality. The book's short poems tell of the emotions that the sanctuary of Arantzazu and the little hawthorn plant have awakened in the poet's heart.

Lekuona offers a clear look at the poetic creation and the product of Gandiaga's artistic research. Gandiaga, deeply rooted in the Basque Country, worked his poems like a goldsmith works metal. Among the most outstanding qualities of his first book, Lekuona's prologue mentions the European inspiration for his aesthetic research, his existentialism, experiments with new metrical structures, and the modernity of his images.

This chapter is not intended as an exhaustive study of Lekuona, but as a brief listing of his most representative articles to demonstrate the interaction between the two sides of his literary production. His poetic originality cannot be explained without examining his literary studies of popular poetry, nor can his literary works of a popular nature be understood without understanding the intuition lent them by his poetic creations. The long years he has dedicated to popular literature have provided him with a great wealth of vocabulary and images, abundant cultural references, and technical resources, just as the act of poetic creation has left him with a mastery of the structures and intuition that is rarely attained without the exercise of creativity.

CHAPTER THIRTEEN

Marcel Jousse and Manuel Lekuona

Two Pioneers of Oral Literature[1]

When we hear the word *literature,* we think exclusively of the written word because of the conditioning imposed upon us by a classical education. As a result, oral literature has remained subordinate to written for many centuries.

Although all languages are basically oral, in the research carried out during the last few centuries, the oral aspect of language has been forgotten while emphasis has been placed on written texts; oral material has been treated like a variation on the written. The very expression "oral literature," so much in vogue today in university and literary circles, instead of clarifying the concept, obscures it because the word *literature* presupposes writing.

Unfortunately, the scholarly community did not accept the hypothesis that an authentic art of the spoken word could exist in preliterary societies, such as the societies that predated the arrival of the Indo-Europeans. Fortunately, this viewpoint is now considered antiquated. Thanks to the research in oral traditions of specialists like Jousse, Milman Parry, Albert Lord, Manuel Lekuona, Jack Goody, Walter J. Ong, Juan Mari Lekuona, and others, the concept of literature is evolving to include forms of oral expression that were ignored in the past.

If we limit ourselves to the Basque Country, we observe that unlike many other nations that set their history down in writing only to see it die, the Basque nation (with its roots in prehistory) did not cement its past in writing. Instead, the Basques inherited Euskara, both the ancient language and the various oral and popular artistic expressions, such as bertsolaritza, the pastorales, ballads, the *xaribari* farces, mascaradas, ancient proverbs, *kopla zaharrak,* and *eresiak* (dirges in verse that female mourners improvised at funerals). Basques in the past shaped their concept of life, their beliefs, and their feelings through different forms of oral expression that for the most part made up for the centuries-long absence of a written culture to interpret their social and artistic environment.

These manifestations of oral literature are the expression of popular, or folk, culture, and they are very useful for acquainting oneself with the character of a nation. In the opinion of Rodney Gallop: "Although all poems and histories taken from the lips of the people do not necessarily contain intrinsic literary beauty, there exists a fascination and true scientific value in copying and studying them, for there are few things in which a nation reveals its personality as well as in its popular literature."[2]

Societies that live according to the rule of an exclusively oral culture possess their own characteristics: The environment appears to be interpreted solely by means of the spoken word; its literature endures only through the cognizant faculties of the sender-receiver pair; and the continuity of the culture depends on the people who transmit the cultural values orally, from one generation to another, through the verbal and collective memory. In this way, the artists themselves take over the function of books, and the collective memory plays the role of new editions. As a result, the true author is the public author, a collective and anonymous entity. Thus we can affirm that this oral literature is created *by* and *for* the people.

The anonymous artist is born among the people and interprets the feelings of the collective. The texts that are heard do not belong to a specific person but to the people as a whole. Those texts are created to change, and on occasion passages are altered. A simple poem created by an anonymous author grows like an embryo in the womb of the people. As a result, what might have been the exclusive and personal work of a single author later becomes a collective work by means of the contributions of innumerable popular creators, who thus give a historical face to the text.

If we move to the reality of the Basque people, we observe that the two major means of oral transmission were the kitchen of the *baserri* (Basque farmhouse) and the church. On long winter afternoons, the baserri would become the principal school of oral literature. After eating a frugal dinner and saying the rosary with *Amona* (Grandmother), family members would listen to the old stories and tales Amona told them while they shucked corn. At other times, Grandfather would sing the bertso-paperak that he had bought in town on market day or after Mass. No less important was the work of the spinners, seamstresses, and menders of fishnets in maintaining the oral tradition. The traditional repertory was thus constantly reviewed and renewed.

The local church was another important place for the transmission of oral literature, since the priests used verses for catechistic purposes. Until the nineteenth century, the majority of Basques were illiterate (but not ignorant). During the sixteenth and seventeenth centuries, no literary work was published in Hegoalde. A few catechisms formed the entire Basque-language production for the greater part of the Basque Country, and even these should be considered within the context of oral literature. Since the common people did not know how to read, the priest would read the text aloud, and the people accepted and preserved the oral religious message by means of memory. Those catechisms were thus written from the perspective of oral popular literature, and they would later enrich the treasury of literature through the collective memory.

There were two great pioneers in the concept of popular oral literature: Jousse (France, 1886-1962) and Manuel Lekuona (Euskal Herria, 1894-1987). In addition to discussing the important roles that each played in his respective country in the field of oral literature, I hope to demonstrate the influence the former had on the latter. To what extent did Jousse's 1925 book, *Le style oral rythmique et mnémotechnique chez les verbo-moteurs,* enrich the knowledge of the young Basque professor who had already published several studies on Basque oral literature?

MARCEL JOUSSE

Oral literature owes a great deal to Marcel Jousse. Ordained as a priest in 1910, he became a Jesuit in 1913. He was a French artillery captain in World War I and a professor for a quarter of a century (1931-1957) at the Sorbonne and other French universities. In *Le style oral,* the product of twenty years of intensive research, Jousse broached the problems of the origin of language and analyzed the spontaneity of human gesture. His most important lines of thought can be summed up thus: he questions the hegemony of a culture based essentially on the writing that society tries to impose on humankind as the only path for culture and civilization. In Jousse's opinion, the spoken word is clutched in the grip of writing, and the richest depths of the human being are thus obscured. The real, living, internal universe of humanity cannot be exclusively reflected in the written word.

Jousse always uses personal experiences as a point of departure—experiences from childhood enriched with the oral tales told by his illiterate mother and grandmother, as well as what he observed on the front during World War I. Later he traveled to the United States, where he spent two years, and contrasted his experiences there with those of Native Americans. Further, he closely observed life on Indian reservations.

Upon his return to Paris in 1922 he continued to confront his theories with facts. He surprises the reader with his constant use of personal stories that support and accept only one master: everyday reality. His maxim would be to faithfully respect that reality, always fearful that the written word and books might deform it in some way.

Jousse was born in Sarthe, in rural northern France. His true first teachers were his grandmother and his mother, who was nearly illiterate but very intelligent. The child Marcel did not know how to read when he started school, nor could he reason, but he knew of many things, as a result of the stories and songs he heard in peasant gatherings until he was five or six years old.

These evening get-togethers and social gatherings, like those Orixe describes in *Euskaldunak,* were usually held during the winter. Warmed by sweet cider and roasted chestnuts, the rural people would tell stories by means of songs. The passing on of news and the power of memory surprised the child Marcel, who for the first time heard of another child who became the great teacher Jesus of Nazareth, the true educator who used physical gestures to preach the Good News.

Jousse's rural childhood is important, because he refers to it constantly to explain his research and his pedagogical achievements. The peasants of Sarthe taught him to mistrust lovely discourse and thick volumes that often served only as library adornments without adding anything to the knowledge and culture of the human race. Leaving aside the idealist philosophy dominant at that time in the French university, Jousse submerged himself in his rural upbringing, where all mechanisms of thought and human expression were in play. When it came time for a profound study of the complexity of human behavior, Jousse did not simply follow the guidelines of traditional philosophy but immersed himself in his own childhood gestures, thus establishing a relationship to Greco-Roman culture that hid a much richer and deeper reality.

Until then much importance had been given to the spoken language but only as an essential expression of the human being. Prior to Jousee, gesture remained limited to the field of asthetics, to the grace of movement and emotional gesture manifested in expressions of happiness, sadness, anger, etc.

The publication of *Le style oral* in 1925 represented a pedagogical and anthropological revolution. Without discarding writing, which will always be a very practical means of communication, Jousse affirmed categorically that "man is gesture; gesture is man." [3] He put humankind's entire anatomy at the service of thought: "Man thinks with his whole body." [4]

His claim that man did not first express himself solely through the mouth but with his body, especially his hands, was a risky challenge in a time when the term "oral style" had not even been coined. As Jousse confesses in *Le style oral,* "it [the book] was a true scandal." [5] In spite of its revolutionary premise, in 1927 Pope Pious XI noted that *Le style oral* was "a complete revolution, but in the good sense of the word." [6]

The scandal Jousse's message caused in the scientific community of linguists, anthropologists, pedagogues, psychologists, and historians reverberated in religious circles, especially Catholic circles, as well, because of his ideas about Jesus of Nazareth. To that point, no one had viewed Jesus as other than a religious figure and apologist. Jousse, on the other hand, situated Christ in His historical context and as teaching according to the pedagogical canons of the rabbis of Israel. Jousse, of course, knew of Christ and the Gospel from childhood, but what really interested him was not the divine aspect of Jesus Christ but the pedagogical one, that is, the physical gestures that lay beneath the surface of the Gospel that narrates the story of the Rabbi Joshua (Jeshua). This character was always for Jousse a scientific obsession.

Jousse mastered several languages, including Latin, Hebrew, Aramaic, and Greek, and conducted a profound study of Homer's two masterpieces, the *Iliad* and the *Odyssey*. He began to compare evenings in Sarthe during his childhood with certain passages in the Old and New Testaments (the Book of Job, the Parables, etc.) and finally with the Homeric compositions, and he concluded that there existed consistent formulas and phrases taken from oral tradition in the Bible and both of Homer's epics. The Bible, the *Iliad,* and the *Aeneid* served as a broad human laboratory where he could experiment and verify specific mechanisms of the human being. For Jousse, both Homer's *Iliad* and Virgil's *Aeneid* were great epic poems and masterworks of the written word. The *Aeneid* was an artificial epic, the elaborate product of a refined civilization that already possessed written books, but the *Iliad* appeared to be a natural, sincere, and true composition, an immortal work by a spontaneous poet who took advantage of popular oral cultural baggage—the expression of the genuine language of the Greek people, the spoken language in which physical gesture played a major role.

Jousse departed from the general tendency to consider the illiterate ignorant and inferior, as if the written language, school, and books were the only source of culture. He believed it was a serious mistake for teachers to indoctrinate children to believe that written language was the true language, to the detriment of spoken language, when in reality the former was nothing but an expression, figure, and image of the latter. In his opinion, illiterate peoples were often very cultured and intelligent. The peasant might not know how to decline *rosa-rosae* in Latin, but, because he looked at them and smelled them, he knew the different kinds of roses with their colors and fragrances better than any Latin scholar did. In the same way, a child is more interested in a rose that he sees, holds, and touches than in observing his or her name written on a piece of paper.

For oralist and anthropologist Jousse, language was essentially physical gesture in its different forms: mime, gesture painted on a wall, and gesture written down in order to be pronounced. Jousse's terminology evolved from "concretism" to "algebraism," and that evolution implied the living gesture, the sound of the larynx, or oral style and its formation, in an algebraic formula that is the written language. Jousse contrasted biblical concretism, which improved traditional decadent pedagogy, with the dryness of the algebraic formulas that poured from abstract intellectualism. Aristotle affirmed that the human being was the animal who gestured the most. In human gesture, people receive the impression of surrounding reality through all the fibers of their bodies. The human organism acts like an accumulator of energy, which is manifested in innumerable gestures, especially manual gestures, that regulate everyday human behavior.

One of the magic words Jousse uses is *intus-susception,* a word with a rich semantic connotation that figures as a key word in *Le style oral.* According to Jousse, the worth of a human being depends on his or her introspection and observation of the inner world. The point of departure for *Le style oral* is the observation of self. Jousse reviewed five thousand books over twenty years, and he chose some five hundred from which to take fragments and phrases that were most appropriate to the reality that he had perceived in gesture. *Le style oral,* composed almost exclusively of citations, is notable for its logical synthesis of different writers.

In Jousse's opinion the laws governing oral style differ from those for written style because the former is retained aurally and is transmitted by memory whereas the latter has weakened memory. In the face of the amnesia books cause, Jousse affirms that there can be no brilliance without the help of a good memory. His apologia for oral literature, physical gesture, and the importance of hands in communication is founded on concrete examples that in his opinion prove and support the objectives outlined in his book. Thus, for example, he cites Spencer and Gillen's description of the Warramunga tribe in Australia, which emphasizes the importance of hands as taking the most forms of all the motor organs of the human body:

> In the Warramunga tribe . . . widows are forbidden to speak, sometimes for as long as twelve months and during that time they do not communicate with others unless they do so by gesturing. They become so expert at it that they prefer communicating with gestures even when not obliged to do so. . . . In female gatherings, absolute silence reigns, and yet they maintain very animated communication by means of fingers, hands and arms. . . . They communicate rapidly and their gestures are difficult to imitate. . . . There is one old lady in the Tenaut Creek Indian tribe who has not pronounced a single word in 25 years.[7]

Maurice Blondel, one of the most famous philosophers of the time, said about *Le style oral:* "The strength of his personal method pleases me."[8] Without a doubt, this work will long be an indispensable reference in the field of oral and anthropological research.

MANUEL LEKUONA (1894-1987)

Manuel Lekuona from childhood had at his disposition a beautiful library willed to his relatives by his uncle Iñarra, who was a priest and a poet. From a very early age, Lekuona was able to keep himself informed about different aspects of Basque culture, especially literature, both written and oral. As a young professor, he gave a lecture on Basque meter in the first session of the Seminario de Gasteiz. In that lecture he described the metrical structure of Basque verse and adopted a definitive position based on the study and scholarly knowledge of the Basque poetic tradition. Using words of praise spoken by Bishop Eijo y Garay of Gasteiz about Basque, Lekuona talked on a subject about which "almost nothing had been said"[9] (rhythm, rhyme, popular poetry, Basque stress, the foot as a unit of Basque verse, etc.) and encouraged those studying to be priests to accept the point in the still incipient but already vigorous Basque cultural movement.

His lecture marks the beginning of the long trajectory of Lekuona the writer, who planted the seed of interest in poetry among those seminarians, such as Aitzol, Etxeberria, Jakakortajarena, F. Loidi, Martin Lekuona, A. Zugasti, Angel Sukia, and Ignacio Otamendi, who years later would become apologists for and creators of Basque literature. For their benefit, Manuel Lekuona founded the Kardaberaz Academy.

His long tenure as professor of Basque (1915-1936) in the Seminario de Gasteiz helped him enter the world of popular literature, as did his contact with two other Gipuzkoan professors, José Miguel Barandiarán and Antonio Pildain, later the bishop of Las Palmas de Gran Canaria in the Canary Islands.

The year 1918 represents a landmark in Basque culture for various reasons. From September 1 to 8 the First Congress of Basque Studies (Eusko Ikaskuntza) was held in Oñati, where Euskaltzaindia was initiated. It formally became an institution in 1919. The congress in Oñati also represented a starting point and a commitment to Basque popular literature by one of the best oralists of the twentieth century. That oralist was Manuel Lekuona.

The First Congress of Basque Studies motivated Lekuona to make a firmer commitment to popular literature, including bertsolaritza. A journalist from Donostia offered him the opportunity to do so:

> But what I will never forget is a communication for the Congress, presented and read by a journalist from Donostia . . . a work that exalted the figure of the German peasant who dedicated Sunday afternoons to drinking in a beer hall and listening attentively to a reading of the great poets Goethe and Schiller, while our peasants in the cider shops listen to the simplicities of the bertsolariak. . . . The qualification of "simplicities" applied to our popular poets pierced me to the

soul. I can say that from that moment I conceived a plan to dedicate myself to mounting a defense of bertsolaritza.[10]

Histories of Basque literature portray Lekuona as a writer who cultivated poetry, theater, and prose. If we carefully examine his vast production, twelve volumes' worth, we observe that his themes are varied and diverse. Most notable are the academic works that predate the Spanish Civil War. I will highlight only his contributions to the fields of decorative poetry, the *kopla zaharrak,* and the knowledge and appreciation of bertsolaritza.

Popular Oral Literature

Lekuona was not the first to study popular oral literature. Even so, no one can doubt the importance of his contribution, as it was he who defined its characteristics and systematized some of the poetic genres. He was able to join studies of Basque folklore with the theories in vogue at the time, especially the methodology of Jousse.

The 1925 publication of *Le Style oral* marked a milestone in Lekuona's study of popular Basque poetry. Several years before *Le Style oral* appeared, Lekuona published works that demonstrated his interest in themes related to orality, popular poetry, bertsolaritza, and so on. But *Le Style oral* no doubt reaffirmed that interest at the same time that it opened the broad panorama of the importance of physical gesture in the origin of the language, by using as a starting point the concrete experiences of childhood enriched by the oral narratives of the elders in the family setting. In this way, Lekuona questioned the hegemony of a culture based principally on the written word.

In September 1930 Lekuona gave an important lecture, entitled "Popular Basque Poetry," at the city hall of Bergara on the occasion of the Fifth Congress of Basque Studies (Eusko Ikaskuntza). On only one occasion was Jousse mentioned, in a bibliographical reference ("La poesia popular vasca" [Basque popular poetry]). In that lecture there appeared clearly defined the three points, or types of poetry, that encompass Lekuona's most personal and original contribution to the wealth of Basque popular poetry: decorative poetry, the *kopla zaharrak,* and bertsolaritza.

After a brief introduction that stresses the importance of popular Basque poetry, he points out its beauty even on those occasions when it is plagued by *erderismos* (words borrowed from Spanish) or by apparent illogicality. Lekuona then applies his theories to Basque popular poetry by projecting the importance of purely decorative poetry that is described as poetry of adornment, without substance—poetry based on rhythmic and musical coordination of articulated sounds that may say nothing to the intellect but that may communicate a stylized message. One of the examples Lekuona cites is Father Donostia's lullaby "Ttunkurrunkuttuna." This type of poetry sometimes combines decoration with intelligible content in spite of the fact that the decorative portions lack any precise meaning. They deal with words stylized because of their foreign origin, because of some deformation, or because of an incorrect order in some of the poet's expressions. Thus, for example, in the first line of "Ttunkurrunkuttuna" we find "xirrixti-mirrixti," and "ikimilikiliklik" in the fourth line:

> Xirrixti-mirrixti, gerrena, plat,
> olio-zopa, kikili-salda,
> urrup! edan edo klik!
> ikimilikiliklik.[11]

> Xirrixti-mirrixti, roaster, platter, oil soup, chicken broth, by sips! drink or swallow! ikimilikiliklik.

Lekuona then analyzes the content of the *kopla zaharrak,* which are curious for their apparent lack of logic—that is, use of non sequiturs—between the focal image and the subsidiary image of the verse. Instead, there exists a relationship between them based on rhetorical transposition. As an example, he cites the first verse of Bereterretxe's famous song:

> Altzak ez dik biotzik;
> ez gaztanberak ezurrik . . .
> Ez nien uste erraiten ziela
> Aitunen semek gezurrik.[12]

> The alder tree has no marrow nor cottage cheese any bone . . .
> I did not believe that a nobleman would lie.

This literal translation of the couplet lacks a logical connection between the subsidiary images ("the alder tree has no marrow, nor cottage cheese any bone") and the focal image ("I did not believe that a nobleman would lie"). Thus, there appears to be incoherence between the two parts of the couplet. When Lekuona translated it, he introduced the comparative phases, which did not appear in the original text: "[it is certain that] the alder tree has no marrow, nor cottage cheese any bone," "[just as certainly] did I believe that a nobleman would not lie." Even though the concept of certainty did not figure explicitly in the verse, Lekuona saw, upon juxtaposing the statements about nature and the nobility, that the poet was as sure of one thing as he was of the other.

Lekuona then disagreed with those who believed that a people did not possess literature because they did not have one in written form. He later analyzed the essence of bertsolaritza, putting special emphasis on improvisation.

Some of these ideas, merely outlined in the lecture at Bergara, were warmly received by Basques interested in oral and popular literature, especially in bertsolaritza, Aitzol being the outstanding example.[13] The impact that Lekuona's new poetic theory had on Aitzol was decisive for the profound change that took place in the latter with regard to poetry. With the firmness of an arbitrator who imposes his law on the field of Basque poetry, Aitzol chose popular oral poetry over the cultured poetry of Lizardi, Orixe, and Lauaxeta and no longer attributed the same importance to cultured poetry that he had in 1930.

Lekuona realized that the current rules regulating the judging of bertsolaritza were not sufficient and that comparing them with the rules used to judge written poetry only led to bertsolaritza's loss of prestige. In 1935, the same year of the first Day of the Bertsolari and the first national bertsolari championship held in Donostia, Lekuona published *Literatura oral euskérika* (Oral Basque literature). In addition to delving more deeply into the themes he mentioned in his 1930 lecture, in this work he also cites many ideas and key words from *Le style oral,* such as "mnemotechnia" (*mnémotechnie*)—the importance of memory in oral literature—the differences between Homer's *Iliad* and Virgil's *Aeneid* with regard to spontaneity and the different sources used by the two authors, the role of primitive assemblies where texts were recited and sung but not read, and some characters from the Old Testament who demonstrated a capacity for poetic improvisation: "Marcel Jousse says quite rightly . . . that just as the use of a watch has killed our faculty for calculating at any time what hour of the day it is, a faculty that primitive man possessed, in the same way the invention of printing and especially the use of writing has made our memory lazy to the point that today it is impossible for us to remember even the names of our most intimate friends."[14]

I should also note that, in the first part of *Literatura oral euskérika,* Lekuona details the fundamental traits of oral literature: rhythmic skill, the development of memory, the rapidity with which the images move, and improvisation.

If the word *pioneer* evokes an image of a "person who takes the first steps in some human activity," then Jousse and Manuel Lekuona are more than pioneers in the field of oral literature. Jousse was aware of the fundamental law of rhythm and physical gesture that accompanies us from birth to death. He delved into the anthropology of human expression until he was convinced that the language of physical gesture was the origin of that expression.

By applying some of Jousse's ideas to oral Basque literature, Lekuona created a theoretical vision of Basque orality with repercussions in literary creation, in the practice of popular poetic expression, and in fieldwork. He applied a methodology that was broadly accepted in his time and left us writings on theoretical formulation that place him at the head of any group of Basque oralists.

NOTES

Introduction

1. In 1942, three years after the end of the Spanish Civil War, the military governor of Gipuzkoa urged his people to speak Spanish. In Bizkaia the civil governor, G. Riestra, ordered the destruction of all tombstones written in Basque.

2. The *cuaderna via* is a stanza of four monorhythmic verses of fifteen syllables each.

3. This difference is noted even in some histories of Basque literature, such as that by Luis Villasante, *Historia de la literatura vasca,* which is divided into two parts.

4. Unfortunately, the articles' publication in this journal made them largely inaccessible to most Basques.

5. Although Larramendi and Sabino Arana y Goiri in Spain did not write much in Basque, they gave impetus to two of the best groups of Basque writers.

6. Luis Michelena (a.k.a. Koldo Mitxelena) says that Orixe is "the most representative figure of one period of Basque letters"; *Historia de la literatura vasca* (Madrid: Ediciones Minotauro, 1960), 148.

7. Mikel Zarate left some sixteen original or translated books published between 1960 and 1979. Among them are critical studies of various writers, in *Euskal literatura,* vols. 7 and 9 (Durango: L. Zugazaga, 1979).

8. In 1958 Koldo Mitxelena published a brief summary of Basque literature in *Historia general de las literaturas hispánicas,* vol. 5, ed. Guillermo Díaz Plaja (Barcelona: Barna, 1958).

9. Luis Villasante also wrote several summaries of the history of Basque literature. Two of the most important are "Lengua y literatura vasca," in *Tesoro breve de las letras hispánicas,* ed. Guillermo Díaz Plaja (Madrid: Editorial Magisterio Español, 1972), 6:15-27; and in *Cultura vasca* by José Miguel de Barandiarán (Zarauz: Erein, 1978). Villasante follows the same method he used in 1961. On the positive side, there appear in these works several contemporary authors who are still living.

10. Mujika has also published two double volumes about two very important poets, Jose Mari "Lizardi" Agirre and Jon Aiphasorho Mirande: *Lizardi-ren lirika bideak,* 2 vols. (Donostia: Haranburu, 1983), and *Mirande-ren poesigintza* (Donostia: Haranburu, 1984).

Chapter One. Survey of Basque Poetry

1. The competition was held at the Euskal Olerki Eguna (Day of Basque Poetry), founded by Aitzol and Euskaltzaleak and held from 1930 to 1936.

2. Bitoriano Gandiaga, *Elorri.* (Oñate: Editorial Franciscana Aranzazu, 1962).

Chapter Two. Bertsolaritza and the Basque Diaspora

1. In 1521 Magellan was assassinated by natives of the Philippines. His assistant, Juan Sebastián Elcano, a native of Getaria, Gipuzkoa, was thus the first to circumnavigate the globe in 1522.

2. The return home is depicted with great emotion in the songs "Ara nun diran" (Jose María Iparragirre, 1828-1891) and "Urrundik" (Elizanburu, 1828-1891).

3. Resurreccíon María de Azkue, *Cancionero popular del País Vasco,* vol. I (Bilbo: Auñamendi, 1968), 76.

4. Ibid., 75.

5. Through the works and verses of Juan Ignacio Iztueta (1767-1845), we know the history and vicissitudes of the Gipuzkoans of the nineteenth century. The same thing happens with modern bertsolariak. See, for example, Ignacio Eizmendi's last book, *Basarri, Kantari nator* (Zarautz: Itxaropena, 1960).

6. Pedro Mari Otaño, *Pedro Mari Otaño'ren bertsoak* (Zarautz: Itxaropena, 1959), 66.

7. Ibid., 67-69.

8. Ibid.

9. Ibid.

10. Ibid., 65-66.

11. Ibid., 103-7.

12. *Pedro María Otaño* audio cassette 101OTS, HG-221K, no. 7762.

13. Ibid.

14. José "Pello Errota" Elizegi, *Pello Errotaren bizitza* (Tolosa: Auspoa, 1963), 127.

15. José "Pello Errota" Elizegi, *Pello Errotak, jarritako bertsoak: Bere alabaren argibideakin* (Tolosa: Auspoa, 1963), 147-48.

16. During the elimination round of the 1985 bertsolari competition in Nafarroa Beherea, Mixel came out a champion. Although the quality of his art does not equal that of his father, he nevertheless won the championship for a second time, in 1989.

17. Fernando "Xalbador" Aire, *Odolaren mintzoa* (Zarautz: Auspoa, 1976), 231-32.

18. Luis de Castresana, *Vida y obra de Iparraguirre* (Bilbo: Gran Enciclopedia Vasca, 1971), 90.

19. Ibid., 96.

20. Ibid., 260.

21. Ibid., 256-58.

22. Ibid., 244.

23. Udarregi was famous for his memory. In one competition in which he ended up tied with another bertsolari, the tie-breaker required him to repeat all the verses he had created that afternoon. Udarregi replied that he could. His opponent could not.

24. Antonio Zavala, *Udarregi bertsolaria* (Tososa: Auspoa, 1966), 20-21.

25. José María Satrústegi, *Luzaide'ko kantiak* (Tolosa: Auspoa, 1967), 131-33.

26. Zavala, *Iru anai bertsolari* (Tolosa: Auspoa, 1968), 73-76.

27. Ibid., 91.

28. Zavala, *Ameriketako bertsoak* (Tolosa: Auspoa, 1984), 80-82.

29. Zavala, *Paulo Yanzi* (Tolosa: Auspoa, 1968), 129-31.

30. Ibid., 134-36.

31. Ibid., 272.

32. Santiago Onaindia, *Milla euskal-olerki eder,* 1154-55.

33. Ibid.

34. *Ameriketako bertsoak,* 109-14.

35. Ibid., 104-5.

36. Ibid., 128.

37. Manuel Lasarte, *Gordean neuzkanak* (Tolosa: Auspoa, 1975), 196.

Chapter Three. Pastorales

1. Zuberoa has a population of about eighteen thousand, most of whom make their living from agriculture and livestock. Sixty percent of the population knows Euskera, although its use is primarily limited to the family and peasant milieus. It is not often heard in the urban centers such as Atarratze (Tardets) and Mauleon (Maule), where half the province's population is located. In Iparralde, Basque is rarely used in the educational system or in government.

2. On July 24, 1988, for the first time the president of the autonomous Basque government in Spain, José Antonio Ardanza, and his minister of culture, Joseba Arregi, were present for the presentation of the pastorale "Zumalakarregi" in Iparralde.

3. Junes Casenave, *Ibañeta* (1978) and *Santa Grazi* (1976).

4. One of the best representatives of Basque popular poetry was Etxahun. He possessed an extraordinary natural talent, but he was a popular, rather than an educated, poet.

5. The Basques have traditionally respected the clergy. An exception to this rule is demonstrated in the poem "Barkoxeko Eliza" (1859), in which P. Topet (Etxahun) attacks Father Schmarsow, the priest of Barkoxe.

6. The same may be said of the other phenomenon of Basque oral literature, bertsolaritza. It required the patient labors of investigators such as

Manuel Lekuona to point out its value. His *Literatura oral euskérika* (Basque oral literature) was a milestone in the study of this genre.

7. Wilhelm Freiherr Von Humboldt, "Diario del viaje vasco," trans. Telesforo de Aranzadi, *Revista Internacional de Estudios Vascos* 14, no. 2 (1923): 249.

8. J. Augustin Chaho, *Voyage en Navarre pendant l'insurrection des Basques (1830–1835)* (Bayonne: P. Lespés, 1865), 333–34.

9. His only pastorale that is not related to Basque topics is *Ximena* (1979), about the life of the wife of El Cid Campeador.

10. Matalas was the parish priest of Moncayolle. In 1661 the people of Zuberoa rebelled against taxation and having to repurchase their lands, which the king had sold to the nobles. The peasants lost their struggle, and their leader, Matalas, was executed. Etxahun and José Mari Iparragirre were two popular poets. The life of the first was full of misfortune. The second was a vagabond who, singing and playing his guitar, traveled in many nations.

11. The first presentation of Urdiñarbe's pastorale, *Agosti Xaho,* took place at night, unusual for a pastorale.

Chapter Four. Bernard Detxepare—Medieval or Renaissance Writer?

1. An earlier version of this chapter was published in *Journal of the Society of Basque Studies in America* 2 (1981): 21–32. It is reprinted with the permission of the editor.

2. Among those who compare Detxepare to Juan Ruiz are Luis M. Mujika, *Historia de la literatura euskerika,* 86; Koldo Mitxelena, "Literatura en lengua vasca," 5: 350; and Luis Villasante, *Historia de la literatura vasca,* 54. The parallel with Rabelais was noted by Julio de Urquijo, "Introducción a nuestra edición 'Linguae vasconum primitiae' de Bernat Dechepare," 667.

3. Only one copy of the first-edition volumes published in 1545 has survived in Paris. Detxepare was mentioned by another writer, Lope de Irasti, for the first time in 1625, but in the following centuries he was forgotten.

4. *Catálogo de obras euskaras* (Barcelona: Tasso, 1891), 5.

5. José M. Huarte, "Los primitivos del euskera: Dechepare y su tiempo," 242.

6. The struggles between the Agramonteses and the Beamonteses are described in the "Song of Berreterretxe." See Santiago Onaindia, *Euskal literatura,* 1: 56.

7. Koldo Mitxelena (ed.), *Olerkiak 1545: Bernat Dechepare* (Donostia: Txertoa, 1978), 48.

8. The writer Alonso de Ercilla (of Bizkaian origin) wrote *La Araucana* in Spanish. Enthusiastic supporters of the Basque language, such as Larramendi and P. P. Astarloa, also wrote in Spanish, as did less-supportive writers like Unamuno and Pío Baroja.

9. Mitxelena, *1545*, 72. See "Dies irae, dies illa," *Liber usualis (Missae et officii)*, 1810.

10. Mitxelena, *1545*, 60

11. Ibid., 88.

12. Ibid., 102

13. Ibid., 104.

14. Ibid., 132.

15. The cruel behavior of the woman toward her lover reminds us of "Les quinze joies du mariage" (The fifteen joys of marriage) by an unknown French writer. In this poem, too, the woman always has an answer for her husband.

16. Mitxelena, *1545*, 156.

17. Karl Orff, *Carmina Burana*, Munster-Druzk, Hannover, Deutsche Gramophone 139.362.

18. Julio Urquijo, "Introducción" 668. See also José Aristimuño, "El primer renacentista y poeta euskaldun," 12.

Chapter 5. Jose de Aristimuño, Alias "Aitzol":
A Martyr to the Basque Cause

1. Jose Mari "Lizardi" Agirre, *Itz-lauz* (Donostia: Euskaltzaleak, 1934), 100-101.

Chapter Six. Nicolás Ormaetxea, Alias "Orixe" (1888-1961):
The Life and Work of a Controversial Writer

1. Luis Michelena, *Historia de la literatura vasca*, 148.

2. Pierre Lafitte, "Lettre ouverte à M. N. Ormaechea," *Gernika* 10 (Jan.-Mar. 1950), 19-20.

3. Federico Krutwig Sagredo, *Computer shock. Vasconia año 2001* (Estella: Gráficas Lizarra, 1984), 451. To familiarize yourself with the different viewpoints of these two authors on the Basque language, also see Orixe's response to Krutwig, "Krutwig yauna euskeraz," *Euzko-gogoa* 11-12 (Nov.-Dec. 1950): 49-52.

4. Andima Ibinagabeitia, "Euzko-gogoa elentxu," *Euzko-gogoa* 11-12 (Nov.-Dec. 1950): 55.

5. Luis Michelena, "Atarikoa," in *"Orixe" omenaldi* (Donostia: Izarra, 1965), 7. For many young writers of the time, among them José Luis "Txillardegi" Alvarez Enparantza, Gabriel Aresti, Joxe Azurmendi, and Joseba Intxausti, Orixe was the master to emulate. When Orixe returned from exile in 1954 he was well received, but soon the debates and controversies began with some of his old admirers, such as Enparantza and Intxausti. See Enparantza, *Euskal kulturaren zapalketa, 1956-1981* (Donostia: Elkar, 1984), 46.

6. Michelena, "Atarikoa," 8-9.

7. Following Basque tradition, the child Nicolás was named after the saint on whose day he was born, in this case, Saint Nicholas.

One of the triplets, Martín, died while very young. As Orixe tells us in *Barne-muinetan* (Zarautz: Itxaropena, 1934), "Jausi zen zure etxe aragiz egiña iru urte baiño len" (Your house of flesh fell before it was three years old) (130).

8. Orixe, *Euskaldunak poema eta olerki guziak* (San Sebastián: Auñamendi, 1972), 172.

9. As a child, Nicolás lived on the Errekalde farm under the care of his adoptive mother, Rosa, and her mother, Asuntxi. Orixe always treated the latter as his grandmother. The old woman was very important in the formation of Orixe's spirituality. (Ibid., 577):

> Ez-jakin jakintsu aren
> ikasle zur nintzala ni! . . .
> Ua lako gurasorik
> otoitzean ez dut kausi.

> I wanted to be like her, illiterate but wise. I never found another spiritual master of her kind in prayer. (ibid., 11)

10. Orixe, "Quito'n arrebarekin," *Euzko-gogoa* 11–12 (Nov.-Dec. 1950): 13.

11. Orixe, *Omenaldi,* 36, 37.

12. A Jesuit passed through Uitzi recruiting young boys who might enter the order. This means of recruiting candidates was common at the time and would be until half a century later. This is how young Orixe was chosen as a candidate. The opinions of his teacher and the village priest played a decisive role in his selection.

Orixe was always slow to elaborate on the problems that caused him to leave the company of Jesus. Keeping in mind the Jesuits' sense of obedience and the poet's accusatory personality, it is no wonder that there were problems. It is also known from other members of the Society, such as Jokin Zaitegi, that the Basque language caused problems inside the religious community. Pablo Iztueta in *"Quito'n arrebarekin" irakurriz* (Donostia: Etor, 1988) confirms what was suspected about the true cause of Orixe's departure from the Jesuit monastery. At the end of his book, Iztueta inserts an unedited letter from Orixe, obtained thanks to the assistance offered by Dr. Antonio Labayen, Orixe's intimate friend. It is an example of correspondence that took place between Orixe and his superiors: "Habiendo desaparecido en el saqueo de mi casa por los falangistas mi correspondencia con los PP. Provinciales y General, debo hablar de memoria de algunos sucesos que no son como olvidados" (405). In these documents, written in 1943 in Saubion, France, Orixe gives us the key to his departure from the convent — he was asked to leave. Iztueta gives us many details about Orixe's health (*"Quito'n arrebarekin,"* 403–33.) He suffered from nasal hemorrhages, terrible headaches, and rheumatoid arthritis. He also mentions the great aversion to Basque that existed in Jesuit secondary schools, seminaries, and convents. Orixe was accused of being a Basque separatist simply because of his fondness for the Basque language. He relates for us the suffering and humiliation he had to endure at the hands of some of his superiors, who were more political than paternal. He was even forbidden to write his relatives in Basque ("*Quito'n arrebarekin*," 37); *Omenaldi*, 37.

13. At this time, Orixe replaced the Bizkaian writer Ebaista Bustintza, known as Kirikiño, on the editorial board of the Basque section of the daily paper *Euzkadi*. He shared his post with the great Bizkaian poet Esteban Urkiaga. He also got to know certain members of Euskaltzaindia. Among those members were Julio Urkijo, Arturo Campión, Luis de Eleizalde, Seber Altube, Juan Bautista Eguzkitza, and Raimundo Olabide. During this time, Orixe deepened his knowledge of oral Basque literature through his friendship with Azkue, Barandiarán, and Manuel Lekuona. This experience was very useful when he began writing *Euskaldunak.*

14. Orixe, "Nota necrológica sobre Azkue," *Gernika* 19 (Apr.-June 1952): 96-97.

15. It is interesting to note that Orixe signed his first poems with the initials "S. J.," used only by ordained members of the Jesuit order. Later he began using the pseudonym Orixe.

16. Luis Michelena, "Asaba zaarren baratza," *Egan* 17, no. 3-6 (May-Dec. 1960): 129.

17. The translation was published in *Euskaldunak poema,* 595-96.

18. Ibid., 598.

19. Ibid., 602-3, 604-9, 610, 601.

20. Juan Eusebio Nieremberg (1595-1658) was born in Madrid to German parents. He was a prolific writer whose most notable works lay within the field of asceticism. He had a serene, persuasive style and did not overuse the dramatic tone popular with many of the religious writers of the period. He possessed a great facility for the use of the language.

21. Nikolas Ormaetxea (Orixe), *Salmutegia* (San Sebastián: Izarra, 1967), vii.

22. Orixe did not like the existing translations of the Charter of the United Nations, so he translated it himself with singular mastery:

> Recientemente he visto un folleto de la ONU impreso en español, ininteligible para el cien por ciento de los españoles, salvo para los leguleyos. Su título es una verdadera atrocidad lingüística. "Declaración universal de los derechos del hombre." No, señor, no es universal, sino de la ONU o de la Revolución francesa. . . . Eso no se puede traducir al vasco, porque las atrocidades no se pueden ni deben traducir a ningún idioma sensato. ("Errores de vascólogos nuestros," *Gernika* 10 (Jan.-Mar. 1950), 18.

23. Nicolás "Orixe" Ormaechea, *El Lazarillo de Tormes. Tormes'ko itsu-mutila* (Bilbao: Verdes Achirica, 1929), 120.

24. Orixe, *Mireio, 21.* This translation was enthusiastically received because of its innovative tone. Josu M. Leizaola, "Orixe agertu zan izkera be-

rri batekin," in *"Jainkoaren billa" gutuna zer da?* (Baiona: Euskal-Kulturaren Alde, 1973); this work was translated into several languages, including Japanese, and inspired an opera by Gounod. Moreover, Mistral won the Nobel Prize for Literature in 1904, sharing it with the work of the Spaniard José Echegaray.

25. Jesús María Leizaola, *Obras completas* (Donostia: Sendoa Argitaldaria, 1981), 1:185.

26. Orixe, "Errores de vascólogos nuestros," 16.

27. Much of the Basque literature produced at the end of the nineteenth century and beginning of the twentieth was heavily influenced by the loss of the *fueros* and Basque liberties.

28. Nikolas Ormaetxea, *Santa Cruz apaiza* (San Sebastián: Loiola, 1929), 8.

29. He did not use the familiar forms as much in this work as he would later in "Quito'n arrebarekin."

30. Orixe and Lizardi had already met in 1928 on the occasion of a talk the former gave in Donostia. Lizardi was in the audience. He encouraged Orixe to write *Euskaldunak.* Despite their very different personalities, they encouraged one other to work on behalf of the Basque language.

Orixe's relationship with his parents was unusual because of their separation. He mentions his father only once in his works, in a dialogue with his sister, a nun: "1931'tik 1936'era! Bitartean aita zanaren eriotza. Etxean gertatu nintxinan" (1931 to 1936! Father died in that interval. While I was at home). "Quito'n arrebarekin" 11-12 (Nov.-Dec. 1950): 13.

31. It is difficult to appreciate to what lengths Franco's ironfisted dictatorship went during this time. Even if there was nothing bad in the Basque books, the fact that they were written in the language was a crime. The same thing happened to other Basque writers like Mitxelena and Etxaide. On more than one occasion, José de Arteche had to appear before the authorities in order to get them to allow the publication of Basque-language books ("Quito'n arrebarekin" 3-4 [Mar.-Apr. 1951], 16).

32. Of this number, Orixe wrote some 10,300 lines. The rest were popular songs or well-known poetry by other Basque writers.

33. Orixe, *Euskaldunak. Los vascos,* 186.

34. Ibid., 182-86.

35. Juan San Martín, "Orixeren poemari buruz," *Jakin* 21 (1966): 68-71; Jokin Zaitegi, "Euskaldunak," in *"Orixe" omenaldi,* 255.

36. In contrast, we have cases such as that of Txomin Aguirre, who wrote his novel *Garoa* (Donostia: Euskaltzaleak, 1935) a quarter of a century earlier. In what is clearly a novel of manners dealing with agriculture, he describes a meeting of workers that took place in Eibar over labor problems (288-89).

Garoa is without a doubt one of the best novels of manners in twentieth-century Basque literature. Nevertheless, it is said to contain excessive idealism (quite normal in a post-Romantic work). Take, for example, the description of Joanes Artzaina, the protagonist, with which Aguirre begins the novel. Also, the dialect used in the novel is Gipuzkoan, although the Bizkaian of Oñati is spoken in that region.

37. *Euskaldunak: Poema eta olerki guziak,* 695.

38. Orixe, "Eusk, Euskadi," *Euzko-gogoa* 3–4 (Mar.–Apr. 1951): 35.

39. *Euskaldunak. Los vascos,* 176.

40. Although not every critic agrees with what Justo Mokoroa (Ibar) says about this, I cite him here as an example of the differences of opinion on this topic: "To put it as graphically as possible, *Euskaldunak* is the race singing to itself about its own life through the mouth of a gigantic interpreter. In contrast to what is narrated in almost all known epic poems, the poet here not only does not invent anything, he also does not include any of himself." *Euskaldunak poema eta olerki guzkiak,* 695.

Orixe admitted that he tried to express things as a farmer would: "Beaztoparen bat arkitzen dudanean, nere buruari galdetzen diot: au nola esango luke gure baserritar batek" (When I run into a problem, I ask myself, How would a farmer say this?) Andima "Elentxu" Ibinagabeitia, "Orixe euskeratzaile," in *"Orixe" omenaldi* (Donostia: Izarra, 1965), 94.

41. Orixe, *Euskaldunak. Los vascos,* 228.

42. Jon Bilbao and A. Onaindia, "Orixe'ren lanak," in *"Orixe" omenaldi* (Donostia: Izarra, 1965), 127.

43. Jose Mari Aranalde, *"Orixe" omenaldi,* 38.

44. Orixe, *Euskaldunak. Los vascos,* 224.

45. To understand this point, it helps to read Pío Baroja's *La leyenda de Jaun de Alzate* (Madrid: R. Caro Raggio, 1922) and Jon Mirande's poem "Euskal Laminei."

46. Orixe, *Euskaldunak. Los vascos,* 368. The behavior of the Church (the pope and the Spanish bishops) during the Spanish Civil War and afterward prompted Orixe to severely criticize certain stands taken by the Church hierarchy.

47. Orixe most often used *mandeulia* (horsefly), *azeri* (fox), *zakur* (dog), *erbi* (hare), *mando* (mule), *oillo* (chicken), *euli* (fly), *suge* (snake), *basakatu* (wildcat), *leoi* (lion), *maskulo* (snail), *basurde* (wild boar), *ardi* (sheep), *beor* (mare), *zerri* (pig), *erle* (bee), *asto* (burro), *katamotz* (lynx), *katu* (cat), *ate* (duck), and *erlabio* (wasp).

48. Orixe translated this book into Spanish but refused to translate the title because it sounded ostentatious in translation: "En las médulas del interior" (In the marrow of the inner being).

49. Orixe, *Barne-muinetan,* 21.

50. Ibid., 28

51. Pascal was one of the greatest writers of prose in French literature. After his conversion, his life was a militant constant with an apologetic projection. True conversion, in his opinion, consisted of *s'aneantir* before God in recognition that nothing could be done without Him. *Barne-muinetan,* 34–36.

52. Faith was Orixe's pillar of support. Although he lived in Betharram, very close to the sanctuary of the Virgin of Lourdes, he went there only four or five times in two years. His faith was not fed by miracles:

Ez nintzan itsatsi
poz-leku artara. Naiago fedea.

I did not cling to that place of consolation. I prefer faith (*Euskaldunak poema*, 589).

53. Orixe, *Barne-muinetan*, 62.

54. Ibid., 68.

55. Ibid., 5. José Mari "Lizardi" Agirre's *Biotz-begietan, olerkiak* (Zarautz: Itxaropena Argitaldaria, 1970) originally published as *Biotz-begietan* (Bilbo: Verdes, 1932) is considered by most critics to be the best example of Basque lyric poetry created in the first part of the twentieth century. Although Lizardi was eight years younger than Orixe, the older man always treated him like a close friend. Occasionally, Lizardi even teased him, calling him "Homero, Anakreonte, Virgilio y Cicerón." The chapter entitled "Donapaule'ra yoan etorria" in Lizardi's *Itz-lauz* is proof of this friendship.

56. Orixe, *Barne-muinetan*, 10.

57. To better understand the atmosphere at that time in Nafarroa, see Marino Ayerra Redín, *No me avergoncé del evangelio* (Bilbao: Amado, 1978).

58. Orixe, *Euskaldunak poema eta olerki guziak*, 586.

59. Dr. Manuel Aranzabal, a priest from Lizarza, Gipuzkoa, obtained Orixe's freedom. "Quito'n arrebarekin" 7–8 (Jul.–Aug. 1951): 42.

60. Aranalde, "Gure iruxki aundia," in *"Orixe" omenaldi*, 37.

61. Raimundo Olabide, *Itun Zâr eta Berria* (Bilbo: Yesu'ren Biotzaren Deya, 1958). Olabide's work is impressive if we keep in mind that he accomplished it as an *euskaldunberri*. Nevertheless, the work is occasionally obscure and hard to understand because of his extremely purist attitude toward vocabulary.

62. There were many devotional books and books of novenas for the Sacred Heart, the Virgin, and the saints. There was even an incomplete missal in existence, *Argi donea*, but there was no complete missal. Orixe, *Urte guziko meza-bezperak* (Askain: Garakoiztar Laguntzaileak, 1949), vii.

63. Orixe, *Urte guziko*, vii.

64. Ibid., viii.

65. In spite of its poor format, *Euzko-gogoa* was the greatest cultural monument erected during the Franco era. It was made possible by the titanic labors of one man, Zaitegi. After Zaitegi's death, Juan San Martín wrote, "In another nation there would be national mourning for a man of his stature." *Landuz* (Izarra: Gipuzkoako Aurrezki Kutxa, 1983). Zaitegi formed a group of excellent writers, including the so-called *Euskal Irutasun Deuna* (Holy Basque Trinity), made up of Zaitegi, Orixe, and Ibinagabeitia. Mirande, Iratzeder, Koldo Mitxelena, Salbatore Mitxelena, Txomin Peillen, Antonio Labayen, Nemesio Etxaniz, Krutwig, and many other young writ-

ers of the postwar period also contributed. The journal was established in 1950, and in 1955 Zaitegi moved his editorial activities to Biarritz. Because of a lack of financial support, it failed in 1959. Among other things, this journal served as a bridge between two generations of Basque writers.

66. Orixe, "Quito'n arrebarekin" nos. 3-4 (Mar.-Apr. 1951): 14.

67. Orixe, *Euskaldunak poema*, 514-15.

68. Ibid., 517-18.

69. Ibid., 531.

70. Ibid., 532.

71. Orixe, "Quito'n arrebarekin" nos. 3-4 (Mar.-Apr. 1951): 15.

72. Ibid., 13.

73. Orixe, *Euskaldunak poema*, 556.

74. This is the original title, but the book is known by only the first part of its title.

Because of his dialogue with his sister, Dionisia, we know that he had begun preparing this work in the Basque Country at the same time he was preparing *Euskaldunak:* "Etzekiñat xuxen zer urtetan, beste lan aundia egiten ari nintzala. Nolanai ere, etxetik aldegiterako egin nenunan sail ederra." (I don't remember in what year exactly, but I was preparing the other massive work. In any case, by the time I had to leave home, I had a good deal of it done). "Quito'n arrebarekin" 5-6 (May-June 1951): 7.

An example of his style is his use of *nition* instead of the traditional *nizkion,* whereby he substitutes the pluralizer *it* for *izk.*

For example, compare the style of this book with that of Orixe's *Santa Cruz apaiza* (Donostia: Loiola, 1929).

75. "Quito'n arrebarekin," nos. 11-12 (Nov.-Dec. 1950): 14-15.

76. Ibid., 5-6 (May-June 1951): 9.

77. Ibid., 1-2 (Jan.-Feb. 1952): 18.

78. Ibid., 7-8 (July-Aug. 1952): 12.

79. ("Aita Urrutia'ri," pp. 8-9); "Quito'n arrebarekin," nos. 9-10 (Sept.-Oct. 1951): 25. Even the "Humani Generis" encyclical of Pius XII was very poorly received in many traditional Catholic circles.

80. Gernika is the sacred capital of the Basques. It was a symbol of the tragedy of a Catholic nation that, because of its loyalty to democracy, preferred to fight against a dictator who used the name of God to advance his military crusade. Neither Rome nor the Catholic world in general could understand the position of the Basques, who while remaining Catholic allied themselves with Republicans, Socialists, and Marxists to defend their old liberties. Seventeen Basque priests were shot. Thus was the promise of General Mola kept: "It is necessary to destroy the capital of a perverted people who dare to oppose the irresistible cause of the national ideal." Joxe Azurmendi, *Zer dugu Orixe-ren alde?* (Oñati: Arantzazu, 1977), 196. Defense of the Basques by French writers and intellectuals, such as Jacques Maritain, Georges Bernanos, François Mauriac, and Gabriel-Honoré Marcel, went unheard.

81. "Quito'n arrebarekin" nos. 7-8 (Nov.-Dec. 1951): 46-47.

82. Orixe, *Euskaldunak poema,* 538-40.

83. Ibid., 539-41.

84. *"Orixe" omenaldi,* 39. In the last years of his life, he was able to exclaim in the tranquil retreat of Añorga, "Jainkoak ekarri nau onera. Orainarte pelota bezela, jo eta tira erabilli ba'nau ere orain atseden apur bat eman didala esango nuke" (God has brought me here. Although until this point he has batted me about like a ball, I would say that now he has given me a chance to rest). Ibid., 53.

85. *Euskaldunak poema,* 581.

86. Ibid., 540.

87. Ibid., 547-48.

88. Ibid., 542.

89. Ibid., 585.

90. Ibid., 573-90.

91. Ibid., 582.

92. Ibid., 581.

93. Zaitegi left the Jesuit Order in 1944. His problems with his superiors were continual and serious. He settled as a parish priest in Guatemala, where he dedicated himself to teaching at the University of San Carlos and the American Institute; in 1951 he started his own center of studies, composed of a lyceum and a residence hall. He entered Guatemala on a passport from Euzkadi.

94. Orixe, "Agur guatemalari," *Euzko-gogoa* 9-10 (Sept.-Oct. 1954): 132.

95. Orixe, *Aitorkizunak* (Zarautz: Itxaropena, 1956).

96. Ibid., 2.

97. Ibid.

98. *"Orixe" omenaldi,* 113.

99. *Jainkoaren billa* (Bilbao: Etor, 1971). Orixe wrote an unpublished manuscript in Spanish on this theme entitled "El trato con Dios" (Estibalitzeko Artxibategia [Archives of Estibalitz Convent], 1959). He extracted material from this book for *Jainkoaren billa.* Baztarrika, "Òrixe,' Jainko-billari purrukatua," in *"Orixe" omenaldi,* 187; *Jainkoaren billa,* 17.

100. Ibid., 18.

101. Ibid.

102. Ibid., 253.

103. Ibid., 160.

104. Orixe was buried in the Polloe cemetery in Donostia until 1988, when his remains were transferred to the cemetery in his native village, Orexa. See Antonio Labayen, "Nicolás Ormaetxea (1888-1961)," in Santiago Onaindia, *"Orixe" omenaldi* (Donostia: Izarra, 1965), 24.

105. Jon Garmendia, "Orixe Euzkaltzain," in Santiago Onaindia, *"Orixe* omenaldi,"* 43.

106. Txillardegi, *Jakin* 21 (1981): 83.

107. See Orixe's defense against Lafitte's attacks: "Aita Mitxelena berri-zaleekin," *Euzko-gogoa* 1-2 (Jan.-Feb. 1952): 24.

108. *Egan* 4-6 (1961): 158.

109. There is not the slightest influence from Lizardi, in spite of Orixe's admiration for him. Nor is there any from the great writers such as Dostoevsky, Ibsen, or Baroja.

110. Domingo Aguirre, "Cultismos, pedantería, barbarie," 14.

111. In 1981, twenty years after Orixe's death, Spain's prime minister, Adolfo Suárez, told *Paris-Match* that the Basque language was not appropriate for teaching nuclear physics. The efforts of certain groups of young Basques, including those responsible for the *UZEI* dictionaries and the magazine *Elhuyar,* are proving that statement false.

112. "Eztogu erderazko itzik aotan erabilli bear, esan gura doguna euskerazko itzakaz esan daikegunean" (We should not use foreign words when we can express what we want to say with Basque words). Txomin Agirre, *Kresala* (Donostia: Itxaropena, 1988?), xiii.

113. Urquijo, "Krutwig jauna euskeraz," 49. *Euzko-gogoa* 11-12 (Nov.-Dec.): 51.

114. Orixe, "Unificación del lenguaje literario," *Revista Internacional de Estudios Vascos* 11 (1920): 59; Garmendia, "Jainkoak ekarri nau onera," in *"Orixe" omenaldi,* 55.

115. Orixe, "Erria, erria!" *Euzko-gogoa* 1-2 (Jan.-Feb. 1951): 11.

116. Txillardegi, "1956-1961: Kultur euskararen bila," *Jakin* 21 (1981): 90.

117. "Krutwig yauna euskeraz," 50; Orixe, "La primera academia vasca," *Gernika* 9 (Dec. 1949): 19; Orixe, "Aita Mitxelena berrizaleekin," *Euzko-gogoa* 1-2 (Jan.-Feb. 1952): 23-25.

118. Koldo Mitxelena, "Orixe-ren eriotzean," *Egan* 19 (July-Dec. 1961): 157.

119. Gabriel Aresti, *Poemak II* (Bilbao: Kriselu, 1976), 76.

120. Nicolás "Orixe" Ormaetxea and Martín de Oyarzabal, *El lenguaje vasco* (San Sebastián: Gráficas Izarra, 1963), 8.

121. Patxi Altuna, *Mitxelenaren idazlan hautatuak* (Bilbao: Etor, 1972), 295.

Chapter Seven. Jose Mari Agirre, Alias "Lizardi": *A Lyric Poet*

1. Among them were Orixe; Lizardi; Lauaxeta; Luis Jauregi, alias "Jautarkol" (1896-1971); Loramendi, Claudio Sagarzazu, alias "Satarka" (1895-1971); Zaitegi, etc.

2. Loramendi began writing in a more modern style in 1930.

3. In the first part of Juan Mari Lekuona's *Muga beroak* (Bilbao: Ed. Mensajero and Gero, 1973), Lizardi's influence is very strong. Bitoriano Gandiaga also openly admits to Lizardi's influence.

4. If asked to point out differences among the three great poets, I would say that Orixe was the most popular and the least influenced by modern

foreign trends in literature and by Arana y Goiri's purism. Lauaxeta was more open to outside influences and was more of a purist than the other two. Lizardi was the most lyrical.

5. Bernat Detxepare, *Olerkiak* (San Sebastián: Txertoa, 1978), 154.

6. Aristimuño, José "Aitzol." "El poeta José María Aguirre. Xabier Lizardi," *Yakintza* 3 (1933): 164.

7. Lizardi's life was not without troubles and misunderstandings. One of his friends criticized his best poem, saying that he did not understand anything but the title, "Negu" (Winter), and he did not wish to waste his time reading any more of it (*Euzkadi*, 8 May 1930). Even today there are critics who do not join in the general praise of Lizardi's poetry: "hari buruz esandako gehienek harropuzkeriak baino ez direla" (The majority of things said about his poetry are nothing but fanfare; Josu Landa, *Gerraondoko poesiaren historia* [Donostia: Elkar, 1983], 15.).

8. Lizardi's literary production was rather scant. In addition to this book of poetry, there is a book of prose, *Itz-lauz*, three plays, and more than one hundred newspaper articles.

9. Luis Mari Mujika, *Lizardi-ren lirika bideak* (San Sebastián: Haranburu, 1983), 1:22.

10. *Euzkadi*, 11-16 Feb. 1930.

11. José Mari "Lizardi" Agirre, *Biotz-begietan* (Bilbao: Verdes, 1932), 162.

12. *Euzkadi*, 25 Sept. 1930.

13. Ibid., 27 March 1932.

14. The poet's initial attempts can be seen in the poems published in the magazine *Karmel*, nos. 180, 181, and 183 (1987), under the title "Lizardi-ren gaztetako olerkiak." He used the pseudonyms "Zarautz'ar Sabin" and "Samaiko Zulo" for these poems.

15. In addition to taking part in several poetry competitions, he helped organize literary festivals and events in support of the Basque language, such as the "III Day of the Basque Language" (1929) celebrated in Andoain in honor of Manuel Larramendi. He also took part in the "I Day of Basque Poetry" (1930) in Errenteria and in the "II Day of the Basque Child" (1930) in Segura.

16. Agirre, *Biotz-begietan*, 193.

17. Agirre, *Euzkadi*, 8 May 1930.

18. José Mari "Lizardi" Agirre, *Itz-lauz* (San Sebastián: Euskaltzaleak, 1934), 58.

19. Lizardi, *Euzkadi*, 13 June 1929.

20. Ibid., 9 Oct. 1927.

21. Lizardi, *El Día*, 5 June 1930.

22. Bonifacio de Etxegarai branded him "odol-berotxo, bazternastalle, eztabaidakari alperrikako, arroxko ta artobero" (hot-blooded, self-involved, pointlessly argumentative, a bit presumptuous, and conceited; *El Día*, 12 Nov. 1930).

23. Aitzol, *Euzkadi*, 6 Jan. 1935.

24. Agirre, *Itz-lauz,* 100-101.

25. Agirre, *Biotz-begietan,* 46-48.

26. Ibid., 84.

27. Ibid.

28. Ibid., 88.

29. Ibid., xxiv.

30. Ibid., 134.

31. Ibid., 134.

32. Ibid., 136.

33. Miguel de Unamuno, *Obras completas* (Madrid: Afrodisio Aguado, 1958), 6:334-36.

34. Ibid., 6:335.

35. Agirre, *Itz-lauz,* 102-3.

36. Agirre, *Biotz-begietan,* 64.

37. Lizardi to Jokin Zaitegi, 10 Dec. 1932. This letter is housed in the Euskaltzaindia library in Bilbo. I obtained a copy with help from assistant librarian José Antonio Arana Martija.

38. Koldo Mitxelena, "Biotz-Begietan. Olerkiak (Poesías vascas con traducción castellana)" *Egan* 2 (1956): 84.

39. Lizardi, *Euzkadi,* 30 December 1931.

40. There has been much discussion about the literary influences in Lizardi's work. This is perhaps the most hidden aspect of his work. There is evidence that his personal library was very small (Nicolás "Orixe" Ormaetxea, "Orixe," *Olerti* 1-2 [1963]: 109). Lizardi was never affected by foreign literary trends, as was Lauaxeta. On the other hand, we do observe in his poetry some influence of the classical poetic rules defended by Oihenart and Arana y Goiri, such as the manner in which synaloephas are handled and the correspondence between phonetic and semantic unity.

Chapter Eight. Esteban Urkiaga, Alias "Lauaxeta" (1905-1937): *A Modern Poet of the Pre-Civil War Period*

1. Among the books I should mention are *Olerki guztiak* (Bilbao: S. Onaindia, 1985) by Onaindia and two books by Jon Kortazar, *Olerkiak* (Donostia: Erein, 1985) and *Teoría y práctica poética de Lauaxeta* (Bilbo: Desclée de Brouwer, 1986), taken from his doctoral thesis, "Teoría y práctica de Esteban Urkiaga, Lauaxeta."

2. It is likely he was convinced that he was not good enough to be a Jesuit. In any case, there is no allusion to this problem in his writings. His decision to leave apparently was not traumatic.

3. The pseudonym Lauaxeta (Place of Four Winds) was undoubtedly inspired by his parents' wind-battered house in Mungia.

4. Esteban "Lauaxeta" Urkiaga, *Olerkiak* (San Sebastián: Etor, 1974), 95.

5. Esteban "Lauaxeta" Urkiaga, "Lauaxetaren azken eskribuak" *Anaitasuna* (June 1977): 43.

6. García Lorca was assassinated by Franco's forces on August 19, 1936.

7. Lauaxeta accepted violence only as a defensive weapon. During the Civil War he took up arms because he believed it was the duty of every Basque to defend his country against enemy attack.

8. Aitzol was the soul of the Basque cultural renaissance that took place in the first third of the twentieth century in the Basque Country, especially Gipuzkoa. See chapter 5 for a discussion of his life and work.

9. Luis de Castresana, *Vida y obra de Iparraguirre* (Bilbao: Editorial La Gran Enciclopedia Vasca, 1971), 256-58.

10. Ibid., 256.

11. Lauaxeta, *Euzkadi,* 10 Oct. 1933.

12. Orixe, "Bide barrijak," *Euzkadi,* Nov. 1931.

13. Lauaxeta, *Euzkadi,* 16 Nov. 1933, 8.

14. Jon Kortazar, *Teoría y práctica poética de Lauaxeta* (Bilbao: Desclée de Brouwer, 1986), 87.

15. Luis Cernuda, *Estudios sobre poesía española contemporánea* (Madrid: Ed. Guadarrama, 1957), 121.

16. Kortazar, *Teoría y práctica poética de Lauaxeta,* 108.

17. Federico García Lorca, *Obras completas* (Madrid: Aguilar, 1967), 425-26.

18. Ibid., 454.

19. He wrote a great deal of prose as a journalist and also wrote short plays.

20. Esteban "Lauaxeta" Urkiaga, "Eztabaida," in *Azalpenak,* ed. Jon Kortazar (Bilbao: Labayru, 1982), 121.

21. Lizardi, "Rumbos Nuevos," *Euzkadi,* Dec. 1931.

22. Urkiaga, *Olerki guztiak,* 236-37.

23. Ibid., 136.

24. Ibid., 156.

25. Ibid., 400-408.

26. Ibid., 110-12.

27. Bernardo Estornés Lasas, *Enciclopedia general ilustrada del País Vasco. Cuerpo B. Arte, lengua y literatura* (Vitoria-Gasteiz: n.p., n.d.), 5:248.

28. Lauaxeta, *Olerki guztiak,* 236-37.

29. García Lorca, *Obras completas,* 453-57.

30. Urkiaga, *Olerki guztiak,* 295.

31. Ibid., 294.

32. Ibid., 314.

33. Ibid.

34. Ibid., 244.

35. Ibid., 248.

36. Ibid., 278.

Chapter Nine. Salbatore Mitxelena and Bitoriano Gandiaga:
The Franciscan School

1. Inurritza is the name of the valley where the poet's farmhouse, which was demolished to make way for a highway, was located.

2. Salbatore Mitxelena, *Idazlan guztiak,* 2 vols. (Arantzazu-Oñati: Jakin, 1977), 1:122.

3. Ibid., 62.

4. Ibid., 121.

5. Ibid., 2:260.

6. Ibid., 1:67.

7. The *kopla zaharrak* are short verses that contain two rhymes, three at most. These verses are accompanied by Basque musical instruments. Logical and rational unity is usually missing. The images in this type of poetry have great strength, and imagination and sentiment play a very important role.

8. Mitxelena, *Idazlan guztiak,* 2:249, song 9.

9. "Bizi nai" appeared in *Euzko Gogoa* (May–Dec. 1955): 66–75. Mitxelena won a competition organized by Zaitegi for publication in this magazine.

10. Mitxelena, *Idazlan guztiak,* 2:11.

11. Ibid., 176.

12. Ibid., 286.

13. Ibid., 258.

14. Ibid.

15. Ibid., 286.

16. Ibid., 256.

17. Ibid., 307.

18. Ibid., 1:247.

19. Ibid., 233. The Agotes were a small ethnic group of unknown origin, different from the Basques. They settled in Navarre and led a rather isolated life.

20. Ibid., 431.

21. Xabier Lizardi, *Olerkiak* (San Sebastián: Erein, 1983), 169; Mitxelena, *Idazlan guztiak,* 1:375.

22. Mitxelena, *Idazlan guztiak,* 1:379.

23. Lizardi, *Olerkiak,* 129.

24. On the basis of some sermons that he was preaching in the parish of Saint Andrew in Eibar, Gipuzkoa, Mitxelena was denounced to the Francoist authorities.

25. Bitoriano Gandiaga, *Elorri* (Arantzazu and Oñati: Ed. Franciscana, 1962), 24.

26. Ibid., 84.

27. Gabriel Aresti, *Obra Guztiak: Poemak I* (Donostia: Kriselu, 1976), 466.

28. On rare occasions, he sent poems to Onaindia to be published. Two of them won prizes in the Carmelite convent of Larrea, in Zornotza, Bizkaia: "Argi oneko poema" in 1963 and "Gaztainadi" in 1969.

29. Gandiaga, *Elorri,* 128.

30. Bitoriano Gandiaga, *Hiru gizon bakarka* (Bilbao: Gero, 1974), 18.

31. See the *Pacem in Terris* in Catholic Church, *Seven Great Encyclicals* (Glen Rock, N.J.: Paulist Press, 1963) and the conciliary document *Gaudium et Spes* in Angel Herrera Oria, ed., *Concilio Vaticano II* (Madrid: La Editorial Católica, 1968).

32. Gandiaga, *Elorri,* 64. Gabriel Aresti wrote *Harri eta herri* (Zarautz: Itxaropena Argitaldaria, 1964), and Xabier Lete wrote *Egunetik egunera orduen gurpilean. Poemak* (Bilbao: Cinsa 101, 1968). Gandiaga's value is especially high if we keep in mind his age when he wrote *Elorri.* Most of it was completed during the years he was studying theology, or when he was between twenty and twenty-four years old.

33. In the four books that he has written since *Elorri,* he uses Unified Basque.

34. Gandiaga, *Hiru gizon bakarka,* 18.

35. Ibid., 98.

36. Ibid., 133.

37. Bitoriano Gandiaga, *Gabon dut anuntzio,* (Arantzazu and Oñati: Ed. Franciscana Arantzazu, 1986), 111.

38. Ibid., 16.

Chapter Ten. Jon Mirande: *A Nonconformist Writer*

1. Among the best studies on Jon Mirande are three articles by Andolin Eguzkitza in *Saioak,* Joxe Azurmendi's *Mirande eta kristautasuna* (San Sebastián: Caja de Ahorros Provincial de Guipúzcoa, 1978), and two volumes by the Basque critic Mujika, *Mirande-ren poesigintza.*

2. The majority of those who knew Mirande are sure that his death was a suicide. Etxaide, an intimate friend, is not so sure, however, and has pointed out the excessive number of sleeping pills that Mirande, who suffered from insomnia, used as a possible cause of accidental death. *Habe* 40 (April 1984): 8.

3. In Hegoalde many consider Aresti to be the pioneer of modern Basque poetry, especially for "Maldan behera (Miren eta Joaneren historiaren bukaera)," beautiful but difficult poetry published in *Euskera* 5 (1960): 189–234. Mirande, however, was using the modern techniques employed by Aresti a few years earlier.

4. Although Etxaide affirms that Mirande's first language was Basque (*Zeruko argia,* 519 [1973]: 7), it seems more likely that it was not. According to Txomin Peillen, Mirande's Basque was not very good in 1947. Furthermore, his family environment in Paris was not ideal for learning Basque. The poet's sister, after spending a few years in Zuberoa, denied having spoken Basque with her relatives. *Jon Mirande-ren idazlan hautatuak* (Bilbao: Gero, 1976), 12–13.

5. On one occasion, the poet had trouble with the French employees be-

cause he spoke Basque on the telephone with Txomin Peillen. The suffocating atmosphere of this job is reflected in the poem "Paris-Beuret." He describes the atmosphere in the Finance Ministry: "Bai naute maite nola deabruak Jainkoa" (They love me the way the devil loves God). Mirande, *Poemak, 1950–1966* (Donostia: Erein, 1984), 69.

6. In spite of knowing so many languages, Mirande habitually wrote only in Basque and in the Celtic tongues. Peillen, *Jon Mirande-ren idazlan hautatuak,* 20.

7. The influence of Arana y Goiri on Basque language and literature was remarkable. He intended for Basque to be pure, without a trace of "lenguas erdéricas" (foreign languages). Many of the best Basque writers were influenced by him, including Lauaxeta, Lizardi, Orixe, Zaitegi, and Ibinagabeitia.

8. The Basque writers who had the greatest influence on this reform movement and on the expansion of the Unified Basque language were Koldo Mitxelena, Txillardegi, Aresti, Villasante, Krutwig, and Xavier Kintana.

9. The majority of modern writers find it difficult to use the classicist Axular's perfect syntax. The effect is similar to what would happen if twentieth-century Spaniards tried to write in the style of Cervantes. The problem is in achieving a beautiful yet spontaneous style. As Koldo Mitxelena says, "Gauzak ederki kontatzen dakien jendea lortu behar da" (We must find people who narrate events in a beautiful manner), *Habe* 45 (June 15, 1984): 6. Unfortunately, some Basque writers lack fluency and elegance. They write as if a corset were pinching them. According to Arantza Urretabizkaia, a supporter of Unified Basque, Axular's writing was taken to be the bible of Basque syntax, and the result was a Basque language that was artificial and difficult. *Deia* (18 Nov. 1981): 11.

10. Mirande and Peillen founded the much-imitated review *Igela* in Paris. Its nonconformist ideology, considered iconoclastic at the time, prevented them from publishing more than a few issues. They were never forgiven for the fact that *Igela* was not a "frog" from "holy water."

11. Euskaltzaindia was founded in 1919. The first attempts to create such an organization took place during the final years of the nineteenth century. In one of the Academy's first sessions, rules for spelling were outlined, but no agreement was reached with regard to the creation of a unified literary language. After many arguments, and in fewer than twenty years, the Academy accomplished for the Basque language what has taken other nations centuries to achieve: literary unification.

12. Seeing the limitations imposed on the ikastolak by even the Socialist government of François Mitterrand, we must admit that Mirande was not wrong. Paris has always considered Iparralde, especially the coast, to be an ideal location for tourism. Folkloric expression is encouraged because it attracts tourists.

13. In spite of his differences with the separatist movement Euskadi Ta

Askatasuna (ETA), caused in large measure by the influence of Marxism, Mirande was a pioneer in accepting the idea of violence. Some of the words he used against his Basque enemies (such as *eho,* to grind) are proof of that.

14. *Mirande-ren poesigintza,* 1:56.

15. Jon Etxaide, "Jon Etxaide: Idazle kontentagaitzaren tristura," *Habe* 40 (April 1984): 9.

16. Mujika, *Mirande-ren poesigintza,* 1:50.

17. Txillardegi, *Zeruko argia* (Feb. 25, 1973): 3.

18. *Jon Mirande-ren idazlan hautatuak,* 16.

19. The exact date of his death is not known. It was probably December 25, 1972. Two weeks later a friend, Gascon Tauriac, found the poet's decomposing body. Mirande was living alone at the time.

20. "Ohiko Jainkoari," in *Mirande poesigintza,,* 2:194.

21. *Mirande-ren eta Kristautasuna,* 19.

22. *Mirande-ren poesigintza,* 2:195.

23. Ibid.

24. Mirande, *Gernika* 23 (April–June 1953): 86.

25. Ortzi is a mythological character representing the ancient sun god; Basajaun is the Basque mythological character who lived like a lord in the forest; Lamia is a Basque mythological character related to witches and druids; Mari of Anboto, a Basque mythological character, is a witch who lived in the cave on the mountain of Anboto, Bizkaia.

26. "Euskaldun zintzoen blada," in *Mirande-ren poesigintza,* 2:171.

27. *Jon Mirande-ren idazlan hautatuak,* 54.

28. Mirande, "Euskaldungoaren etsaiak," *Gernika* 23 (April–June 1953): 85–87.

29. Mirande to Extaide, *Saioak* 3 (1979): 238.

30. *Mirande-ren poesigintza,* 1:120.

31. During a tribute by the Catalonians and the French to L. Companys, the assassinated president of the Catalonian Generalitat, Mirande called the French "assassins" because of their government's collaboration with the Gestapo and with Franco. When everyone stood up to sing the "Marseillaise," Mirande remained seated. He scorned the French tricolor, calling it an *ipurzapia* (cloth for wiping one's bottom.) His reaction was similar to that of Basques from Hegoalde. At one Aberri Eguna (the Basque Country national holiday) celebration, he began shouting hurray for Franco and Spain to demonstrate his nonconformity with the upright and democratic Basques present at that patriotic gathering (*Jon Mirande-ren idazlan hautatuak,* 278–79).

32. Mirande encountered difficulties in publishing some of his poems and his novel *Haur besoetakoa* (Donostia: Lur, 1970). The latter was published in 1970, long after he had completed it. By that time, he felt deceived, and not even the publication of his novel could lift his spirits. He even had problems with Koldo Mitxelena, director of the magazine *Egan,* when he tried to publish a poem in that review: "*Egan*'en ez dutelako nai izan

ene idazlan bat publikatu, aski konformista ez zelako noski" (They did not want to publish my writing in *Egan*, because it was not sufficiently conformist). *Saioak* 3 (1979): 234.

33. *Mirande-ren poesigintza*, 1:34, from a letter written to Tauer from Paris on February 9, 1970.

34. *Jon Mirande-ren idazlan hautatuak*, 362.

35. *Mirande-ren poesigintza*, 2:171.

36. Ibid., 1:51, from a letter written to Tauer on August 21, 1995.

37. Ibid., 1:55.

38. In 1953 the Franciscan I. Berriatua founded the review *Anaitasuna* as a monthly publication. In 1968 it was a biweekly publication and was edited in Bilbo. It ceased publication in 1980. *Anaitasuna* 8 (1971) 15:5.

39. *Mirande-ren idazlan hautatuak*, 23.

40. When the "Goncourt" literary prize was awarded to the Romanian Vintila Horia for *Dieu est né en exil*, it was subsequently withdrawn because of pressure exerted by French Jews. Mirande did not accept the withdrawal and wrote a short article condemning the award (*Egan* 13 [1960]: 237–39.). A reader named Aginaga condemned his anti-Semitic position in *Egan* (no. 13 [1961]: 69) the following year. This provoked a harsh reaction from Mirande, who complained that no one had defended him against the lies Aginaga spouted about his Basque "Nazi" ideas.

41. Mirande, *Saioak* 3 (1979): 240.

42. *Gure Herria* 44 (1972): 281.

43. Arrue, "Cuatro poetas vascos actuales" (Iratzeder, Mirande, Gandiaga, and Aresti), *Euskera* 8–9 (1963–1964): 189.

44. Mirande,"Olerkariarenean," *Gernika*, 23 (Apr.–June 1953): 100.

45. Among some of the best modern poets, I should point out Gandiaga, Juan Mari Lekuona, Mikel Lasa, Lete, Joxean Arce, Koldo Izagirre, Sarrionandia, and Bernardo Atxaga.

46. *Haur besoetakoa*, 104.

47. Ibid., 6.

48. The first Basque novel to use modern techniques and to deal with the modern concept of time was written in 1969 by Ramón Saizarbitoria, *Egunero hasten delako* (Donostia: Hordago, 1969). A review of this novel can be found in *World Literature Today* 58, 4 (autumn 1984): 645.

49. *Haur besoetakoa*, 63.

50. Ibid., 8.

51. Ibid., 102.

52. Today some bertsolariak touch on love themes in a crude fashion. See Amuriza-Peñagarikano in *Bertsolari txapelketa 1982* (Bilbo: Euskaltzaindia, 1983), 170–72.

53. *Haur besoetakoa*, 18–19.

54. Ibid., 55.

55. Mirande, "Neskutxak" *Gernika* 16 (July–Sept. 1951): 43.

56. Mirande, "Amsterdameko orhoitzapen bat," *Egan* 12 (1959): 121–22.

57. Mirande, *Poemak, 1950–1966,* 124.

58. Ibid., 82.

59. *Olerkiak 1545. Bernat Dechepare,* 104: "Munduian ezta gauzarik // hain eder ez plazentik, // nola emaztia gizonaren // petik buluzkorririk (There is nothing more beautiful and pleasing in the world than a naked woman beneath a man).

60. *Mirande-ren poesigintza,* 2:196.

61. Unfortunately, the original Basque version of this essay has been lost. There exists a French translation, which has been translated into Basque by Peillen.

62. Jon Mirande, "Eder bati," in *Ene Jainko-eidol zaharra, lur!* (Donostia: Elkar, 1984), 61–62.

63. "Olerkariarenean," *Gernika* 23 (April–June 1953): 100.

64. *Mirande-ren poesigintza,* 2:194.

65. *Mirande-ren idazlan hautatuak,* 363.

66. Ibid., 365–66.

67. "Kattalin," *Mirande-ren poesigintza,* 2:190.

68. Mirande, "Nil igitur mors est," *Egan* 1 (1952): 13–14.

69. Krutwig, *Euzko-gogoa* 5–6 (1952): 1.

70. Mirande, "Zakur hil bati XX," in *Poemak, 1950–1966* (Donostia: Erein, 1984), 103. Black humor is also found in Mirande's "Ametsa," *Gernika* 19 (April–June 1951): 106–9, and in "Maitarien ardoa, "*Euzko-gogoa* 7 (1956): 16.

71. *Ene Jainko-eidol zaharra, lur!* (Donostia: Elkar, 1984), 82.

72. *Haur besoetakoa,* 109.

73. *Mirande-ren poesigintza,* 2:166. Telesforo Monzón, an advocate of independence and a Basque writer, wrote a famous poem called "Batasuna," which was later made into a song. It is curious that in his poem, the wolf (*otso*) is used to represent the enemy from whom the shepherd (the Basque people) must defend his flock (Euskal Herria) with his staff. In Mirande's work, the wolf is the Basque who must grind the bones of his enemies between his teeth.

74. While Larramendi, Astarloa, and nineteenth-century writers composed apologia in defense of Euskara in Spanish, Mirande preferred to demonstrate the excellence of the Basque language by writing in Basque. Mirande, "Olekariarenean," *Gernika* 23 (April–June 1953): 98–102.

75. "Kattalin," *Mirande-ren poesigintza,* 2:190.

76. "Gabon-abestia," in S. Onaindía, *Milla Euskal-olerki eder* (Amorebieta: n.p., 1954), 2:676.

Chapter Eleven. Gabriel Aresti: *The Poetry of a Fighter*

1. Gabriel Aresti, *Gabriel Arestiren literatur lanak,* vol. 2 (Bilbao: Susa, 1986), 2:67.

2. Gabriel Aresti, *Obra guztiak. Poemak II* (Bilbao: Kriselu, 1976), 464.

3. Gabriel Aresti, *Obra guztiak. Poemak I* (Bilbao: Kriselu, 1976), 454.

4. For example, "Gehientasun haundiari," "Eskatzen dut bakea eta hitza," "Biotz-begietan," "Majoria haundiarekin," and "Bigarrenez Gabriel Zelaiarekin."

5. Blas de Otero, "On the death of my good friend, the Basque poet Gabriel Aresti," *Poesía con nombres* (Madrid: Alianza Editorial, 1977), 92.

6. Fernando "Xalbador" Aire, *Odolaren mintzoa* (Tolosa: Auspoa, 1976), 83. The bertsolari from Urepel speaks of "Izana eta izena" (The being and the name).

7. Gabriel Aresti, "Nire aitaren etxea defendituko dut" (I will defend my father's house), *in Poemak I*, 466–68.

8. Aresti, *Poemak II*, 92.

9. Aresti, *Gabriel Arestiren literatur lanak*, 2:79.

10. Ibid., 205.

11. Ibid., 93.

12. Otero was very fond of the language of his ancestors, but he did not write in Basque because he never mastered it.

13. Aresti, *Gabriel Arestiren literatur lanak*, 2:21.

14. Aresti, *Poemak I*, 492.

15. Aresti, *Poemak II*, 400.

16. Koldo Mitxelena, "Miscelánea filológica vasca [II]," *Fontes Linguae Vasconum*, 30 (Sept.-Dec.): 407. Originally, this phrase was coined by Ibon Sarasola, and later on Koldo Mitxelena adopted it.

17. Aresti, *Poemak I*, 118–77.

18. Nazim Hikmet spoke out in favor of the independence of his country, Turkey, between 1919 and 1923. The Basque Aresti and the Turk Hikmet had many things in common: Marxism, use of poetry as a weapon, concern for the working classes, the alienation of humankind, exaltation of popular poetry, free verse, and the use of their respective languages as poetic themes.

Tomás de Meabe (1879–1915) was born in Bilbo. As an adolescent he was a fervent Catholic and an enthusiast of Basque nationalism, but he turned to socialism and distinguished himself for his anticlerical and antinationalist campaigns. He was an ardent polemicist with an ironic, fiery style. He wrote a great deal as a journalist, and he also wrote fables, some of which are preserved in *Fábulas del errabundo* (Madrid: Leviatan, n.d.).

Gabriel Celaya (1911–1991) was born in Hernani, Gipuzkoa. He finished his studies in industrial engineering in 1935, but personal inclination led him to writing books of poetry. In Celaya's opinion, a poet was a man first, and as such he was responsible both to his own conscience and to his peers.

19. Aresti, *Gabriel Arestiren literatur lanak*, 2:109.

20. Ibid., 75.

21. Ibid., 41.

22. Mitxelena, "Miscelánea filológica vasca," 413.

Chapter Twelve. Juan Mari Lekuona: *A Bridge Between*
Cultured Poetry and Popular Literature

1. Juan Mari Lekuona, *Ideario ascético-pastoral de Fray Bartolomé de los Mártires O.P. (1515–1590)* (Gasteiz: Eset, 1968); Juan Mari Lekuona, *Mindura Gaur* (Donostia: Ed. Seminario de San Sebastián, 1966); Juan Mari Lekuona, *Muga Beroak* (Bilbao: Ed. Mensajero and Gero, 1973); Juan Mari Lekuona, *Ilargiaren Eskolan* (Donostia: Erein, 1979); Juan Mari Lekuona, *Ahozko Euskal Literatura,* (Donostia: Erein, 1982); Juan Mari Lekuona, *Mimodramak eta Ikonoak* (Donostia: Erein, 1990).

2. In addition to Iñarra, Manuel Lekuona, and Juan Mari Lekuona, I should also mention Martín Lekuona (1908–1936) (brother of Manuel) and two brothers of Juan Mari, Andoni (b. 1932) and Julián (b. 1938), both known in the fields of Basque literature and Basque music.

3. Euskaltzaindia. *El libro blanco del euskara. Basque* (Bilbao: Real Academic Española de la Lengua Vasca, 1977), 11.

4. For an explanation of bertso-paperak, see Aulestia, *Improvisational Poetry from the Basque Country* (Reno: University of Nevada Press, 1995), 53–54.

5. Franco Manca, "Battista Guarini," in *Critical Survey of Drama* ed. Frank Magill (Englewood Cliffs, N.J.: Salem Press, 1985), 841–48. This statement by Juan Mari Lekuona agrees with Manca's ideas on the pastorale in Italy.

6. Juan Mari Lekuona, "Oralidad y poesía," in *Euskaldunak. La etnia vasca,* ed. Enrique Ayerbe (Donostia: Etor, 1985), 5:135.

7. This lecture was given in Basque under the title "Herri-lirika XVIII. Mendean" at the Second World Basque Congress, held in Gasteiz, October 5–9, 1987.

8. For an explanation of 8 *txikia,* see Aulestia, *Improvisational Poetry from the Basque Country,* 24.

9. Lekuona's four other prologues appear in the following books: Joxe Manuel Arriola, *Nekez bada ere* (Arrasate: Euskalgraf, 1981); Inaxiomari Atxukarro, *Irriparrezko printzak* (Donostia: Sendoa, 1982); Zaldubi et al., *Bapatean 89* (Donostia: Elkar, 1989); and Gorka Aulestia, *Bertsolarismo* (Bilbao: Diputación Foral de Bizkaia, 1990).

Chapter Thirteen. Marcel Jousse and Manuel Lekuona:
Two Pioneers of Oral Literature

1. Originally published in Spanish in *Revista Internacional de los Estudios Vascos,* year 42, vol. 39, no. 1 (1994): 27–40. Dedicated to Manuel Lekuona on the hundredth anniversary of his birth.

2. Rodney Gallop, *A Book of the Basques* (London: Macmillan, 1930), 109.

3. Marcel Jousse, *Le style oral rythmique et mnémotechnique chez les verbomoteurs* (Paris: Gabriel Beauchesne, 1925), 20.

4. Marcel Jousse, *L'Anthropologie du geste* (Paris: Gallimard, 1981), 17.

5. Jousse, *Le style oral,* 20.

6. Ibid.

7. Ibid., 73.

8. Ibid., 24.

9. Manuel Lekuona, *Idaz-lan guztiak,* vol. 1: *Ahozko Literatura* (Tolosa: Librería Técnica de la Difusión, 1978), 1:153.

10. Ibid., 8:368.

11. Ibid., 1:197.

12. Ibid., 205.

13. In 1928 the International Congress on Popular Art was held in Prague. In the Basque Country the public attitude toward the bertsolari was changing. The works of Makazaga, reprinted in *Bertsolariya* (Rentería: Eusko Bib., 1931–1932), *Otaño Pedro M^a. Olerki Onenak Alkar* (Donostia: Iñaki Deuna, 1930), and the works of Lekuona all played an influential role in Aitzol's shift toward a greater appreciation of bertsolaritza and helped the public attitude change as well.

14. Lekuona, *Idaz-lan guztiak,* 1:266. In the opinion of oralist and poet Juan Mari Lekuona, his uncle Manuel became familiar with Jousse's book through Gasteiz native Jesús Enciso Viana, his companion in the seminary and later the bishop of Ciudad Rodrigo and Palma in Majorca. Enciso attained the title of doctor of theology at the Gregorian University in Rome, and there he discovered the work of Marcel Jousse.

BIBLIOGRAPHY

Agirre, José Mari "Lizardi." *Biotz-begietan.* Bilbao: Verdes, 1932 (2nd ed. Zarautz: Itxaropena, 1970).

———. *Itz-lauz.* San Sebastián: Euskaltzaleak, 1934.

———. *Kazetari-lanak.* Donostia: Erein, 1987.

———. *Olerkiak.* San Sebastián: Erein, 1983.

Aguirre, Domingo. *Garoa.* Donostia: Euskaltzaleak, 1935.

Aire, Fernando "Xalbador." *Odolaren mintzoa.* Zarautz: Auspoa, 1976.

Aitzol. *See* Aristimuño, José.

Altuna, Francisco M. *Etxepareren hiztegia.* Bilbao: Mensajero, 1979.

———. *Mitxelenaren idazlan hautatuak.* Bilbao: Etor, 1972.

———. *Versificación de Dechepare.* Bilbao: Mensajero, 1979.

Amenabar, Joan, ed. *Euskal poesia kultoaren bilduma.* 2 vols. Donostia: Elkar, 1983.

Amuriza, Xabier. *Menditik mundura.* Bilbao: Printzen, 1977.

Arana y Goiri, Sabino. *Obras completas.* Buenos Aires: Ekin, 1965.

Aranalde, Joxe Mari. *Xalbador Pertsularia.* Oiartzun: Sendoa, 1996.

Aresti, Gabriel. *Gabriel Arestieren literatur lanak.* Vol. 2. Bilbao: Susa, 1986.

———. *Harri eta herri.* Zarautz: Itxaropena Argitaldaria, 1964.

———. *Obra guztiak. Poemak I.* Donostia: Kriselu, 1976.

———. *Obra guztiak. Poemak II.* Donostia: Kriselu, 1976.

Aristimuño, José "Aitzol." *La democracia en Euzkadi.* Donostia: Itxaropena, 1935.

———. *Idaz-lan guztiak. Obras completas.* 6 vols. Donostia: Erein, 1988.

———. *Lucha de idiomas en Euzkadi y en Europa.* Donostia: Euskaltzeak, 1935.

———. "La muerte del euskera o los profetas de mal agüero." El Día (Donostia). 1921. November.

———. "El poeta José Maria Aguirre. Xabier Lizardi." *Yakintza* 3 (1933): 163-77.

———. "El primer renacentista y poeta euskaldun." *Yakintza* 1 (1933): 12-20.

Arrue, Antonio. "Cuatro poetas vascos actuales." *Euskera* nos. 8-9 (1963-1964): 179-98.

Ataun, Bonifacio de. "Linguae vasconum primitiae." *Boletín del Instituto Americano de Estudios Vascos* 6 (1955): 115-27.

Atxaga, Bernardo. *Etiopia.* Bilbao, Hauzoa, 1978.

———. *Ziutateaz.* Donostia: Kriselu, 1976.

Aulestia, Gorka. *Bertsolarismo.* Bilbao: Diputación Foral de Bizkaia, 1990.

————. "Breve historia del bertsolarismo." In *Los escritores,* edited by Gorka Aulestia, 15–82. Vitoria: Fundación "Caja Vital Kutxa," 1996.

————. "Dos poetas pioneros: 'Lauaxeta' y Jon Mirande." In *Congreso de Literatura,* edited by Jesús María Lasagabaster, 255–70. Madrid: Castalia, 1989.

————, ed. *Los Escritores vascos.* Vitoria: Fundación "Caja Vital Kutxa," 1996.

————. *Improvisational Poetry from the Basque Country.* Reno: University of Nevada Press, 1995.

Ayerra, Marino. *No me avergoncé del evangelio.* Bilbao: Amado, 1978.

Azkue, Resurreccíon María de. *Cancionero popular del País Vasco.* Vol. 1. Bilbao: Auñamendi, 1968.

Azurmendi, Joxe. *Mirande eta kristautasuna.* Donostia: Caja de Ahorros Provincial de Guipúzcoa, 1978.

————. "Miranderen kritika iraultza Frantsesari." *Jakin* 52 (1989): 69–87.

————. "Miranderen kritika iraultza Frantsesari." *Jakin* 53 (1989): 81–114.

————. *Schopenhauer, Nietzsche, Spengler Mirande-ren pentsamenduan.* San Sebastián: Susa, 1989.

————. *Zer dugu Orixe-ren alde?* Oñati: Arantzazu, 1977.

————. *Zer dugu Orixe-ren kontra?* Oñati: Arantzazu, 1976.

Balzola, Francisco. *Argi donea.* Zarautz: Itxaropena, 1932.

Baroja, Pío. *La leyenda de Jaun de Alzate.* Madrid: Caro Raggio, 1922.

Basarri. *See* Eizmendi, Ignacio.

Baudelaire, P. Charles. *Les fleurs du mal.* Paris: Marcel Didier, 1961.

Bertsolari txapelketa 1965–1-1. Tolosa: Auspoa, 1965.

Bertsolari txapelketa 1967. Tolosa: Auspoa, 1967.

Bertsolari txapelketa 1982. Bilbao: Jagon-1, 1983.

Bertsolari txapelketa Nagusia. Tolosa; Auspoa, 1980.

"Bertsolaritza." *Jakin* 14–15 (1980): 6–29.

Bilbao, Jon, and Santiago Onaindia. "Orixe'ren lanak." In *"Orixe" Omenaldi,* edited by Euskaltzaindiaren Ardurapean Argitaratua, 71–85. Donostia: Izarra, 1965.

Bilintx. *See* Bizkarrondo, Indalecio.

Bizkarrondo, Indalecio "Bilintx." *Bertso ta lan guztiak.* Tolosa: Auspoa, 1961.

Breton, André. *Manifeste du surréalisme.* Paris: J. J. Pauvert, n.d.

Casenave, Junes. *Ibañeta.* Oñati-Arantzazu: Jakin, 1978.

————. *Santa Grazi.* Oñati-Arantzazu: Jakin, 1976.

Castresana, Luis de. *Vida y obra de Iparraguirre.* Bilbao: Gran Enciclopedia Vasca, 1971.

Cernuda, Luis. *Estudios sobre poesía española contemporánea.* Madrid: Ed. Guadarrama, 1957.

Chaho, A. *Biarritz entre Les Pyrénées et l'Océan, itinéraire pittoresque.* Baiona: A. Andreossy, 1855.

————. *Voyage en Navarre pendant l'insurrection des Basques (1830–1835).* Baiona: P. Lespés, 1865.

Cortázar, Nicolás de. *Cien autores vascos.* Donostia: Auñamendi. 1966.

Detxepare (Etxepare), Bernat (Bernard). *Olerkiak.* San Sebastián: Txertoa, 1978.

Diharce, Jean "Iratzeder." *Biziaren olerkiak.* Bilbao: Gero, 1983.

Eguzkitza, Andolin. "Jon Mirande elaberrigile: 'Haur besoetakoa'-ren egiturazterketa." *Saioak* (1979): 227-53; (1980): 99-122; (1983): 115-36.

Eizmendi, Ignacio "Basarri." *Kantari nator.* Zarautz: Itxaropena, 1960.

———. *Bertsolaritzari buruz.* Tolosa: Auspoa, 1984.

———. *Laugarren txinpartak.* Tolosa: Auspoa, 1966.

———. *Sortu zaizkidanak.* Tolosa: Auspoa, 1973.

Elentxu. *See* Ibinagabeitia, Andima.

Elizegi, José. *Pello Errotak, jarritako bertsoak: Bere alabaren argibideakin.* Tolosa: Auspoa, 1963.

———. *Pello Errotaren bizitza.* Tolosa: Auspoa, 1963.

Enbeita, Balendin. *Nere apurra.* Tolosa: Auspoa, 1974.

Enbeita, Kepa "Urretxindor." *Bertso-lanak Osorik.* Buenos Aires: Ekin, 1971.

———. *Euskalerriko bertsolarien txapelketa 1960.* Zarautz: Itxaropena, 1961.

Enparantza, José Luis Alvarez "Txillardegi." *Euskal kulturaren zapalketa 1956-1981.* Donostia: Elkar, 1984.

———. "1956-1961: Kultur euskararen bila." *Jakin* 21 (1981): 75-90.

———. *Peru Leartza'ko.* Donostia: Elkar, 1979.

Ercilla, Alonso de. *La araucana.* Madrid: P. Cossio, 1569.

Erzibengoa, Joshe, and Patxi Ezkiaga. *Euskal literatura.* Bilbao: Gero, 1975.

Estornés Lasa, Bernardo. *Encyclopedia general ilustrada del País Vasco.* Vols. 1-5. Donostia: Auñamendi, 1981.

Etxaide, Jon. *Amasei seme Euskalerriko.* Zarautz: Itxaropena, 1958.

Etxaniz, Nemesio. "Unamuno ta Abendats." *Euzko-gogoa* 10 (1959): 110-12.

Etxenagustia, Karmelo. *Euskal idazleen lorategia.* Donostia: Izarra, 1969.

———. *Iparraldeko euskal idazleak.* Bilbao: Labayru, 1981.

Etxenagustia, Karmelo, Jon Kortazar, and Aitor Etxebarria. *Euskal idazleak bizkaieraz: antologia, testu azterketak, ariketak.* Bilbao: Labayru, 1980.

Etxepare, Bernard. *Linguae vasconum primitiae, 1545-1995.* Bilbo: Euskaltzaindia, 1995.

Euskaltzaindia. *El libro blanco del euskara.* Bilbao: Real Academia de la Lengua Vasca, 1977.

———. *Euskalerriko bertsolarien txapelketa (1960).* Zarautz: Itxaropena, 1961.

Euskaltzaindiaren Ardurapean Argitaratua. *"Orixe" omenaldi.* Donostia: Izarra, 1965.

Gandiaga, Bitoriano. *Denbora galdu alde.* Donostia: Erein, 1985.

———. *Elorri.* Arantzazu and Oñati: Ed. Franciscana, 1962.

———. *Gabon dut anuntzio.* Arantzazu and Oñati: Ed. Franciscana Arantzazu, 1986.

———. *Hiru gizon bakarka.* Bilbao: Gero, 1974.

———. *Uda batez Madrilen.* Arantzazu and Oñati: Jakin, 1977.

Garamendi, M. A. *El teatro popular vasco. Semiótica de la representación.* Donostia: Gipuzkoako Foru Aldundia, 1991.

García Lorca, Federico. *Obras completas.* Madrid: Aguilar, 1967.

Garmendia, Jon. "Orixe Euzkaltzain." In *"Orixe" Omenaldi,* edited by Euskaltzaindiaren Ardurapean Argitaratua, 41-44. Donostia: Izarra, 1965.

Garriga, Gabino de. "El léxico del primer libro euskérico." *Boletín del Instituto Americano de Estudios Vascos* 3 (1952): 150-54.

Gil Bera, Eduardo. "Prefacio." In *La ahijada,* edited by Eduardo Gil Bera, 9-78. Iruñea: Pamiela, 1991.

Gullón, Ricardo. *Estudios sobre Juan Ramón Jiménez.* Buenos Aires: Ed. Losada, 1960.

Haritschelhar, Jean. "Bihotz-begietako Euskal Herria Lizardirengan." In *Euskal linguistika eta literatura,* edited by Jose Antonio Artamendi, 369-92. Bilbao: Universidad de Deusto, 1981.

————, ed. *Être Basque.* Toulouse: Privat. 1983.

————. *La pastorale. Théatre populaire basque en Soule.* Baiona: Lauburu, 1987.

Harriton de Alaiza, C. A. "Santa Grazi Pastorala." Ph.D. diss., University of California, Los Angeles, 1978.

Hérelle, Georges. *Le répertoire du théâtre tragique.* Paris: Champion, 1928.

————. "Les Sources de pastorales et la méthode de travail des pastorales." *Gure Herria* 2 (1922): 691-701.

Huarte, José M. de. "Los primitivos del euskera. Dechepare y su tiempo." *Euskalerriaren alde* 271 (1926): 241-46.

Humboldt, Wilhelm von. "Diario del viaje vasco." Trans. Telesforo de Aranzadi. *Revista internacional de estudios vascos* 14, no. 2 (1923): 249.

————. *Guillermo de Humboldt y el país vasco.* San Sebastián: Eusko Ikaskuntza, 1925.

Ibinagabeitia, Andima "Elentxu." "Euzko-gogoa." *Euzko-gogoa* 11-12 (November-December 1950): 52-59.

————. "Jainkoak ekarri nau onera." In *"Orixe" omenaldi,* edited by Euskaltzaindiaren ardurapean argitaratua, 53-59. Donostia: Izarra, 1965.

————. "Olerkariarenean." *Gernika* 23 (April-June 1953): 98-102. Donostia: Izarra, 1965.

————. "Orixe euskeratzaile." In *"Orixe" Omenaldi,* edited by Euskaltzaindiaren Ardurapean Argitaratua, 87-117. Donostia: Izarra, 1965.

Irastorza, Tere. *Hostoak.* Bilbo: Aurrezki-Kutxa, 1983.

Iratzeder. *See* Diharce, Jean.

Irazu, Jose. *See* Atxaga, Bernardo.

Irigaray, Angel. "Mirande olerkaria, haren idaz lanak." *Egan* 32 (1972): 90-93.

Iztueta, Pablo. *"Quito'n Arrebarekin" irakurriz.* Donostia: Etor, 1988.

Jáuregui, Luis. *Xenpelar bertsolaria: Bizitza ta bertsoak.* Zarautz: Itxaropena, 1958.

Jesus'en biotzaren deya (journal). Bilbao: Mensajero del Corazón de Jesús, 1917-1931.

Jiménez, Juan Ramón. *Libros de poesía.* Madrid: Aguilar, 1957.

Jousse, Marcel. *Le style oral rhythmique et mnémotechnique chez les verbo-moteurs.* Paris: Gabriel Beauchesne, 1925.

Juaristi, Jon. *Literatura vasca.* Madrid: Taurus, 1987.

Kortazar, Jon, ed. *Azalpenak.* Bilbao: Labayru, 1982.

———. *Laberintoen oroimena.* San Sebastián: Baroja, 1989.

———. *Literatura vasca. Siglo XX.* Donostia: Etor, 1990.

———, ed. *Olerkiak.* Donostia: Erein, 1985.

———. *Teoría y práctica poética de Lauaxeta.* Bilbao: Desclée de Brouwer, 1986.

Kortazar, Jon, Lurdes Otaegi, Anjel Zelaieta, Juan Mari Lekuona, and Anjel Lertxundi. "Lizardiren Olertia." *Jakin* 29 (October–December 1983): 5-117.

Krutwwig Sagredo, Federico. *Computer shock Vasconia año 2001.* Estella: Lizarra, 1984.

Labayen, Antonio María. "Nicolás Ormaetxea (1888-1961)." In *"Orixe" Omenaldi,* edited by Euskaltzaindiaren Ardurapean Argitaratua, 15-24. Donostia: Izarra, 1965.

———. "Salbatore Mitxelena, gizon eta olerkari." *Aránzazu* 58 (1978): 54-55, 74-76.

Lafitte, Pierre. *Le Basque et la littérature d'expression basque en Labourd, Basse-Navarre et Soule.* Baiona: Aintzina, 1941.

———. *Eskualdunen loretegia.* Baiona: Laserre, n.d.

———. "Lettre ouverte à M. N. Ormaechea." *Gernika* 10 (January–March 1950): 19-20.

Lafon, René. "Etchahoun et Dechepare." *Gure Herria* 34 (1962): 69-73.

———. "La Langue de Bernard Dechepare." *Boletín de la Real Sociedad Vascongada de Amigos del País* 7 (1951): 308-38.

———. "Notes pour une edition critique et une traduction française de *Linguae vasconum primitiae,* de Bernard Dechepare." *Boletín de la Real Sociedad Vascongada de Amigos del País* 7 (1952): 139-80.

———. "Sur la versification de Dechepare." *Boletín de la Real Sociedad Vascongada de Amigos del País* 13 (1957): 387-93.

Lakarra, Joseba, et al. *Euskal Baladak.* 2 vols. Donostia: Hordago, 1983.

Landa, Josu. *Gerraondoko poesiaren historia.* Donostia: Elkar, 1983.

Larrea, Jose María. *Miranderen lan kritikoak.* Iruñea: Pamiela, 1985.

Lasa, Amaia. *Nere paradisuetan.* San Sebastián: Ediciones Vascas, 1979.

Lasarte, Manuel. *Gordean neuzkanak.* Tolosa: Auspoa, 1975.

Leizaola, Jesús María de. *Estudios sobre la poesía vasca.* Buenos Aires: Ekin, 1951.

———. "Gure olerkariak. Mitxelena, erri-abots olerkariya. N. Etxaniz, Iratzeder." *Euzko-gogoa* 7 (May–June 1956): 24-28.

———. "Literatura vasca." In *Enciclopedia Universal Ilustrada Europeo-Americana.* Vol. 21. Barcelona: Espasa, 1923.

———. *Obras completas.* Vol. 1. Donostia: Sendoa, 1981.

Leizaola, Josu M. *"Jainkoaren billa" gutuna zer da?* Baiona: Euskal-Kulturaren Alde, 1973.

Lekuona, Juan Mari. *Ahozko euskal literatura*. Donostia: Erein. 1982.

———. "Ahozko literaturaren historiaz." In *Euskal Herria. Historia eta gizartea,* vol. 1, edited by Lan Kide Aurrezkia, 127-222. Donostia: Lan Kide Aurrezkia, 1985.

———. "Aita Santi Onaindiaren olerkigintza." Foreword in *Olerki guztien bilduma,* edited by Santiago Onaindia, xi-xxvi. Larrea-Zornotza: Karmel Sorta 2, 1989.

———. "Arriolaren bertsozko lana." Foreword in *Nekez bada ere,* by Joxe Manuel Arriola, 15-20. Arrasate: Euskalgraf, 1981.

———. "Atari gisa." Foreword in *Lengo egunak gogoan,* vol. 1, by Manuel "Uztapide" Olaizola, 11-20. Donostia: Auspoa, 1974.

———. "Aurkezpen bat egin asmoz." Foreword in *Irriparrezko printzak,* by Inaxiomari Atxukarro. Donostia: Sendoa, 1982.

———. "Barrutiaren metrikaz." Foreword in *Gabonetako ikuskizuna,* by Pedro Ignacio de Barrutia, 207-27. Gasteiz: Arabako Foru Aldundia, 1983.

———. "Basarriren bertsolari proiektua." *Iker* 6 (1992): 283-96.

———. "Beneditarren eragina euskal liturgia berrian." *Jaunaren Deia* 72/73 (1980): 294-304.

———. "Bertsolariak historian: Sailkapen saioa." *Jakin* 14/15 (1980): 6-15.

———. "Bertsolarien estrofa-motak hegoaldeko usarioan." *Euskera* 27 (1982): 333-59.

———. "Bilintxen bertsogintza." In *A los 100 años de su muerte. Bilintx (1831–1876),* edited by Miguel Pelay Orozco, 166-85. Gasteiz: Eset, 1978.

———. "Bordariren olerki laburrak." Foreword in *Bakoitzak berea,* vol. 2, by Fernando Artola "Bordari," 9-22. Donostia: Sendoa, 1982.

———. "'Elorri,' argitaraldi berrian." Foreword in *Elorri,* by Bitoriano Gandiaga, 7-24. Oñati: Arantzazu, 1989.

———. "Erdi-ahozkotasunaren literatur estiloaz." *Euskera* 34 (1989): 17-51.

———. "Erri literatura. Atsotitzak eta esaerak." Foreword in *Lekuona'tar Manuel Jaunaren omenezko idazki bilduma III,* edited by Juan José Garmendia, 253-58. Gasteiz: Kardaberaz Bilduma 21, 1977.

———. "Euskal erromantzeen atarian." Foreword in *Euskal linguistika eta literatura: Bide berriak,* edited by Universidad de Deusto, 293-319. Bilbao: La Editorial Vizcaina, 1981.

———. "Euskal herriko ahozko literatura." *Albistaria* (UNESCO) 9 (1985): 33.

———. "Euskaltzaindiaren laguntzaileak 1933." *Euskera* 36 (1991): 491-500.

———. "Ezkontzetako eskari-otoitzak bertsotan." *Jaunaren Deia* 78 (1982): 60-68.

———. "Gandiagari omenaldia. Poesiagintza eta kanta gerraostean." *Jakin* 5 (1978): 123-30.

———. "Gipuzkoako herri-ipuin idatziak." *Euskera* 37 (1992): 449-61.

————. "Hemen doa gaur." Foreword in *Hego haizearen konpasean,* by Mikel Arregi, 7-20. Donostia: Kriselu, 1975.

————. "Herri-poesia eta Oteizaren ulerkuntza estetikoa." In *Oteiza esteta y mitologizador vasco,* 3-16. Donostia: Aurrezki-Kutxa Munizipala, 1986.

————. "Hitzaurrea." Foreword in *Euskal alfabetatzeko literatura,* by Enrike Zabala, i-vi. Lazkao: Pax, 1979.

————. "Hitzaurrea." Foreword in *Ibiltari,* by Paulo Iztueta, 5-14. Donostia: Elkar, 1969.

————. "Hitzaurrea." *Jakin* 75 (March–April, 1933): 11-16.

————. "Hitzaurrea." Foreword in *Bertsolarismo,* by Gorka Aulestia, 10-11. Bilbao: Bizkaiko Foru Aldundia, 1990.

————. *Ibilaldia. Itinerario.* Leioa: Universidad del País Vasco, 1996.

————. *Ideario ascético-pastoral de Fray Bartolomé de los Mártires, O.P. (1514-1590).* Gasteiz: Eset, 1968.

————. *Ikaskuntzak euskal literaturaz (1974-1996).* Donostia: Deustuko Unibertsitatea, 1998.

————. *Ilargiaren eskolan.* Donostia: Erein, 1979.

————. "Iparragirre eta bertsolaritza." In *Iparragirre,* edited by Euskaltzaindia, 109-33. Bilbao: Euskaltzaindia, 1987.

————. "Izaera eta ofizio bereziko pertsonaien erretaula 'Euskaldunak' poeman." *Euskera* 34 (1989): 131-52.

————. "Jendaurreko bertsolaritza." *Jakin* 14/15 (1980): 99-113.

————. "Kontapoesiaren modulu metrikoak Hegoaldeko usarioan." *Euskera* 36 (1991): 825-52.

————. "La lírica popular vasca en el siglo XVIII." In *Congreso de literatura,* edited Jesús María Lasagabaster, 495-525. Madrid: Castalia, 1989.

————. "Literatura oral vasca." In *Cultura vasca II,* 59-109. Zarautz: Erein, 1978,

————. "Literatura oral vasca." In *El libro blanco del Euskara,* 155-78. Bilbao: Elkar, 1977.

————. "Lizardiren eskema metrikoak eta puntuak." *Jakin* 29 (1983): 53-88.

————. "Manuel Lasarteren gordairua." *Zeruko Argia* 663 (1975): 8.

————. *Manuel Lekuona Etxabeguren.* Donostia: Eusko Ikaskuntza, 1995.

————. "Manuel Lekuona Etxabeguren (1984-1987)." *Jakin* 45 (October-December 1987): 169-72.

————. "Manuel Lekuona, kulturlari euskalduna." *Euskera* 34 (1988): 45-51.

————. "Manuel Lekuonaren literatur Kreazioa." *Eusko Ikaskuntza Izkuntza eta Literatura* 3 (1984): 115-42.

————. *Mimodramak eta ikonoak.* Donostia: Erein, 1990.

————. *Mindura gaur.* Donostia: Ed. Seminario de San Sebastián, 1966.

————. *Muga beroak.* Bilbao: Ed. Mensajero and Gero, 1973.

————. "Orixeren liturgi olerkiak." In *Memoriae L. Mitxelena Magistri Sacrum,* edited by Joseba Lakarra, 1201-15. Donostia: "Julio de Urkixo" and Euskal Filologi Mintegia, 1991.

———. "Orixeren mistika-lanez oharkizunak." In *Gentza, teologia eta pastoraltza ikastetxea,* 34–44. Donostia: n.p., 1976/1977.

———. "Poesigintza eta Kanta gerraostean." *Jakin* 5 (1978): 123–30.

———. "Salmoen olerki alderdia." *Jaunaren Deia* 48/90 (1974): 149–54.

———. "Sarrera gisa." Foreword in *Zortziko hautsiak,* by Luis M. Mujika, 7–35. Donostia: Ed. Vascas, 1978.

———. "Sarrera modura." In *Uda batez Madrilen,* by Bitoriano Gandiaga, xv–xxix. Arantzazu-Oñati: Jakin, 1977.

———. "Sintesis unean landuriko poemak." Foreword in *Bertso-paper Printzatuak,* by Joxe Austin Arrieta, 9–26. Donostia: Elkar, 1986.

———. "Tankalaren leloa." Foreword in *Jatorriaren Errotik,* by Martin Ugarte, 105–10. Zarautz: Legazpiko Udal Kultur-Etxea, 1986.

———. "Temas y estructuras." *Los cuadernos del norte* (1986): 139–42.

———. "Txirrita eta Basarri: Bi belaunaldien arteko tenka." *Euskara* 20 (1975): 333–39.

———. "Usariozko euskal olerkigintza." In *Euskaldunak. Euskal Etnia,* vol. 5, 127–22. Donostia: Etor, 1988.

———. "Uztapideren bapateko bertsolaritza." *Oiartzun* 14 (1984): 25–27.

———. "Xalbadorren ekarriaz." *Garaia* 12 (November 18, 1976): 38–39.

Lekuona, Manuel. *Idaz-lan guztiak.* Vol. 1. *Ahozko Literatura.* Tolosa: Librería Técnica de la Difusión, 1978.

———. *Literatura oral euskérika.* Donostia: Beñat Idaztiak, 1935.

———. "Paralelo entre la pastoral suletina y el teatro griego." In *Idaz-lan guztiak.* Tolosa: Librería Técnica de la Difusión, 1978.

Lete, Xabier. *Bigarren poema liburua.* Bilbao: Gero, 1974.

———. *Egunetik egunera orduen gurpilean. Poemak* Bilbao: Cinsa, 1968.

———. "Vinculación y desarraigo en la obra literaria de Jon Mirande." *Garaia* 1 (1976): 33–34.

———. *Xabier Lizardi olerkari eta prosista.* Arantzazu: Jakin, 1974.

Liber usualis (Missae et officii). Tournai: Desclée, 1953.

Lizardi. *See* Agirre, José Mari.

Lizardi, Xabier. *Olerkiak.* San Sebastián: Erein, 1983.

Lizarditar, X. (Jabier de Lizardi). *Biotz-begietan.* Zarautz: Itxaropena, 1970.

Lizarralde, Jose Adriano. *Historia de la Virgen y del Santuario de Aránzazu.* Oñati: Ed. Aránzazu, 1950.

Loramendi. *Olerki ta idatzi guziak.* Zarautz: Itxaropena, 1960.

Loti, Pierre. *Ramuntcho.* Paris: Société du Livre d'Art, 1908.

Michel, Francisque. "Bernard d'Echepare." In *Le Pays Basque sa population, sa langue, ses moeurs, sa littérature et sa musique.* Paris: F. Didot, 1857.

———. *Le Pays Basque, sa population, sa langue, ses moeurs, sa littérature et sa musique.* Paris: F. Didot, 1857.

Mirande, Jon. *Ene Jainko-Eidol zaharra, lur!* San Sebastian: Elkar, 1984.

———. *Gauaz Parke Batean.* Donostia: Elkar, 1984.

———. *Haur besoetakoa.* Donostia: Lur, 1970.

———. *Ilhun-argiak.* Claroscuros, Leioa: Euskal Herriko Unibertsitatea, 1992.

———. *Jon Mirande-ren idazlan hautatuak,* Bilbao: Gero, 1976.

———. *Orhoituz.* Donostia: L. Haranburu Altuna, 1976.

———. *Poemak 1950–1966.* Donostia: Erein, 1984.

Mirande, Jon, and Txomin Peillen. *Peillen, Txomin. Igela.* Donostia: Hordago, 1979.

Mistral, Frédéric. *Mirèio. Pouemo Prouvencau.* Paris: Charpentier, 1864.

Mitxelena, Koldo. "Asaba zaarren baratza." *Egan* 17, no. 3–6 (May–December 1960): 121–34.

———. "Biotz-Begietan. Olerkiak (Poesías vascas con traducción castellana)" *Egan* 2 (1956): 84–86.

———. *Historia de la literatura vasca.* Madrid: Minotauro, 1960.

———. "Literatura en Lengua Vasca." In *Historia general de las literaturas hispánicas,* vol. 5, edited by Guillermo Díaz Plaja. Barcelona: Barna 1958.

———. "Miscelánea filológica vasca." *Fontes Linguae Vasconum* 30 (Sept.-Dec.): 389–413.

———. "Orixe'-ren eriotzean." *Egan* 19, no. 4–6 (July–December 1961): 157–63.

———, ed. *Olerkiak 1545.* Bernat Dechepare. San Sebastián: Txertoa, 1978.

Mitxelena, Salbatore. *Idazlan guztiak.* 2 vols. Arantzazu-Oñati: Jakin, 1977.

Moguel, Juan Antonio. *El doctor Peru Abarca catedrático de la lengua bascongada en la Universidad de Basarte o Diálogos entre un rústico solitario bascongado y un barbero llamado Maisu Juan.* Durango: J. de Elizalde, 1981.

Monzón, Telesforo. *Gudarien Egiñak.* In *Hitzak eta idazkiak,* vol. 4, edited by Koldo Izagirre, 93–146. Zarautz: Itxaropena, 1986.

———. *Urrundik.* Mexico City: Ekin, 1945.

Mozos, Iñaki. "Las pastorales." In *Los escritores,* edited by Gorka Aulestia. Vitoria: Fundación "Caja Vital Kutxa," 1996.

Mujika, Luis M. *Historia de la literatura euskerika.* San Sebastián: Haranburu, 1979.

———. "Influentzi aztarna batzuk Lizardiren Lirikan." *Jakin* 25 (1982): 131–51.

———. *Lizardi-ren lirika bideak.* 2 vols. San Sebastián: Haranburu, 1983.

———. *Mirande-ren poesigintza.* San Sebastián: Haranburu, 1984.

Muxika, Gregorio. *Pernando Amezketarra.* Donostia: Iñaki Deunaren Irarkola, 1927.

Oihartzabal, B. *Zuberoako herri teatroa.* Donostia: Haranburu, 1985.

Oihenart, Arnauld. *Art poétique basque.* Bayonne: Gure Herria, 1967.

———. *Les proverbes basques recueillis par le sieur d'Oihenart, plus les poésies basques du même auteur.* Paris: Bibliotheca Colbertina, 1657.

Olabide, Raimundo. *Itun Zâr eta Berria.* Bilbao: Yesu'ren biotzaren Deya, 1958.

Olaizola, Manuel "Uztapide." *Lengo egunak gogoan.* Tolosa: Auspoa, 1974.

———. *Noizbait.* Tolosa: Auspoa, 1964.

————. *Sasoia Joan da gero.* Tolosa: Auspoa, 1976.

Omaechevarria, Ignacio. *Euskera.* Zarautz: Itxaropena. 1959.

Onaindia, Santiago. *Enbeita oleskaria (1878–1942).* Zarautz: Itxaropena, 1966.

————. *Euskal literatura.* 6 vols. Bilbao: Etor, 1972.

————. *Gure bertsolariak.* Bilbao: Gráficas Bilbao, 1964.

————. *Milla euskal-olerki eder.* Zarauz: Karmeldar Idaztiak, 1954.

————. *Olerki Guztiak.* Bilbao: S. Onaindia, 1985.

————. *Olerki guztien bilduma.* Larrea-Zornotza: Karmel, 1989.

Orixe. *See* Ormaetxea, Nicolás.

Ormaetxea, Nicolás. "Agur Guatemalari." *Euzko-gogoa* 9–10 (September-October 1954): 131–32.

————."Aita Mitxelena berrizaleekin." *Euzko-gogoa* 1–2 (January–February, 1952): 23–25.

————. "Aita Urrutia'ri." *Euzko-gogoa* 7–8 (July–August, 1952): 8–10.

————. *Aitorkizunak.* Zarautz: Itxaropena, 1956.

————. *Barne-muinetan.* Zarautz: Itxaropena, 1934.

————. "Bide barrijak." *Euzkadi* (November 1931).

————. "Cultismos, pedantería, barbarie." *Gernika* 22 (January–March, 1953): 14.

————. "Erria, erria!" *Euzko-gogoa* 1–2 (January–February, 1951): 10–12.

————. "Errores de vascólogos nuestros." *Gernika* 10 (January–March, 1950): 15–19.

————. "Eusk, Euskadi." *Euzko-gogoa* 3–4 (March–April, 1951): 34–37.

————. *Euskaldunak. Los vascos.* Bilbao: Auñamendi, 1950. Reprint, Donostia: Auñamendi, 1976.

————. *Euskaldunak poema eta olerki guziak.* San Sebastián: Auñamendi, 1972.

————. "Euskaldun bipilak eta Manchatar bizkorrak izan zuten burrukaldi Lazgarriaren ondarra." *Revista Internacional de Estudios Vascos* 20 (1929): 6–9.

————. "Euskal-literatura'ren atze edo edesti laburra." *Euskalerriaren Alde* 285 (1927): 191–93.

————. "Gizonaren eskubidegai guzietaz aitorkizuna" ("Declaration of Human Rights of the United Nations). *Euzko-gogoa* 3–4 (March–April, 1950): 33–36.

————. *Jainkoaren billa.* Bilbao: Etor, 1971.

————. "Jainkozko biziera ta ongienera eldutzeko lasterbide bikaina." *Jesusen Biotzaren Deya* 1, no. 11 (November 1917): 338–43. Translation of Juan Eusebio Nieremberg, *Vida divina y camino real de grande atajo para la perfección,* Biblioteca de Autores Españoles 103. Madrid: Atlas, n.d.

————. "Krutwig yauna euskeraz." *Euzko-gogoa* 11–12 (November–December 1950): 49–52.

————. *Lati-izkuntzaren joskera.* Sestao: Bayo, 1966.

————. *El Lazarillo de Tormes. Tormes'ko Itsu-mutila.* Bilbao: Verdes Achirica, 1929.

————. *El lenguaje vasco.* San Sebastián: Izarra, 1963.

————. *Mireio.* Bilbao: Verdes Achirica, 1930.

———. "Nota necrológica sobre Azkue." *Gernika* 19 (April–June, 1952): 93–100.

———. "Orixe." *Olerti* 1-2 (1963): 106-14.

———. "La primera academia vasca." *Gernika* 9 (December 1949): 1823.

———. "Quito'n arrebarekin." *Euzko-gogoa* 9-10 (September–October 1951): 25.

———. "Quito'n arrebarekin." *Euzko-gogoa* 3-4 (1951): 13-19.

———. *Salmutegia.* San Sebastián: Izarra, 1967.

———. *Santa Cruz Apaiza.* Donostia: Loiola, 1929.

———. "El trato con Dios." Unpublished, Archives of Estibalitz Convent, 1959.

———. "Unificación del lenguaje literario." *Revista Internacional de Estudios Vascos* 11 (1920): 53-61.

———. *Urte guziko meza-bezperak.* Askain: Garakoiztar Laguntzaileak, 1949.

Ormaetxea, Nicolás, and M. Oyarzabal. *El lenguaje vasco.* Donostia: Izarra, 1963.

Ormaetxea, Nicolás (Orixe), and Jaime Zugasti Kerexeta. *Itun berria, lau ebangelioak.* San Sebastián: Izarra, 1967.

Orpustan, Jean-Baptiste. *Précis d'historire littéraire basque. 1545–1950.* Baigorri: Izpegi, 1996.

Otaño, Pedro Mari. *Pedro Mari Otaño'ren bertsoak.* Zarautz: Itxaropena, 1959.

Oteiza, Jorge de. *Quousque tandem . . . !* San Sebastián: Txertoa, 1971.

Peillen, Txomin. "Jon Mirande-ren gelako irudi grabatua: Albrecht Dürer-en 'Melencolia.'" *Maiatz* 3 (1982): 4-13.

Ramos Gil, Carlos. *Claves líricas de García Lorca.* Madrid: Aguilar, 1967.

Reicher, Gil. "Bernard Dechepare a-t-il subi des influences litteraires?" *Gure Herria* 30 (1958): 311-17.

———. "Le grand poete basque Bernard Dechepare." *Gure Herria* 29 (1957): 33-49.

Saizarbitoria, Ramón. *Egunero hasten delako.* Donostia: Mordago, 1969.

San Martín, Juan. *Escritores euskéricos.* Bilbao: La Gran Enciclopedia Vasca. 1968.

———. "Jon Mirande, orhoituz." In *Gogoz,* 389-92. Donostia: Caja de Ahorros Provincial de Guipúzcoa, 1978.

———. *Landuz.* Izarra: Gipuzkoako Aurrezki Kutxa, 1983.

———. *Literaturaren inguruan.* Donostia: Hordago, 1980.

———. "Orixeren poemari buruz." *Jakin* no. 21 (1966): 65-72.

———. "Salbatore Mitxelena, aberriminak eragindako poeta." *Egan* 37 (1977): 95-99.

S. Aureli Augustini confessionum libri tredecim. Germany: M. Skutella, 1934.

Sarasola, Ibon. *Euskal literatura numerotan.* Donostia: Kriselu. 1975.

———. Historia social de la literatura vasca [Euskal literaturaren historia]. Madrid: Akal, 1976.

———. "Lizardi-ren poemagintzaren alde formalen estudio batetarako." In

Homenaje a Julio Baroja, by Ibon Sarasola, 953-63. Madrid: Centro de Investigaciones Sociológicas, 1978.

Sarrionandia, Joseba. "Haur besoetakoa eta beste ninfula batzu." *Maiatz* 4 (1983): 3-8.

———. *Izuen gordelekuetan barrena.* Bilbao: Bilbao Aurrezki-Kutxa, 1981.

Satrústegui, José María. *Bordel bertsolaria.* Tolosa: Auspoa, 1965.

———. *Luzaide'ko kantiak.* Tolosa: Auspoa, 1967.

Sorarrain Ogarrio, Genaro. *Catálogo de obras euskaras.* Barcelona: Tasso, 1891.

Tellería, Pello. "Gandiaga, plazara." *Aránzazu* 57 (1977): 384-85.

Thalamas Labandibar, Juan. "El sentimiento cosmovital en las poesías de Lizardi." *Boletín de la Real Sociedad Vascongada de los Amigos del País* 1-2 (1974): 193-222.

Torrealday, Joan Mari. *Euskal idazleak, gaur: Historia social de la lengua y literatura vasca.* Oñati: Jakin. 1977.

Txillardegi. *See* Enparantza, José Luis Alvarez.

Ugalde, Martín de. "El exilio en la literatura vasca: problemas y consecuencias." In *El exilio español de 1939,* 6:217-83. Madrid: Taurus, 1976.

Unamuno, Miguel de. *Obras completas.* Vol. 6. Madrid: Afrodisio Aguado, 1958.

Urkiaga, Esteban "Lauaxeta." *Olerkiak.* San Sebastián: Etor, 1974.

Urkizu, Patri. *Euskal teatroaren historia.* Donostia: Kriselu, 1975.

———. *Lengua y literatura vasca.* Donostia: L. Haranburu, 1978.

Urquijo, Julio de. "Introducción a nuestra edición 'Linguae vasconum primitiae' de Bernat Dechepare." *Revista Internacional de Estudios Vascos* 24 (1933): 668.

Urretabizkaia, Arantza. *Maitasunaren magalean.* Donostia: Gipuzkoako Aurrezki Kutxa Probintziala, 1982.

Vélez de Mendizabal, Josemari. *Jokin Zaitegi.* Arrasate: Izarra, 1981.

Verlaine, Paul. *Oeuvres complètes.* Vol. 1. Paris: Albert Messein, 1947.

———. *Oeuvres poétiques complètes.* Paris: Gallimard, 1962.

Villasante, Luis. *Historia de la literatura vasca.* 2nd Oñati: Aránzazu, 1979.

———. "Lengua y literatura vasca." In *Tesoro breve de las letras hispánicas,* edited by G. Díaz Plaja, 6:15-27. Madrid: Magisterio Español. 1972.

———. "Literatura vasca escrita." In *Cultura vasca,* edited by Euskal Unibertsitatea, E.U.T.G., 2:111-36. Donostia: Erein, 1978.

———. "Lizardi en la literatura y en la poesía vasca." *Fontes Linguae Vasconum* (May-Aug. 1975): 227-36.

Webster, W. "Les Pastorales basques." In *La tradition au Pays Basque,* by W. Webster, 243-65. Paris: Bureaux de la Tradition Nationale, 1899.

Xalbador. *See* Aire, Fernando.

Zabala, Enrique. *Euskal literatura alfabetatzeko.* Lazkao: Pax, 1979.

Zarate, Mikel. *Bizkaiko euskal idazleak.* Bilbao: Derio, 1970.

———. *Euskal literatura.* Vol. 7. Durango: L. Zugazaga, 1977.

———. *Euskal literatura.* Vol. 9. Durango: L. Zugazaga, 1979.

Zavala, Antonio. *Ameriketako bertsoak.* Tolosa: Auspoa, 1984.

———. *Bilintx/Indalecio Bizcarrondo (1831–1876): Bizitza eta bertsoak (vida y poesías)*. Donostia: Caja de Ahorros de Guipúzcoa, 1978.

———. *Bosquejo de historia del bertsolarismo*. San Sebastián: Auñamendi, 1964.

———. *Iru anai bertsolari*. Tolosa: Auspoa, 1968.

———. *Paulo Yanzi*. Tolosa: Auspoa, 1968.

———. *Pello Errotaren bizitza. Bere alabak kontatua*. Tolosa: Auspoa, 1963.

———. *Pello Errotaren itzala*. Tolosa: Auspoa, 1965.

———. *Txirritaren bertsoak I*. Tolosa: Auspoa, 1971.

———. *Txirritaren bertsoak II*. Tolosa: Auspoa, 1971.

———. *Udarregi bertsolaria*. Tososa: Auspoa, 1966.

———. *Xenpelar: Bertsolaria*. Tolosa: Auspoa, 1969.

———. *Zepai bertsolaria (Akilino Izagirre Amenabar) (1906–1971)*. Tolosa: Auspoa, 1971.

INDEX

Anaximenes, 86
Anboto, Lady of. *See* Mari of Anboto
angels, 47
anti-Semitism, 157, 160, 229n. 40
Antzerki Eguna, 61
Aozko literatura (M. Lekuona), 8
Arana, Juan ("Loramendi"), 13-14, 63, 98
Aranalde, José Mari, 88
Arana y Goiri, Sabino, 3; Aitzol and, 60;
 Aresti and, 179; Basque language and,
 227n. 7; Basque nationalism and, 158;
 Euskadi concept and, 155; Lauaxeta and,
 118; Lizardi and, 99-100, 113, 222n. 4;
 Orixe and, 76
Aranburu, David, 38
Arantzazu, 133, 136, 138. *See also* Virgin of
 Arantzazu
Arantzazu, euskal sinismenaren poema
 (S. Mitxelena), 14, 136, 137-39
Arantzazu, poem of Basque faith (S. Mitxe-
 lena). See *Arantzazu, euskal sinismenaren
 poema*
"Ara nun diran" (Iparragirre), 119
Aranzabal, Manuel, 218n. 59
Aránzazu (magazine), 42
Arce, J. A. ("Hartzabal"), 15
Ardanza, José Antonio, 211n. 2
Aresti, Gabriel, 231n. 18; adaptation of
 Detxepare's poems, 52; Basque lan-
 guage and, 94, 173-74, 177-78, 180;
 Bizkaitarrak, 180; death of, 174; *Harri eta
 herri*, 144, 145, 173; literary influences
 on, 173, 176, 179-80; *Maldan behera*,
 179-80; notions of truth and, 178-79;
 on Orixe, 96; poetic style of, 180-82;
 "rupturist" movement and, 15; sig-
 nificance of, 172, 182; social poetry of,
 172-73, 174-77, 178-80
Argentina: *bertsolaritza* in, 19-22, 25-26,
 29-30, 39-40; Orixe and, 82
Argi oneko poema (Gandiaga), 225n. 28
Aristimuño, Jose de ("Aitzol"), 13, 60-64,
 80, 99, 103, 125, 189, 206-7
Aristotle, 203
Arrats-beran (Lauaxeta), 13, 117, 121, 125,
 128-32, 194
Arraun eta amets (S. Mitxelena), 142
Arregi, Joseba, 211n. 2
Arrese Beitia, Felipe, 12
Arrue, Antonio, 161
Arteche, José de, 216n. 31
Art poétique (Oihenart), 10
Art poétique (Verlaine), 121
Artzai mutilla (Otaño), 19

Artzain gorri (pastorale), 50
As evening approaches (Lauaxeta). See
 Arrats-beran
"Asking for a kiss" (Detxepare), 56
Asociación Libre de Ensayos Artísticos
 (ALEA), 117
Astarloa, P. P., 212n. 8
At sunset (Lauaxeta), 13
Atxaga, Bernardo, 16
Augustine, Saint, 90-91, 127
Australia, 40-41
autobiographical poems, 56-57
Axular. *See* Daguerre, Pedro
azken pheredika, 48
Azkue, Resurrección María de, 67-68

Baal, 168
"Bacchus," 188
ballads, 191-92. See also *bertsolaritza;* oral
 poetry; songs; troubadours
Baltzategi, Rodrigo, 137
bapateko bertsoak, 188
Barandiarán, José Miguel de, 61, 195, 204
"Barkoxeko Eliza," 211n. 5
Barne-muinetan (Orixe), 64, 78-80, 98,
 103, 115
Baroja, Pío, 156, 158, 170, 212n. 8
"Barruntza-Leioan" (Loramendi), 14
Basajaun, 228n. 25
Basarri, 189, 192, 193
"Basarriren bertsolari proiektua" (J. M.
 Lekuona), 192
"Basarri's bertsolari project" (J. M.
 Lekuona), 192
baserri, 199
"Baso-Itzal" (Lizardi), 63
Basque Center (Paris), 158-59
"Basque Country and America" (Iparra-
 girre), 31
Basque Country and Liberty. *See* Euskadi
 Ta Askatasuna
Basque culture (J. M. Lekuona), 185-86
*Le Basque et la littérature d'expression basque
 en Labourd* (Lafitte), 7
Basque flag, 50
Basque language: Aitzol and, 61-62;
 Arana y Goiri and, 227n. 7; Aresti and,
 173-74, 177-78, 180; Axular and, 227n.
 9; Detxepare and, 54, 57, 99; Lauaxeta
 and, 118; Lizardi and, 99, 100, 101-2,
 108-10; Mirande and, 153-55, 159, 160,
 170, 171, 226n. 4, 230n. 74; Mitxelena
 and, 134, 135, 138; neologisms and, 11,
 85, 94-95, 113, 146; Orixe and, 69, 73-

Goncourt literary prize, 229n. 40
"Good-bye" (Lizardi), 103
"Good-bye to my beloved mother" (Iparragirre), 29
Gorrotoa lege (Etxaide), 3
Gospel, 70, 202
grammars: by Orixe, 92–93
Greek poets: classical, 122; Homer, 70, 202, 207
grief: in Lizardi's poetry, 105–8
"Grown" (Otero), 176
Guatemala, 90, 220n. 93
Gudarien egiñank (Monzón), 14
Guruzbidea (S. Mitxelena), 136

hamarreko txikia meter, 19
Haritschelhar, Jean, 8
Harri eta herri (Aresti), 144, 145, 173
Hartzabal. *See* Arce, J. A.
Hatred is law (Etxaide), 3
Haur besoetakoa (Mirande), 153, 156, 162–64, 168, 228n. 32
Hawthorn (Gandiaga). *See Elorri*
Hegoalde, 2; emigration and, 17; historical survey of poetry in, 12-14, 15
hemistiches, 57
hendecasyllable, 57
Hérelle, Georges, 44, 46, 49–50, 51
heroes, 46–47, 50
herrimin. See nostalgia
Hikmet, Nazim, 180, 231n. 18
Hipona, Bishop of, 127
Hiru gizon bakarka (Gandiaga), 15, 145, 148-49, 196
Historia de Arantzazu (Lizarralde), 136
Historia de la literatura euskerika (Mujika), 6–7
Historia de la literatura vasca (K. Mitxelena), 6
Historia de la literatura vasca (Villasante), 6
History of Basque literature (Sarasola), 3
Holy Basque Trinity, 218n. 65
Homer, 70, 202, 207
homesickness. *See* nostalgia
homosexuality, 166
Horace, 69
Horia, Vintila, 229n. 40
Hot frontiers (J. M. Lekuona), 16
Huarte, José M., 53
Humboldt, Wilhelm von, 49

Ibinagabeitia, Andima, 116, 154, 159, 218 n.65
Idazlan guztiak (S. Mitxelena), 134

Idirin, Maite, 52
"Igan beti nire lelo" (Orixe), 87, 89-90
Igela (magazine), 154, 227n. 10
Ignatius of Loyola, Saint, 77, 86
"Ihauteen epaiketa eta kondenazioa," 188
I have a Christmas message (Gandiaga), 150–51
ikurriña, 50
Ilargiaren eskolan (J. M. Lekuona), 16, 194–95
Iliad (Homer), 70, 202, 207
imagery: in Aresti's poetry, 174, 175–77; in Gandiaga's poetry, 148; in Lauaxeta's poetry, 132; in Lizardi's poetry, 113–14
immigration. *See* emigration
Iñarra, Miguel Antonio, 184
In defense of leisure (Gandiaga). *See Denbora galdu alde*
Index Expurgatorius, 141
indianos, 29, 30–31
In Quito with my sister (Orixe), 84, 85–87
In search of God (Orixe), 91–92
intelligence, 124
International Congress on Popular Art, 233n. 13
"In the beginning" (Otero), 174, 178
In the eyes of the heart (Lizardi). *See Biotz-begietan*
In the lunar school (J. M. Lekuona), 16, 194–95
In the marrow (Orixe). *See Barne-muinetan*
"In the mirror" (television program), 183
In the school of the moon (J. M. Lekuona), 194–95
intus-susception, 203
Intxausti, 94
Inurritza, 225n. 1
Iparragirre, José María, 14, 29–31, 119, 212n. 10
Iparralde, 2, 5, 11–12, 17, 211n. 1, 227n. 12
Iparraldeko euskal idazleak (Etxenagusia), 5
Irasti, Lope de, 212n. 3
Irastorza, Tere, 16
Iratzeder. *See* Diharce, Jean
I request peace and the word (Otero), 174
irrationality, 125–26
"Ispiluan" (television program), 183
Itun berria, lau ebangelioak (Orixe), 70
Itz-lauz (Lizardi), 103
"I will defend my father's house" (Aresti), 174-75
"Izadi abestia" (J. M. Lekuona), 193
Iztueta, Juan Ignacio, 210n. 5
Iztueta, Pablo, 214n. 12

93; Manuel Lekuona on, 204-7; means of transmission, 199-200; scholarly recognition of, 198. *See also* oral poetry
Oral literature (M. Lekuona), 8
"Oral literature of the Basque Country" (J. M. Lekuona), 189
oral poetry: Aitzol's defense of, 64; Aresti and, 180; historical survey of, 11-12; Lauaxeta and, 129; J. M. Lekuona on, 189-90; Manuel Lekuona on, 61. *See also* oral literature
Orexa, 74-80
Organisation Armée Secrète (OAS), 160
Orixe. *See* Ormaetxea, Nicolás
Ormaetxea, Nicolás ("Orixe"), 5; *Aitor-kizunak*, 90-91, 93; Aitzol on, 103; on Azkue, 67-68; *Barne-muinetan*, 64, 78-80, 98, 103, 115; Basque Country, return to, 90-93; Basque dialects and, 68, 70, 71, 72, 73, 81, 95; Basque language and, 69, 73-74, 76, 93-95, 214-15n. 12; "Berraondo'ko Meza," 82-83; in Bilbo, 70-74; birth and childhood, 66, 214n. 9; burial of, 220n. 104; character of, 95-96; compared to other poets, 221-22n. 4; criticism of, 65-66; cultural and religious upbringing, 67-70; education of, 67; *Euskaldunak. Los vascos*, 13, 63, 65, 74-78, 115, 138-39, 216n. 30; *Euskal Irutasun Deuna* and, 218n. 65; "Euskal-literatura'ren atze edo edezti laburra," 2, 92, 93; Euskaltzaleak society and, 61; in exile, 81; faith of, 77, 78-80, 218n. 52; "Getsemaní," 87-89; *Gizonaren esku-bidegai guzietaz aitorkizuna*, 70; "Igan beti nire lelo," 87, 89-90; influences on, 215n. 13; *Itun berria, lau ebangelioak*, 70; "J. S. Bach'i Elizan," 82, 83; *Jainkoaren billa*, 91-92, 220n. 99; Jesuits and, 67, 77, 214-15n. 12; *Lati-izkuntzaren joskera*, 92-93; in Latin America, 82-90; on Lauaxeta, 121-22, 123; J. M. Lekuona and, 194; *El lenguaje vasco*, 92; literary production of, 13; Lizardi and, 80, 102, 216n. 30, 218n. 55; K. Mitxelena on, 65, 66, 93, 97, 209n. 6; in Orexa, 74-80; prizes and awards of, 93; *Quito'n arrebarekin*, 84, 85-87; religious poetry of, 68, 76-77, 78-80, 82-83, 87-90; religious prose of, 84, 85-87, 91-92, 220n. 99; *Salmutegia*, 70; *Santa Cruz apaiza*, 72-74; significance of, 65, 66, 96-97, 115; Spanish Civil War and, 80-81; translations by, 68-72, 81-82, 90-91; *Urte*

guziko meza-bezperak, 68, 81-82; writing style of, 77-78, 89, 93-95
Orphaned poems (S. Mitxelena), 134
Ortzi, 157, 158, 228n. 25
Oskorri, 52
Otaño, Jose Bernardo, 184
Otaño, Pedro Mari ("Katarro"), 184
Otaño, Pello, 19-25
"Otartxo utsa" (Lizardi), 103
Oteiza, Jorge de, 145, 195
Otero, Blas de, 117, 174, 175, 176, 177, 178

paganism, 157-58, 160-61, 168
"Pansart," 188
Pantagruel (Rabelais), 54, 57
Papadiamantópoulos, Yánnis, 123
parades, 48
Paris: Mirande and, 153, 158-59, 170; tourism to Iparralde, 227n. 12
"Paris-Beuret" (Mirande), 227n. 5
"Paris'ko txolarrea" (Lizardi), 103
Parnassianism, 119, 120
paroemiology, 187-88
Pascal, Blaise, 91, 217n. 51
Past is already gone, The (Etxaide), 3
pastorales, 9; bipolarization and, 45, 47; characteristics of, 45-48; origins and history of, 44, 48-51, 188, 189; plot structure, 48; popularity of, 44, 51. *See also* popular theater
patriotic poetry, 12
Le Pays Basque (Michel), 7
pedophilia, 156, 164-65
Peillen, Txomin, 154, 155, 156, 159, 160, 167, 226n. 4, 227n. 10
Pello, Pantxo ta, 52
Pello Errota. *See* Elizegi, José
Per Leartzza-ko (Txillardegi), 96
Peru abarca (Moguel), 74, 138
Peter farm shoe (Moguel). *See* Peru abarca
Petrirena, Juan F. ("Xenpelar"), 25, 193
Pido la paz y la palabra (Otero), 174
"Pigalle" (Mirande), 165
Pildain, Antonio, 204
Pious XI, 201
Plato, 120
Pléiade literary group, 57
Plotinus, 86
Poe, Edgar Allan, 168, 170
Poema del cante jondo (García Lorca), 130
"Poem of the Basque traveler" (Lizardi), 103, 108-9
poesía pura, 123-24
"Poesía y oralidad" (J. M. Lekuona), 189

Urdiñarbe, 212n. 11

Urkiaga, Esteban ("Lauaxeta"): Aitzol and, 63; *Arrats-beran,* 13, 117, 121, 125, 128-32, 194; *Bide-barrijak,* 13, 62, 98, 115, 117, 120, 122, 126-28; death of, 14, 80, 115, 118; *Euzkadi* magazine and, 117, 215n. 13; García Lorca and, 125-26, 129, 130; Juan Ramón Jiménez and, 123-24; J. M. Lekuona and, 194; life and poetic career of, 116-18; literary influences on, 116, 118-26, 127, 128-29, 130; Lizardi and, 112, 222n. 4; S. Mitxelena and, 136; Oihenart and, 10; pseudonyms of, 117; significance of, 132; violence and, 223n. 41

Urkijo, Julio. *See* Urquijo, Julio de

Urkizu, Patri, 7

Urquijo, Julio de, 95, 188

Urretabizkaia, Arantza, 16

Urrundik (Monzón), 14

"Urte giroak ene begian" (Lizardi), 103, 104

Urte guziko meza-bezperak (Orixe), 68, 81-82

Uruguay, 30

"Usariozko euskal olerkigintza" (J. M. Lekuona), 189

UZEI. *See* Unibertsitate Zerbitzuetarako Euskal Ikastetxea

Uztapide. *See* Olaizola, Manuel

Valéry, Paul, 116, 124

Vega, Garcilaso de la, 57

Verlaine, Paul, 119, 121, 170

"Verses sent to Uncle José Bernardo from America" (Otaño), 22-23

Vida divina y camino real del grande atajo para la perfección (Nieremberg), 69

Villasante, Luis, 6, 94, 154, 209nn. 3, 9

Villon, François, 11

Vinson, Julien, 49

violence, 125; Mirande and, 227-28n. 13

Virgil, 69, 122, 202, 207

Virgin Mary, 55

Virgin of Arantzazu, 42, 133; in Gandiaga's poetry, 143; in Mitxelena's writings, 136, 137, 138, 142

Virgin of Lourdes, 218n. 52

Warm borders (J. M. Lekuona), 193-94

Warramunga tribe, 203

While wasting time (Gandiaga). See *Denbora galdu alde*

"White Book of Euskara" (J. M. Lekuona), 185

wine: *txakoli,* 148

"Winter" (Lizardi), 222n. 7

witches, 137. *See also* Mari of Anboto

women: in Lauaxeta's poetry, 131; *pastorales* and, 51; poetry of Juan Ruiz and, 58; poets, 16

Writers from Iparralde (Etxenagusia), 5

Xabier de Lizardi. *See* Agirre, Jose Mari

"Xabiertxoren eriotza" (Lizardi), 105-7

Xalbador. *See* Aire, Fernando

Xavier, Saint Francis, 77

Xenpelar. *See* Petrirena, Juan F.

Ximena (pastorale), 51

"Xori ori ez baita Jainkoaren obra" (Aire), 27-28

Yakintza (journal), 61, 62, 64

Yanzi, Pablo, 36

"Young girls" (Mirande), 164

"You stroll happily in the morning" (Lauaxeta), 131

Zaitegi, Jokin: Aitzol and, 63; *Euzko-gogoa* and, 82, 90, 218-19n. 65; "Generation of Aitzol," 60; Jesuits and, 214n. 12, 220n. 93; Lauaxeta and, 116; Lizardi and, 111; Mirande and, 154

"Zaldia" (Orixe), 69

Zalduby. *See* Adema, Gracian

Zarate, Mikel, 4

"Zazpi Eskualherriek" (Adema), 12

"Zeruko bizia" (Orixe), 69

Ziutateaz (Atxaga), 16

zortziko txikia, 192

Zuberoa, 11; description of, 211n. 1; Matalas and, 212n. 10; *pastorales* and, 44, 48; popular theater in, 195

Zuberoan dialect, 10, 11; Mirande and, 155; in *pastorales,* 45

Zugarramurdi, 77

"Zumalakarregi," 211n. 2